P9-DOC-564

THE MUNICIPAL BOND INVESTMENT ADVISOR

TAX-EXEMPT
INVESTING FOR
HIGH-BRACKET
INDIVIDUALS

WILSON WHITE

PROBUS PUBLISHING COMPANY
Chicago, Illinois

Library of Congress Cataloging in Publication Data Available

ISBN 1-55738-190-9

Printed in the United States of America

BB

1   2   3   4   5   6   7   8   9   0

DEDICATION
To Martha

TABLE OF CONTENTS

SECTION III *THE MANAGED FUNDS*

SECTION IV *DIRECT INVESTING*

SECTION V *DELEGATED ASSET MANAGEMENT*

Preface

Back in 1986, lacking a commercial publisher, I self-published my first book, *The Municipal Bond Market: Basics*. I thank the some seven thousand people who have bought it. *Basics* was designed primarily for bond professionals, but since there are so few works available on tax-exempts, many of the sales have been to individual buyers.

I have written the present book specifically for the private investor. Municipal bonds are certainly the most complex investment vehicle bought by individuals and I hope to show how they originate, how their markets work, and how to purchase them properly. Rather than go into fine detail about their credits, you will see that I emphasize the importance of timing, what the workings of their markets are, and when and how to pick the best deal.

My entire career has been spent in tax-exempts. I started in 1954 as an assistant trader with a small New York municipal bond firm, when state and local bonds were in a quiet backwater of finance. I had my own bond-dealing company for many years, including the tumultuous times of the well-known New York bond crisis. During the roaring Eighties I traded the bond markets actively, first down and finally up. We will see that one typical good move in bonds is five *basis points*, .05%, of interest. In 1980 and 1981, I traded bonds that dropped more than a thousand basis points, from 5% to 15%, and from a price of 100 down below 50, credit unchanged. Perhaps you can see why I am so wary of losses from interest rate changes.

I've had a share in dealing with credit troubles as well, such as the now infamous WHOOPs bonds. Their declines were so great we don't even measure them in yield. Now *there's* a move. Maybe when I caution readers about over-concentration you will see it's from more than abstract reasoning.

Now I am a consultant with Barre and Co., headquartered in Dallas. I spend a few hours a week trading and advising, but most of my time is devoted to writing.

Conventional widsom says that a person should write about what he or she knows. After thirty years in the business, I figured I really *did* know enough and produced *Basics,* drawing from my own experience. For this book, however, I've had to restudy the municipal bond industry, not for new issues and trading, which I had been doing myself, but by delving into the quite distinct topics of trusts and funds.

I've had plenty of help in writing this book. First and foremost, I've been greatly encouraged by the number of people who bought my first one. Then there's Peg Webb, who has sent out all the copies and kept the accounts straight. Mia Scanga was my able researcher for over a year. Mike Lipper both allowed me free range of his company's data and also answered many statistical queries. Steve Nathan helped me with the Zotti's taxes. Peter Fugiel and Carl Keller aided me with U.I.T.s. Cary Anderson, Dave Dowden, and Jim Kochan, all of Merrill, have steered me through state tax and other information. The Investment Company Institute, especially Betty Hart, has provided information about the various bond packages. *The Bond Buyer*, particularly my pen pal Joe Mysak, has been invaluable, statistically and editorially. William Blase of Scudder, Stevens and Clark has provided data permitting me to use one of their funds as an example. Jim Lebenthal made valuable suggestions. Vita Nelson, honcha of *The Moneypaper,* has even printed a chapter, her style. Special thanks to all the dealers who have let me make lists of their names for investor referral. A.M.B.A.C. and M.B.I.A., good customers of my first book, have encouraged my doing this one. Chris Taylor, head of the Municipal Securities Rulemaking Board, and ditto the Public Securities Association, have provided well placed guidance. Loukas Hriston of Tucker, Anthony, who I'd recommend as anyone's customer's man, always helped when needed. Peter C. Trent guided me firmly on trust topics. Moody's and Standard & Poor's publications are used throughout this work. Last, but not least, Probus has been a delightful publisher.

Wilson White

Section I
The Fundamentals

THE FOUR WAYS TO TAX-EXEMPT INVESTING

The Three Prerequisites

Ten million Americans now benefit from tax-exempt income and if you're not among them maybe it's time to join the crowd. However, municipal bonds are not for everyone; before investing in them, you should be able to answer yes to three prerequisite questions.

First: *Do you have enough cash in reserve?* Before making any long term investment, you should have at least six months' living expenses stashed away in immediately available funds. So you can pay your regular bills, swing a new car, and meet health emergencies without bothering your investments. It's expensive to turn long term bonds into cash, so don't count on your municipal bonds for liquidity unless something really unforeseeable comes along. Investing is serious business and the seats are hard, so keep a comfortable cash cushion handy.

Second: *Is your income high enough?* Currently, most personal earnings are taxed at just three Federal rates: 15%, 28%, and 31%. Unless you've reached the upper brackets you're usually better off with higher yielding taxable investments (bank CD's or corporation bonds, for instance). Why pay for an exemption you don't need? However, if you're paying at the higher rates you will almost always come out better by investing in municipals. Top bracket 15%? Buy taxables. Top bracket 28% or 31%. Buy tax-exempts.

3

Third: *Do you really want to put your money in municipal bonds?* Let's assume that the timing is correct (see Chapter 3 for specifics) but that the highest rate available on good municipals is 8%. Could you buy some real estate or invest in a business you are sure will return more than 8%, after taxes, year after year? Or do you know of a stock practically certain to go up a lot? If so, consider one of these carefully. Although this book concentrates on municipals, they are by no means the only way to go. If you know of something better, great, go get it. However, in the short, medium, or long run, tax-exempts are hard to beat.

☞ *WILSON ADVISES*

Before you buy municipals check the prerequisites:
1.) Six months of living expenses in reserve.
2.) Federal income tax in the upper brackets.
3.) No better investments available.

Choosing the Right Bond Vehicle

Now that you're ready for tax-exempt investing, what comes next? Some investors are considering tax-frees for the first time, while others have been accumulating them for years. Many people choose to buy their bonds and hold them until they come due. More aggressive investors need to grasp the wheel of fortune, actively switching their assets around, straining for the highest yield, as the world turns. No matter what your style, there are four quite different paths to investing in municipal bonds. You can buy *unit investment trusts, managed funds, unpackaged individual bonds,* or you can *delegate* the whole job to others. Here's a brief summary of each.

U.I.T.S

Many people's first investment in tax-exempts is through a unit investment trust. U.I.T.s are a security which dealers create by selecting and bundling together a fixed package of different municipal bonds which stay permanently in the trust. Units in the U.I.T. are then sold to investors at a marked up price, usually by about 5%. U.I.T.s first appeared in 1961, when just $20 million were sold. By 1979 sales had risen to $3 billion and in 1985 reached almost $16 billion, though since then sales have tapered off. Sponsors certainly aren't shy about pushing trusts' strong points and the $90 billion now outstanding attests to their popularity.

The typical U.I.T. household has one and a half incomes totalling $50,000 per year. They often add on to their holdings, rarely sell them and now hold about $25,000 worth. Why are U.I.T.s so popular? Because they provide diversification, professional bond selection, after-tax return, and, perhaps most important of all, great convenience. 12% of all outstanding tax-exempts are held in U.I.T.s.

The Managed Funds

Managed funds are also composed of bundles of tax-exempt bonds put together by dealers and sold to the public. Their chief distinction from U.I.T.s is that the managers can sell any of the bonds in the portfolio and replace them with others that may represent better values. Funds first appeared in 1976 and by 1981 the public was buying $4 billion worth a year. Now they are huge—in 1990 the public held $125 billion worth. Managed funds provide most of the features of U.I.T.s—diversification, bond selection, tax-exempt return, and convenience. As can be expected, the fund runners also solicit new customers vigorously, and no doubt you have seen and heard their ads many times. Investors in funds have somewhat larger and more diversified portfolios than U.I.T. buyers. About two and a half million households own them, with the average holding around $35,000. Managed funds now hold 18% of all tax-exempts.

Direct Investing

Some individual buyers of tax-exempts prefer to pick their own bonds and many are happy with their results. Among them are some small buyers, but there is more traffic from the medium and large sized investors. How do you go about investing independently? Suppose your eye catches an ad in *The Wall Street Journal* like the one in Chapter 20, Figure 20.3. Perhaps the 7% bonds due in 2001 at a price of 100 seem right for your purposes. How can you buy them? Call your regular broker or bank and simply direct them to buy them for you. If these particular bonds are still available, your order will no doubt be honored. Often you may see different kinds of dealer ads, or you may ask your broker to suggest other, unadvertised bonds. If this sort of approach appeals to you, by all means try it, with caution. One piece of advice right now: *Know your dealer.* See Chapter 19 for more about this. About 50% of outstanding municipal bonds are held directly by investors.

Delegated Asset Management

The fourth path in the municipal bond investment field leads to different territory—where you delegate asset managing to someone else. There are four principal sets of investment experts who make their living minding other people's money—*financial planners, dealer managers, bank trust departments,* and *regulated investment companies.* See Chapter 28 for details on how this slice of the investing public is served.

A Map of the Book

Where do you go from here? If you're curious about all four ways through tax-exempt territory you may wish to march straight through the book, and I invite you to do just that. Here is the lay of the land.

Section One–Fundamentals (Chapters 1–4). The basics of investing. After an overview of U.S. finance, we go on to taxes, followed by a chapter on the general principles of bond investing, and then a visit with an imaginary investing couple.

Section Two–U.I.T.s (Chapters 5–12). Covers the unit investment trusts, their structure, their finer points, and also their drawbacks, and how to choose among them.

Section Three–Managed Funds (Chapters 13–18). Treats the municipal bond funds, their design and management, their advantages and disadvantages, finishing with how to select the most appropriate one for you.

Section Four–Direct Investing (Chapters 19–27). Describes the dealer market in municipal bonds, shows how do your own research, and how to pick the best buys around.

Section Five–Delegated Asset Management (Chapter 28). Presents the various kinds of professional portfolio advisors, their advertised functions, and how to get them to work for you.

How to Proceed

Instead of reading straight through you may prefer to graze around. For instance, if you are already thoroughly experienced in finance you'll probably jump over the basics of Section One. Unless fixed bond bundles especially appeal to you, you may want to pass the sections devoted to U.I.T.s and managed funds. In any case, my best wishes for a pleasant and rewarding trip!

CHAPTER 1

BOND BASICS

Bonds

We will be talking about bonds throughout this book, sometimes when they are packed together, sometimes standing alone. What exactly are *bonds*? Bonds are a kind of I.O.U. or a loan. Technically, bonds are legal evidence, called a *debt instrument,* that proves a certain sum of money is owed. The U.S. Treasury, many larger corporations and most municipalities borrow money by issuing bonds. Most of these borrowings are split into investor-sized units, typically of $5,000. Each issuer gets access to many investors' money, while lenders take just the amount they need. Bonds are part of a larger category—*fixed income securities*—which includes bonds, bank certificates of deposit, and preferred stock. The essential features of fixed income securities are these: a binding contract between issuer and investor; a defined date of repayment; and an agreed rate of interest.

☞ *A DEFINITION*

Bond

A debt instrument by which a government or corporation borrows money at an agreed rate of interest and promises to repay a set amount.

Interest

Along with fixed income securities come *interest* payments, priced at such and such *annual percentage rate* (A.P.R.). "Priced" gives the right idea, because the price of borrowing money is its interest rate. Economists call interest a form of rent, which they define as payment for the use of capital over time. If you mortgage your house for $100,000 at an interest rate of 10%, you contract to pay the lender $10,000 a year just for renting you the money, with principal payments extra. When you do the lending, it's the other way around. $100,000 worth of bonds paying 8% interest will return you, the lender, $8,000 every year.

U.S. Government Bonds

The Constitution grants our federal government the power to borrow money, which it currently does with great frequency, and in enormous quantities. Through its financing arm, the U.S. Treasury, the government borrows by selling short term obligations, called *bills,* every Monday. The Treasury borrows more permanently several times a month by issuing long term bonds, paying interest and repaying principal on them like any other debtor. Interest on U.S. obligations is subject to federal income tax, but is exempt from state and local taxation. There is an active market for Treasury bonds which is conducted over-the-counter, not on an exchange. Its participants include securities dealers and banks and, indirectly, you, their customers.

Corporations

Corporations are an element of the American economic system which goes back to medieval England, where people in certain communities were granted powers by a king, including the right to borrow money. During the nineteenth century the corporation idea was greatly expanded and traveled well to the United States, where over 90% of all businesses are organized as corporations. Corporations are created by selling pieces of their equity (ownership) to shareholders. These shares of *common stock* representing units of ownership may either be held closely, as in doctors' associations, or by the general investing public, as are the shares of Xerox and E.I. DuPont. An investor who now holds 670 shares of DuPont common stock owns about .0001% of the company and will share in its fortunes, and dividends, in the same proportion. Approximately 25,000 different stock issues trade every business day, most visibly on the New York Stock Exchange.

☞ *A DEFINITION*

Common Stock

Shares of equity representing percentages of ownership of a corporation.

Corporate Bonds

Both stocks and bonds are *negotiable instruments*, that is they can be freely transferred from one owner to another. Otherwise, they are quite different. When you buy stocks you own part of a company; when you buy bonds you are lending money, and no ownership is involved. Stocks you own. Bonds you loan. Stockholders invest for profits and dividends; most bondholders invest for income. When Dow Chemical needs to raise some money to build a new plant it may go to its investment bankers in New York—presently Goldman, Sachs, Merrill Lynch and First Boston—who may recommend issuing more common stock, thereby increasing the company's equity. Or, they may suggest a new issue of bonds, thus increasing its debt. In either case these investment bankers may then offer Dow Chemical securities to investors, providing the corporation with cash, the public with investments, and (if they judge the situation well) themselves with a profit. As with Treasuries, bond dealers also trade older issues of corporate bonds in the secondary market. The interest on corporate bonds is freely taxed both by the states and by the Federal Government.

The Constitution (Amendment X) provides that the powers not specifically reserved for the federal government belong to the states. The states in turn authorize their municipal governmental units to set and enforce their own laws, and to levy and collect taxes. One other community power is vital, the right to borrow money. Enter municipal bonds.

Municipal Bonds

Back in the early nineteen hundreds U.S. municipalities began to issue bonds. In 1817, the State of New York saw that it needed improved transportation, but the cost was beyond its immediate means. It financed the Erie Canal by selling long term bonds to the investing public, giving as security the full faith and credit of the state. The project was completed successfully and the bonds were gradually retired. This kind of municipal bond is called a general obligation.

Figure 1.1
BONDS OUTSTANDING—1990
ALL MATURITIES

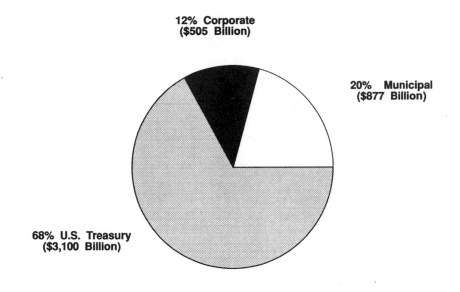

12% Corporate
($505 Billion)

20%   Municipal
($877 Billion)

68% U.S. Treasury
($3,100 Billion)

Municipal Bond Dealers

We have briefly mentioned the dealers who conduct the U.S. and corporate bond markets. Another sector of Wall Street is run by the *municipal bond dealers*, who we will see at work through the rest of this book. They operate both in the new issue (primary) market, helping state and local governments raise money for capital needs, and also in the trading (secondary) market, buying and selling previously issued bonds.

Municipal Bond Tax Exemption

During the early years of debate about imposing a national income tax a delicate question arose—whether or not the federal government could tax interest on state and local bonds. Deciding a long and eloquently argued suit (Pollock vs. Farmers Loan and Trust Company, U.S. 803, 1895), the U.S. Supreme Court ruled it could not, referring to Franklin, Hamilton, and even the father of our

Figure 1.2
BONDS OUTSTANDING—1990
MATURITIES 5 YEARS OR LONGER

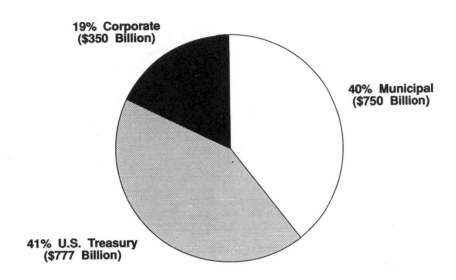

19% Corporate
($350 Billion)

40% Municipal
($750 Billion)

41% U.S. Treasury
($777 Billion)

country along the way. The Court flatly stated that "The tax in question is a tax on the power of the states and their instrumentalities to borrow money, and consequently repugnant to the constitution." This ruling held firm for over ninety years and under its protection over $1.5 trillion municipal bonds were issued, securely tax-exempt. Then, in 1988, in South Carolina vs. Baker, the Supreme Court reversed itself. It stated unequivocally that tax-exemption is a matter for Congress, and not the judiciary, to decide, and that Congress is free to tax the income from state and local government bonds. Federal legislation maintains the exemption of municipal bonds from taxation, and present opinion favors it, but some day this may change. If so, precedent strongly suggests that the outstanding bonds would stay exempt.

Where does that leave us? Treasury bonds are exempt from state and local taxes. State and local bonds are still definitely exempt from federal taxes, with two minor exceptions, to which we will return in Chapter 2. Naturally, this exemption makes municipal bonds especially attractive to individual savers looking for a good return. Ten million people have put their savings into municipal obligations, an impressive vote of confidence.

General Obligation Bonds

General obligation bonds, G.O.'s for short, are unconditional obligations, payable from all the resources of a community, including its property taxes. Each of the fifty states has legislated enabling acts which authorize local government units to levy real estate taxes and sell general obligation bonds. Real estate taxes constitute a lien on property worth many times the bonds issued against it and provide an exceptionally reliable source of income to repay the debts. G.O.'s remained the principal form of municipal security until quite recently and are still many people's favorite sort.

General obligation bonds typically finance capital projects which benefit all, or at least a sizeable majority, of a municipality's citizens. Over the years, Huntsville, Alabama has come to the bond market regularly in order to help pay for school building, drainage improvements, and civic center construction, among other municipal projects. Property taxes go up a few mils to pay for servicing each issue, but the entire community is served. In recent years new issues of G.O.'s have been selling at an average rate of about $30 billion per year, and there are now almost $350 billion outstanding.

Revenue Bonds

The development of *revenue bonds* marked the beginning of the modern municipal bond era. Revs are also solemn municipal obligations, but are usually issued for particular community purposes, benefiting some, but not all of the citizens. For instance, Huntsville, which, owns and operates its own water and electric utility systems sends bills their customers, rather than to all taxpayers. When the revenue comes in, it first goes to pay the expenses of operating and maintaining the projects, then to service the bond issues.

When it becomes necessary to extend or improve its water system, Huntsville may sell more revenue bonds. The city meters and bills businesses and households, collects and segregates the revenue, pays expenses, and its bonds' debt service (principal and interest). In August 1990, Huntsville expanded its operations by creating an authority which negotiated an $87 million new issue to finance a waste disposal facility. The authority will operate the plant, and if all goes well, pay interest on the bonds and gradually retire them. In the past ten years, U.S. communities have been selling about $85 billion of all kinds of revenue bonds annually, and there are about $450 billion outstanding.

Notes

Most governmental units experience irregular flows of income and expense, both seasonal and from year to year. When they need cash, they often borrow for the short term by selling *notes,* a municipal security due in a few weeks or months. Notes are secured by anticipated property taxes or other income, or by expected funding from permanent bond issues, and are often also general obligations of the community. Communities such as Huntsville will sell a note issue, retiring it with when the next round of property taxes comes in, or by its next bond issue.

Federal Regulation

Until 1975 the municipal bond market functioned quite well according to its own lights, but then Congress, led by Senator Harrison A. Williams of New Jersey, decided it should be regulated. Competition still determines prices and profits and dealers maintain the ethical standards; but now, like most businesses, it is subject to federal overview. Municipal bond dealers operate under regulations set by the Municipal Securities Rulemaking Board (M.S.R.B.), with Securities and Exchange Commission (S.E.C.) approval. These rules are enforced by the self-regulating National Association of Securities Dealers (N.A.S.D.).

I wouldn't blame you if you find some of these descriptions of financial processes bewildering, because dealers routinely work *with* the stuff that other people work *for*, money. Finance can indeed appear mysterious, and in fact, some Wall Streeters cultivate the seeming enigmas. However, try to think of money as something to use, like cement, or lumber, or memory chips—just another kind of raw material. You can't build a municipal water system without money, any more than you can without pipes.

Money is just another commodity, and Wall Streeters aren't as strange as they sometimes seem. Even bond dealers watch in wonder at a television program showing liquid gold flowing into ingot molds. And when they read that two rare pennies, both struck in the same year, are auctioned off, one bringing $100,000 and the other only $35,000, they are just as fascinated, and perplexed by the explanations as anyone else.

That's a broad view of finance, with hundreds of millions of shares, and billions and billions of dollars worth of bonds trading every day. But fundamentally it's not much different from the way my daughter operates her store. She orders up a stock of fresh seafood, picks it up at the local airport, and then sells it in small packages. In fact, she and I frequently comment on the similarities between our two businesses. She buys clams and shrimp in bulk and sells them retail, while I buy blocks of San Antonio, Texas electric and gas revenue bonds from a wholesaler and then try to distribute them, often in smaller lots. In the process I help communities raise money and also give investors access to tax-exempt income. My purpose? To make the middleman's profit. Most of my business is at risk, and my profits average under 1% of principal. I wish I had Bea's markup, and she wishes she had my volume.

SUMMARY ** CHAPTER 1 ** SUMMARY

Bond Basics

- Bonds represent debts of a corporation or government.

- Stocks represent shares of a business.

- Bonds you loan. Stocks you own.

- State and local governments raise money by issuing municipal bonds to build public projects.

- These bonds are then repaid gradually, with interest.

- General obligation bonds are backed by property taxes.

- Revenue bonds are paid from the income stream of the project financed.

- Specialized securities companies deal in municipal bonds.

CHAPTER 2

MUNICIPAL BONDS AND THE TAX LAWS

FEDERAL TAXES

U.S. income taxes are, of course, the result of federal legislation, and most of the present provisions were thoroughly revised by the Tax Reform Act of 1986, to which we will be referring often. First we'll look at federal income and other tax laws, then at some state and local levies. Tax laws change frequently and many exceptions obtain. I sincerely advise you to consult your own professionals for interactive advice.

The History of Income Taxes

Constitutional Amendment XVI authorized a U.S. national income tax system. Signed by President Wilson in October, 1913, the first legislation levied a rate of 1%. This taxing system remained fairly simple, although rates rose as high as 40% in the thirties, and to over 90% during World War II. Then, starting in the 1950's, Congress began to add special features to it in almost every session; countless loopholes were legislated, modified, closed, and partially reopened. As a result, by 1970 people and corporations with the same levels of income began to pay wildly differing I.R.S. bills; tax-sheltering had become big business. Suddenly, lifelong East Coast suburbanites would own herds of cattle fattening up in Colorado or almond groves in Florida they would never see.

Tax Reform—1986

After a giant struggle, Congress passed and President Reagan signed the Tax Reform Act of 1986, radically reducing the massive clutter. The treatment of municipal bonds entered the proceedings in Washington a number of times, and at one point their market was disrupted when a misguided suggestion was made to tax their interest. This was quickly withdrawn and normalcy returned.

The 1986 law affected municipal bond holders in three main ways. 1.) The new and lower brackets made owning municipals less valuable, since tax rates on other taxable investments would be dropping. 2.) The elimination of loopholes left municipals the last significant shelter. 3.) Restrictions were placed on the issuance of many types of tax-exempts, thus reducing their future supply. The net effect was to make tax-exempt bonds more attractive and their prices rose sharply.

Income Tax Rates

The first column in Figure 2.1 shows that up to $34K, joint filers are, as of 1991, taxed at 15%. The next column shows that it takes a *taxable* investment of 9.41% *to equal a tax-free 8%*. In other words, in this bracket the government gets 15% and you keep 85%. 85% of the taxable 9.41% is 8%. It's been pretty easy in the past few years to find safe taxable return in the 9% range, so people

---

Figure 2.1
1991 FEDERAL INCOME TAX RATES AND EFFECTS

Joint Filers			Single Filers		
Income	Tax	Taxable Equivalent of Tax Free 8%	Income	Tax	Taxable Equivalent of Tax Free 8%
$ 0 - 34,000	15%	9.41%	$ 0 - 20,000	15%	9.41%
34 - 82,000	28%	11.11%	20 - 49,000	28%	11.11%
82 - 150,000	31%	11.59%	49 - 100,000	31%	11.59%
150 -	33-31%	11.94-11.59%	100 -	33-31%	11.94-11.59%

in the 15% bracket are not greatly better off buying tax-exempt bonds. When we come to the 28% bracket, where you get to keep only 72%, things change. At the same tax-free 8%, the equivalent is a taxable 11.11%. In recent years that high a return has only been found in junk bonds where the extra yield is achieved at considerable extra risk. This gets close to the main point about investing in municipals. *Tax-free bonds usually provide the high-bracket individual fixed-income investor with the highest available spendable returns.*

There is also another way of calculating taxable equivalent yields. Start with the after tax government yield, and compare it to municipals. In the 28% bracket the I.R.S. takes 28 cents per dollar, leaving you 72. 9% taxable becomes only 6.48% spendable (9% x .72 = 6.48%). So anything over 6.48% tax-exempt will beat a taxable 9%. In recent years 7% and higher rates on good grade municipals have been easy to come by, explaining tax-exempts' great popularity. Tax free interest is *not* reported by brokers on their 1099-INT reports to the I.R.S., but taxpayers are supposed to list it on their 1040 income tax form, Line 8b.

Deductions

Many personal deductions were curtailed in 1986. However, three categories significant to municipal bond holders continue to be fully deductible: *real estate taxes* and *state and local income taxes.*

Real estate taxes constitute about one-quarter of all local government revenues. The deductibility of these property taxes was retained leaving the federal subsidy for this source of municipal bond backing unimpaired.

After a substantial battle, the deductibility of state and local income taxes was retained. The effect of eliminating these might have been severe on citizens of high-tax states, whose leaders fought hard to keep it, and won. This strengthened municipal income streams, and high tax states are still busily multiplying the spoils. However, state sales taxes are no longer deductible and the trend is, of course, to raise the subsidized state income taxes and keep non-deductible state sales taxes at the old rates.

Municipal Bonds

Congress took a good look at the tax-exempt bomb shelter during the Reform Act deliberations, but decided not to drop anything on it directly. However, the new law cut back on many abuses of the tax-exempt privilege, limiting the tax-exemption to issues which serve a genuine *public purpose*. No already issued bonds were retroactively subjected to tax. However, the exemption of new issues sold to finance corporate enterprises, private nursing homes and apartment buildings was severely restricted or eliminated. In anticipation of the reforms to come, tens of billions of dollars worth of municipals were hastily issued and sold in 1985 and '86, and new bond sales surged to almost twice their normal volume, many of them with definitely questionable purposes. New flotations then returned to their longterm patterns of growth and the market now rests on firmer ground. In any case, there are plenty of bonds for everyone, tax-exempt as usual, with a couple of minor exceptions.

Federal Taxes on Municipal Bonds

Although we often call them tax-exempts, that term isn't 100% accurate. The I.R.S. collects taxes from owners of municipals in three ways: on *capital gains* when they are sold at a profit; in certain exceptional cases on their *interest;* and at *estate* time. In addition, many states also tax them, as treated shortly.

Capital Gains

Profits registered when securities are sold are treated separately from ordinary income. This includes profits on municipal bonds. If you buy a municipal and later sell it or let it mature at a higher price, you owe tax. Capital gains rates are presently identical to the regular rates, but there is always talk about changing this. For details, see your tax people.

Alternative Minimum Tax

Bonds issued to finance authentic public purpose projects, the traditional municipal improvements such as roads, colleges, and water facilities, are 100% federally tax-exempt. However, many dodges, such as bonds floated solely to earn arbitrage profits, are now denied tax-exemption, and rightly so. Between these two categories—clearly public purpose bonds and the now prohibited abusers—falls a gray area, bonds which are both public in purpose, but don't quite meet the new and stringent requirements. For instance, in August 1990, although it could not qualify for full tax-exemption, the Pennsylvania Housing Finance Authority went ahead and sold $80 million of single family mortgage revenue bonds.

Bonds such as these are subject to the *alternative minimum tax*. What is the A.M.T? A levy designed to tax people with special deductions (such as for passive activity farming or oil drilling losses) so high that they escape paying income tax at the regular rates. If you deduct over $30,000 a year for such preference items, including incentive stock option plans, then interest on A.M.T. municipal bonds is subject, in 1991, to a 24% tax. If you're in this class, watch out that the A.M.T. doesn't get you. Otherwise, A.M.T. bonds can offer the rest of us tax-exempt bargains. Also, a very few communities have decided, for one reason or another, to deliberately issue *taxable municipal bonds*, which are designed mostly for institutions and are not exempt at all.

Estate and Social Security Taxes

The principal worth of municipal bonds is included in estate calculations, and a tax may be due on the market value. At present no tax is paid on estates under $600,000. Over that the rate gets up to 37% in a hurry and reaches 55%. Estate planning is for experts.

People receiving Social Security benefits have to include municipal bond interest in most income tax calculations, in effect paying some tax on state and local bonds. Some close figuring may be necessary for recipients to determine if naturally lower yielding municipals are worth holding.

STATE TAXES

State Income Taxes

That's the good news—no federal tax on most state and local bond interest. But the bad news is that states are free to tax each other, and their levies often markedly reduce holders' out-of-state bond yields. As of 1991, forty-one states levy some form of tax on out-of-state municipal bond interest. In addition, a few tax their residents on the income from bonds issued by some, or all, of their own communities. The formulas for calculating these yield losses are rather complicated, but see the box for a rough rule.

☞ *WILSON ADVISES*

To find out how many basis points in yield you lose on interest from a non-state-exempt bond, multiply your own top state tax rate by 5.

Basis points is a technical term you've probably seen used. A basis point is 1/100 of one per cent of *interest,* or .01%. So if a percentage yield changes by one basis point from 7.44% it goes to 7.45%, or 7.43%. Figure Oregon's income tax is 9%, so their citizens who own out-of-state bonds give up about five times nine basis points or .45% in yield. The loss would be even higher except for the indirect U.S. subsidy—it's allowance of state income tax as a federal deduction. An apparent 8% yield to an Oregon resident holding a New Mexico bond will be reduced to 7.55% (8% minus .45%) by state income taxation. New Jersey's bitterly opposed newly hiked rate of 7% reduces my yield on Indiana bonds by about .35%, after the federal deduction.

There is one set of bonds immune to any income taxes at all—federal, state or local. The interest on bonds of U.S. affiliated issuers, primarily Puerto Rico, but also including the Virgin Islands and some Pacific territories, are exempt by an Act of Congress dating back to 1917. So in Oregon, New Jersey, and all the other states, an apparent 8% on a Puerto Rico bond is a real 8%, 100% tax-free. Some trust and fund managers have taken advantage of this provision. For example 7.4% of Merrill Lynch's giant New York Municipal Bond Fund was placed in Puerto Rico electric, highway, and other of that island Commonwealth's bonds.

True Yield

In addition, any profits you make selling or redeeming securities are often subject to state and local capital gains taxes. You have to deduct the effects of these taxes in order to arrive at a true, after-all-tax yield. Brokers report any sales or redemptions of securities, municipal bonds included, to the I.R.S. on their Form 1099-B.

All in all, the new tax laws are a big improvement, and although state and local bond issuance has been trimmed back, I'm glad to see the municipal business return to its function of supplying capital for projects in the legitimate public interest. I believe that the new taxing system has cut down on tax shelter drag, encouraging a more sensible deployment of assets. In any case, the new laws have taken away almost all the other shelters, leaving intact just one big exception—tax-exempt municipal bonds.

SUMMARY ** CHAPTER 2 ** SUMMARY

Municipal Bonds and the Tax Laws

There are now three personal income brackets, 15, 28 and 31%. Most personal income, including interest on corporate and U.S. Government bonds is taxed at these rates.

- Interest earned on most municipal bonds is 100% Federally tax-exempt.

- Forty-one states also tax personal income with top brackets averaging 6%. Most states exempt interest earned on their own bonds but not on those of other states.

- It takes about a taxable 11% return to equal a tax-exempt 8%.

CHAPTER 3

STRATEGY FOR LONG TERM INVESTING

THE *TIME* TO BUY

Many individual investors tell their sales representatives that they want the safest municipal they can get. The salesperson then usually jumps to thinking Triple A, or insured, or gilt edge, making the job of selling bonds easier. This may be an easy way to part a customer from his money, but I prefer the approach epitomized by the sign on my favorite shoe store's wall. "Don't ask for a size, ask to be fitted." Thinking safe about bonds is like approaching safety on the highway and thinking, "Watch out for the bicycles", when plenty of cars and trucks are whizzing left and right. *When* you buy a bond is much more important than *what* you buy. *Ten* times more important. I know that conventional bond investing advice dwells almost exclusively with safety of principal at maturity—the bicycles on the municipal bond road. But overemphasizing credit is the biggest mistake most people make in buying bonds. Don't get me wrong—credit quality does count. But it's relatively easy to pick strong bonds. Good timing, timing the levels of future interest rates and inflation, is a lot harder, and far more rewarding. We return to bond credit analysis in Chapter 25. First let's look at the cars and trucks on the municipal bond highway—interest rates and inflation.

23

Federal and Municipal Bond Interest Rates

Our federal government is perennially the world's largest borrower and long term municipal bond values generally move up and down with Treasuries. Figure 3.1 shows this powerful correlation. When do interest rates tend to rise? When the economy experiences faster growth, creating more demand for money and the Federal Reserve tightens the money supply. As we will see in more detail in Chapter 3, higher rates automatically bring loss of market value for existing bonds. If you hold some bonds paying 7% and similar ones become available at 8%, then naturally your old 7's become less attractive and will be worth less than the 8's. A perfectly sound long term 7% tax-exempt bought at 100 will probably sink in the marketplace to 90 cents on the original dollar, a decline of 10%.

In the other direction, interest rates tend to fall and bond values rise when the economy slows down and the Fed loosens up on money. Then, good long 8% bonds will probably go up in price, perhaps from 100 to 110 cents on the face amount, up 10%. In both cases the bond's security stays stable but its market value fluctuates sharply with the rise and fall of interest rates.

Buy Them When Their Yield Is Right

What can an individual do in the midst of such cosmic forces? Make an estimate about future interest rates. This may sound like an impossible task, but there are several guidelines. In the 1980's long term municipal bond interest rates fluctuated between 5 1/2% and 13% and averaged around 8 1/2%. In the 70's they went from a low of 5% to a high of 7%, and averaged out at about 6%. So, overall, tax-exempt bonds have returned something like 7 1/2% annually in the usable past. *If long term municipal bond interest rates fall under 8%, I don't like them.* Over 8%, and I am much more positive. Perhaps the best price guide is *The Bond Buyer* 40 bond index, which appears in many newspaper financial sections. This average reflects the yields on a basket of long-term upper-medium quality tax-exempts. When you can buy bonds like these at yields of 8% or higher, they have usually been good buys. At under 7% long maturity municipal bonds have most often proved poor performers. I see this trend continuing for the foreseeable future. These yields apply to U.I.T.s, to managed funds, and to direct investing, as discussed in each section. See figure 26.1.

This formula may sound easy, but there's a catch. The 8% guideline is only valid in hindsight, and has to be revised as conditions change. No one can predict where interest rates will go, we can only feel our way along. But at 8% they feel good to me.

Figure 3.1
LONG TERM U.S. AND MUNICIPAL BOND YIELDS

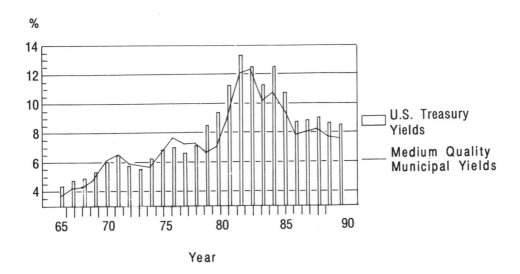

Year

So this is the first safety sign on the highway for long term investing—8. Look at Figure 3.1. See that 8% is slightly higher than the average yield level in the past twenty years. Follow the municipal line onward from 8% and see that yields tend down, sometimes a few years later. Follow the line from 7%. Afterwards, yields usually go up. Here's where I take a stand—8% on good grade, long term tax-exempts.

You will probably find that this is the point where salespeople will resist you most. *Now* is always their idea of when to buy. Now, now, now. Explain this theory and you'll get a thousand arguments to the contrary—here's a special value, the market is turning up, you can lock in a *sure* 6% forever, etc., etc. Don't listen. Watch. Watch what happens below and above 8% and see for yourself. Don't buy long term municipal bonds unless you get 8%, on *good* bonds, not the junk you will probably be offered once a salesperson finds out you have some 8% tax-exempt money to spend NOW.

☞ WILSON ADVISES

Avoid long term municipal bonds when they yield less than 8%.

Yield - Inflation = Real Rate of Return

What is bond principal's other big enemy? Inflation. In 1978, $6,000 could buy you a standard Chevrolet, while the same amount now only buys a couple of snowmobiles. Such shrinkage shows the threat of inflation to hard-earned savings. Inflation at 5% a year eats up bond purchasing power at that rate. This is twenty times worse than defaults at their average of less than 1/4% annually.

Let's take the measure of this persistent foe, this indiscriminate attacker of both interest and principal, and see how to defend yourself. To do so accurately, you're going to have to figure what the rate of inflation will be in the foreseeable future. As one guide, the Consumer Price Index has gone up an average of about 5% annually in the past twenty years, once reaching 13 1/2%. Even a 10% income doesn't help much when prices are rising at 12%, so more important to us is the *real rate of return*. The real, spendable interest rate is defined as *yield minus inflation*. Which is higher, a 12% yield or an 8% yield? It depends. Even a tax-exempt 12% minus 12% inflation is a zero real return, nothing for your money. But if you can get a 9% yield when inflation is at 6%, you have bought a much better deal. 9% minus 6% leaves a real income of 3%.

When long-term tax-exempts holders have received 3% more than inflation, they usually have achieved good investment results. Bonds at 8%, take away inflation at 5%, and you have a 3% true, after-inflation, return. This is the second signal for an open tax-exempt highway. *A 3% true return*. The managers of the American economy, especially the Federal Reserve, seem to have learned a lot about controlling inflation, but don't count on it too heavily. If you can buy good municipals at 8% and figure that the rate of inflation during the life of the bonds will be 5%, then you will have a 3% true yield, and a good long-term return. *8, 3*.

No one has a reliable crystal ball and no one can dependably predict future inflation rates. However, if you figure that inflation is going up, beware of long-term bonds, municipal or other. When you can again get a 3% real return, then you'll have a better chance of achieving your savings goals.

Figure 3.2
MUNICIPAL BONDS—PRICES AND YIELDS VS. CPI CHANGES

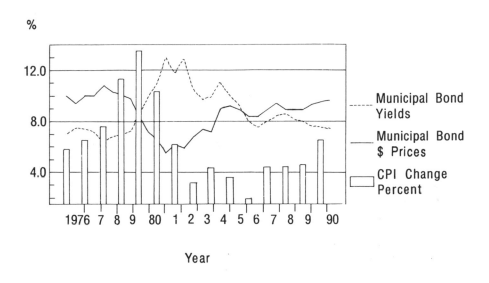

☞ *WILSON ADVISES*

Avoid municipal bonds unless their yield is at least 3% higher than inflation.

The Tax-exempt/Treasury Spread

The third bond signal is an interest rate spread. Tax-frees usually move with governments: one up, the other up, and vice versa. However, they don't move like riders on a bicycle built for two, always at the identical distance from each other—they're more like two regular bikers traveling together. Governments always pedal on ahead, yielding more, while their municipal companion trails behind. However, the distances between them vary, with municipals sometimes almost catching up, and sometimes falling far behind. We measure this differential by taking a percentage—good grade tax-free yields divided by long term Treasury yields.

83 is our third and last guideline number. In the usable past, when returns on long term, good quality (A-rated) municipal bonds are 83% or higher than the rates on long Treasuries, their holders have done well. When, for instance, long U.S. bonds are offered at 10%, and you can buy good grade municipals at 85% of that (8.50%), it's a pretty favorable time to buy them. Why? Because higher percentages come from either temporary over-supply or under-demand for tax-frees, usually making them good buys. The higher the percentage, the better the deal. If municipal yields rise to 90% of Treasuries, their investors usually come out really well; under 80%, less well; under 70% of Treasuries, they have performed poorly. Again, the handiest tax-exempt yield gauge is the *Bond Buyer* 40 bond index which appears in most financially oriented newspapers.

☞ *WILSON ADVISES*

Avoid long term tax-exempts unless they return at least 83% of the long term U.S. bond yield.

Capital Losses

I realize that many investors aren't used to thinking about losses on their municipals. People ask what difference it makes if their bonds go down in the market—they still get the yield they contracted for, right? Right. A bond bought to yield 7% will return that average annual percentage when held to maturity. However, if prices go down in the meantime, these things go wrong: 1.) You lose the opportunity to obtain the new, higher returns. 2.) The marketing cost (the selling and replacing charges) can be high, often equalling a year's interest income. In a sense, good municipal bonds are virtually loss-proof if you wait until they mature. But who wants to wait for 30 years to get even? The time to think about price changes is before you buy. Afterward, you may find yourself just watching the prices go up or down, until you finally decide you've had enough. Don't invest and forget, it's a costly practice.

Problems With Existing Portfolios

Speaking of losses, let's take a moment to apply some of these ideas to existing tax-exempt portfolios. Over 90% of municipal purchases are made by investors who already own tax-frees. Therefore, the greatest risks and the biggest losses are incurred in *existing* portfolios of bonds. If you are already invested in the long term municipal market, immediately review your position and your holdings. If the market background is favorable—8, 3, 83—and if your bonds suit your investment criteria, then stay on the tax-exempt road, you're in good shape. If not, if the market signals are unfavorable, or your holdings unsuitable, start planning how to improve your position. One possibility is to sell the old, inappropriate holdings and replace them with bonds offering better values. You can find specifics on how to sell each of the tax-exempt categories—U.I.T.s, managed funds, and unbundled bonds—in the various sections following, especially Chapter 26.

PICKING THE RETURN

Current or Total Return?

Now let's divide you municipal bond buyers into two groups—those who invest for income now and those who invest for later. *Current return* investors and *total return* investors. In the first group go people who need extra income now, for this month's and this year's bills, and who can't afford to wait until, next century to maximize their investment returns. In the second go those who are in a position to save their current income and reinvest it.

Most people who can't make ends meet comfortably with their ordinary earnings choose to spend their investment income right now. However, you can usually get a better overall return by investing in bonds that yield less now and more later. A household with enough other income to meet present expenses can reasonably invest for the long-term, earning the highest possible eventual return, compounded. Even zero coupon bonds might be the ideal vehicle for this group.

Which One Are You?

Which group are you in, the income now or the income later investors? A quick answer can be found in how you handle your interest coupons and dividends. Do you deposit them right into your checking account to spend immediately, or do

Figure 3.3
CURRENT YIELD AND TOTAL YIELD

Amount Invested	Investment Type	Price	Total Yield	Annual Income	Current Yield
$50,000	Money market fund	100	5.00%	$2,500	5.00%
50,000	Medium term bond	100	6.50%	3,250	6.50%
50,000	Long term bond	100	8.00%	4,000	8.00%
50,000	Long term discount	50	8.50%	3,100	6.20%

you let them ride, reinvesting in more securities? Some people do both, spending part and investing part, but to the extent that you spend these checks you are an income investor, and you should be earning a maximum return now. To the extent that you save and reinvest your investment income, you should be putting it to work for maximum *total* return. Note that we're not talking about getting the best overall investment deal, just whether you need to maximize your bond income for spending today, or whether you can afford to get a higher eventual return by letting your income accumulate and compound for years to come.

Investing for Current Income

Which of the tax-exempt investments listed in Figure 3.3 provides the maximum *current* income, income to spend today? Definitely the third one, with an 8% coupon paying $4,000 annually. If you need the cash this year look at this kind of investment first.

Investing for Total Return

Which of tthese investments is most suitable for people who can afford to seek the highest *total* return? The last one, the long term discount investment at a 8.50% yield. At the cost of lower yield now those who can afford to wait to see their low coupon bonds bought at 50 cents on the dollar and eventually mature at 100 will get the higher overall return. We dealers call this a spread of fifty *basis points* in favor of the discount investment (8.50% vs. 8%), with one basis point equalling 1/100% in yield. How does the skimpy 6.20% now yield grow to 8.50%? A combination of the 6.20% current income and the slow growth to full value, 100, at maturity.

SHORT TERM INVESTING

Let's picture permanent municipal bond investing as a busy highway, an Interstate representing long term tax-exempts. Alongside the highway runs a quieter, local road—short term tax-exempts. Most individual bond investors should plan eventually to get on the high-speed high-yield Interstate, in long term bonds. But first, make sure the going is good, that the market is favorable. If traffic on the Interstate is bumper-to-bumper, with low yields and low real returns, put your savings into highly liquid, short dated municipals by sticking to the local road. Then, when the Interstate clears, when the signals read 8, 3, 83, put your money into long term municipals. In the meanwhile, follow Cervantes advice—'patience and shuffle the cards'.

Short Term Tax-exempt Investments

We touched on municipal *notes* earlier, whereby issuers borrow for a few months to temporarily finance a local government need. These obligations (and also other tax-exempts originally issued with longer maturities and nearing their payoff dates) are available for investors whose needs are temporary. The easiest way to invest in these is through one of the many tax-exempt money market funds such as described in Chapter 15, which hold portfolios of good grade notes and bonds. Bonds issued by the state of Florida and due within four months can be counted on to mature on schedule. Money market funds invested in them and similar obligations will surely pay 100% of your investment back, with interest, on demand. We say that such securities have *high liquidity*.

There are several ways short term municipals fit into investment strategies. 1.) If you owe some money on a certain date, such as for taxes due April 15, it would be foolish to put it in long term bonds, where a decline in price might impair your ability to pay what you owe. 2.) If you don't trust the long term bond market. When the signals are 7, 2, 83, for instance, and not 8, 3, 83. In either case, short term, highly liquid securities may suit you, on the slow but steady local road when Interstate 2031 is jammed. Why ever get off this safe road? Because the speed limit is so low there. In exchange for high liquidity you get lower income.

Intermediate and Long Term Bonds

So, highly liquid short term bonds and funds are almost loss-proof and carry low yields. They are ideal resting places when the market is unfavorable for long term buyers. When the signals are fine, you can ease onto the highway, in either its slower intermediate maturity (due in 10 to 15 years) lane, or directly into the more volatile *long term maturity* fast lane.

Some U.I.T.s, many managed funds and plenty of unpackaged bonds, offer intermediate maturity tax-exempts. For instance, when money markets return 5%, intermediate bonds might return 7%. In a period of sharply rising rates instead of being loss free, bonds due in 10 years or so can typically suffer declines averaging something like 25% of principal. On U.I.T.s, managed funds or plain bonds with maturities of 20 or more years you can lose even more, up to 30 to 40% of your principal. On the other hand the longest bonsbring in the highest yields. We shall return to risks and rewards in Chapters 11, 17 and 25.

The Yield Curve

Here we see a fundamental fact of bond life emerging—the *yield curve*. We just talked about how yields rise—as from 5%, to 6.5% to 8%—as maturity lengthens. Short dated bonds usually pay the lowest available interest rates; medium term bonds carry higher rates; and longest bonds still higher, producing an *upward sloping, positive yield curve,* our most usual bond market pattern. More years, more yield. See figure 3.4 for three different curves

Why do the yield curves usually slope upward with length of maturity? Supply and demand. Usually there are more long term municipal bonds in the market than short, and usually more people want short bonds than long. So both supply and demand drive short term yields down. Why do more people usually want short terms? Because they carry less market risk. It works similarly with managed funds. Short funds yield less, and are less volatile than intermediate maturity funds, which in turn yield less and fluctuate less than long terms. In municipals liquidity and maturity are virtually identical.

Now let's see where we are. We have divided investing into two parts— one with a short time frame and one that commits for many years. To reach goals that are only months away take the local road, of limited maturity tax-exempts. If your goal is more distant, first take the local road, temporarily investing in tax-exempt money market funds until the highway is clear. Then, onto the long term higher yield roadway, saving and compounding your way to success. Tax-exempt rates 8%? Yields minus inflation 3%? 83% ratio? If so your longterm results should be better than average. Not riskless, but you should have an excellent chance of making good time.

Figure 3.4
THE MUNICIPAL BOND YIELD CURVES

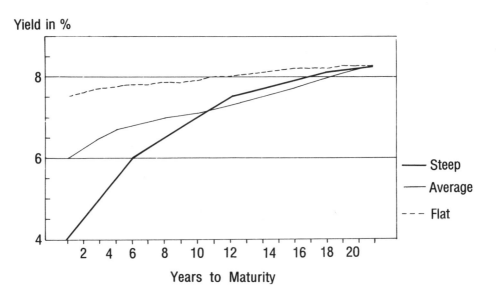

Dollar Cost Averaging

If you are investing regularly, every year or so as the money comes in, then maybe you are practicing *dollar cost averaging* without even realizing it. However, if you have suddenly acquired a large amount of money, from insurance or other sources such as the sale of a business, invest only *part* of your assets in long term bonds. When market conditions are favorable, invest just a fraction, no more than a third at one time. This is *dollar cost averaging*, a tried and true way to minimize market risk. You automatically buy more when prices are cheap and fewer when they're high, thus producing superior results. If conditions are not favorable, then wait, keeping your money loss-proof until the highway traffic is moving well. In the meanwhile, patience. Over the longest horizons investing in riskless short term bonds has given individuals perfectly

Figure 3.5
THE PATH TO SUCCESSFUL TAX-EXEMPT INVESTING

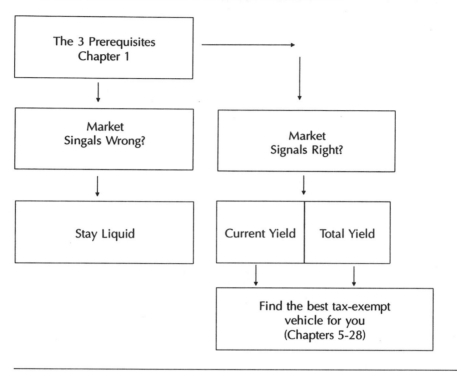

acceptable total returns. Stay out of traffic jams. Then, when the way is clear, zoom into the fast lane.

So that's my strategic outline. Check your prerequisites for buying tax-exempts. Wait until the bond market is in a favorable phase. Figure which you want to emphasize—yield now or a higher yield eventually. Keep highly liquid in short terms. Then pounce on good long term tax-exempts. We cover pouncing in the sections on U.I.T.s, managed funds and plain, unbundled bonds.

SUMMARY ** CHAPTER 3 ** SUMMARY

Strategy For Long Term Investment

- Good bonds are easy to pick; good timing is harder.
- *When* you buy is ten times more important than *what* you buy.
- The biggest losses in bond values are caused by inflation.
- The second biggest are from rising interest rates.
- Aim for either high current return or high total return.
- The longer the bond the greater the risk.
- The longer the bond the greater the return.
- Wait until long term municipals yield 8%.
- Wait until long term municipals yield 3% more than inflation.
- Wait until long term municipals yield at least 83% of U.S. Treasuries.
- Then pounce.

CHAPTER 4

AN INDIVIDUAL INVESTOR CASE EXAMPLE—PART 1

The Unit Investment Trusts

Now let's look at two strictly imaginary investors, Marci and Joe Zotti, to see what questions might be asked about tax-exempt bonds. They will ask a lot—too much for a typical investor, commented Jim Lebenthal after he reviewed this work—but please bear with their inquiries for the educational effect. In 1991 the Zottis were living and working in New York City and one day Joe told Marci how he had made his first investment back in Ohio some years earlier. He had seen an advertisement for something describing itself as a *unit investment trust* which was promising tax-exempt income. The ad was obviously aimed at small investors like himself, so he mailed in its coupon and soon a salesman telephoned him. Joe listened to his pitch, was assured that these unit investment trusts were extremely safe, paid 7.2% income, and really were tax-exempt. Joe had saved $19,000 and calculated that if he invested $14,000 that would leave a comfortable $5,000 in his money market account.

The salesman went on to explain that not only was the U.I.T. diversified, but that it contained fifteen different issues of bonds. Joe asked if he could

37

invest just $14,000, and the salesman said sure, since they were selling at exactly $1,000 a unit, fourteen units would cost him $14,000. He said that this would give him a yearly income of $72 per unit, or $1,008, and Joe agreed to invest the $14,000. After giving the salesman his Social Security number and a lot of other information he inquired about the prospectus the ad had advised him to read before investing. The salesman said he would send him one, it was just the fine print, and reminded him to mail in his check promptly and that was that.

Joe told Marci that he had wanted to ask *why* the trust was exempt from Federal income tax, among other questions, but had not. It was pretty hard sell, he thought. But he had made the commitment, so he filled out some forms when they arrived and returned them along with his check. He soon received a certificate of trust ownership for fourteen units of *Gamma National Tax-Exempt #31* and a 56-page prospectus. Soon he began to receive his monthly income as promised. It was a start.

Joe had checked out what rate of interest he was getting at $1,008 a year. He simply divided this by the investment, $14,000, and came up with .072. He calculated that this was 7.20% a year and according to one method of figuring, *current yield*, he was right.

☞ *A DEFINITION*

Current Yield

The annual percentage return on an investment, excluding any gain or loss of principal. In U.I.T.s, yearly income divided by unit price.

Current Yield

The return you will receive on your money every year is its *current yield*. It's your *now* yield, your investment's annual production of income, ignoring any eventual gain or loss of principal. Current yield is an overall term applying to stocks, bonds, and other securities, in fact sometimes it's called *stock yield*, and can be seen as one column in the stock pages of most newspapers. To calculate current yield divide income by price. At a price of exactly $1,000 it's easy. Suppose a U.I.T. pays $80 a year per unit, and its price is $1,000. $80 divided by $1,000 is .08, or a current yield of 8%. If the same trust paid only $64, this divided by $1,000 produces 6.40%, etc. Joe's fourteen units paid $1,008 a year;

dividing this investment of $14,000 gave him the correct current yield, 7.20%, as advertised.

Premium Trusts

What happens when the price is higher than $1,000, or at what is called a premium? If Joe had paid $1,010 for each unit instead of $1,000, it would still be paying $72 a year; but by applying the same formula, $72 divided by $1,010 produces a lower current yield, 7.13%. The income distribution ($72) stays fixed; however, since the amount invested is $10 higher than before, the current yield falls. This makes sense—if you put up more money to get the same income every year, then you are getting a poorer deal—and the lower current yield shows it. At $1,020 the current yield would be 7.06%, at $1,030, 6.99%, and so on.

Another fundamental of investing has surfaced right here—*prices and yields move inversely,* that is, they move in opposite directions. This applies to all securities—bonds, stocks, trusts, funds, etc. So *when prices go up, yields go down and when prices go down, yields go up,* automatically. Price up? Yield down. You can't get away from it.

Figure 4.1
CURRENT YIELD

Principal Amount	Invested Amount	Percentage Price	Annual Income	Current Yield
$ 1,000	$ 1,000	100	$ 72	7.20%
1,000	1,010	101	72	7.13%
1,000	980	98	72	7.35%
1,000	1,000	100	80	8.00%
50,000	50,000	100	4,000	8.00%
100,000	100,000	100	8,000	8.00%
100,000	101,000	101	8,000	7.92%
100,000	95,000	95	7,500	7.89%

Discount Trusts

At $1,000, U.I.T.s currently yield their payout rate exactly; at a premium they yield less; finishing the picture, under $1,000 they yield more. If Joe paid $990 for the same trust returning $72 a year, then the current yield would be 7.27% (72 divided by 990 = 7.27%); at $980 the current would be 7.35%, etc. When the price goes down, the yield goes up. And, as the yield goes up, the price comes down, it's automatic.

U.I.T.s used to be sold priced by their current yield, abusively. Now they are sold according to a fairer gauge, *long-term return,* which adds in gains or losses of principal. For a further discussion of yield see Chapter 20.

Joe told Marci that the Gamma prospectus contained a lot of dire warnings about what might happen to the bonds in the trust. It even seemed to say that Cleveland had defaulted a few years back, which sounded strange to him, and he figured that these were just explanations put in for the protection of the trust sponsors. Back then it was all too complicated and technical to understand, and so he put the prospectus away with the certificate. For about a year the investment firm kept sending literature offering a variety of stock and bond mutual funds, but he never heard from that salesman again, which was fine with him.

Second Thoughts

Joe's first encounter with unit investment trusts is a typical one. It introduced him to a perfectly good security yielding a tax-exempt 7.20%. However, the service he received was poor—how could he depend on a company that sold him and forgot him?

By 1991 Joe and Marci's picture had changed. They were earning a lot more, about $60,000 a year each, and had saved over $100,000. They figured that with $10,000 a month coming in they were well off financially. However, when they began to talk about taxes, the mood changed.

The Zottis were definitely in the top income brackets, and would be paying about $30,000 to the I.R.S. plus plenty to New York State and New York City. It's true that their state and local income taxes were a deductible item on their federal filing, but on the last dollars coming in, their discretionary investment income, they were paying 39%. They figured that investment income comes in last, since they would continue their careers regardless of how much money their investments brought in. Counting Social Security payments, their tax bill was a depressingly large amount. Marci suggested getting some professional tax or financial planning help, but Joe thought they could do it better themselves, and learn a few things too. So they decided to put everything down on paper, as shown in Figures 4.2 and 4.3.

Figure 4.2
MARCELLA AND JOSEPH ZOTTI, JR.
INVESTMENTS - 1990

	Market Value	Before Taxes		After Taxes	
		Rate	Income	Rate	Income
Certificate of Deposit	$45,000	7.75%	$3,488	4.75%	$2,139*
Money market accounts	10,000	6.5%	650	3.99%	399*
Common stock mutual fund	36,000	3.6%	1,296	2.21%	798*
U.S.Treasury Bond	20,000	7.2%	1,440	4.97%	994**
Gamma Nat. Tax-Exempt #31	14,000	7.2%	1,008	6.65%	931***
Totals	$125,000	6.31%	$7,882	4.21%	$5,261

* Federal (31%), New York State (7.7%) and New York City (3.4%) taxes, after crediting Federal deduction, leave 61% to spend.

**Federal leaves only 69% to spend.

***State and city leave only 92% to spend.

The couple had accumulated some of their savings through a periodic mutual fund purchase plan, but the investment results never seemed satisfactory. They felt that their money was not growing fast enough and cast about for a place to invest away from securities, in a business opportunity, but couldn't come up with anything reasonable. They saw that the little U.I.T. left them a higher return after tax than any of their other investments, providing them more food for thought about tax-exempts.

Over the next few days and weeks both Joe and Marci began to notice the many magazine and newspaper articles and television programs about tax-free products. Many kinds seemed to be available—U.I.T.s and managed funds, as well as individual bonds, like those of the Port Authority of New York, or The New York State Dormitory Authority. In fact, they got a call from a bond salesman on the phone one night but his approach was so crude they preferred to struggle on themselves.

Figure 4.3
MARCELLA AND JOSEPH ZOTTI, JR.
INCOME AND TAXES

	Federal	*New York State*	*N.Y.C.*
Earned Income	$132,000	$132,000	$132,000
Investment Income	6,874	6,442	6,442
Total Income	138,874	138,442	138,442
Adjustments (IRA)	4,000	4,000	4,000
Adjusted Gross Income	134,874	134,442	134,442
Deductions			
New York State Income Tax	8,969	0	0
New York City Income Tax	3,939	0	0
Other	8,000	9,500	9,500
Exemptions	4,000	0	0
Taxable Income	109,666	124,942	124,942
Tax	$ 27,112	$ 8,969	$ 3,939

Source: Nathan & Roccamo, C.P.A., Forest Hills, New York

The yields they saw were fair enough, but they wanted to know more before they made a substantial investment. The great variety confused them so thoroughly they even considered the easy way out—keeping their savings in money market accounts or buying the C.D.s their bank was always pushing.

Investment Decisions

Joe and Marci's predicament is a common one, shared by many younger Americans, and some not so young as well. As outlined in the Introduction, they qualified for municipal bond buying. They had accumulated worthwhile savings, their income was far above average, and neither of them knew of any profitable private investment deal. Confused as they were they persisted—the advantage of tax-exemption is a powerful attraction. Now let's see if we can find some answers to their questions, starting with U.I.T.s.

SUMMARY ** CHAPTER 4 ** SUMMARY

An Individual Investor Case Example—Part 1

- Current yield is income divided by investment.

- It is the now yield, this year's return.

- Reliable information on tax-exempt products is hard to find.

Section II
Unit Investment Trusts

WHITE'S INVESTMENT RATING : *

CHAPTER 5

INTRODUCTION TO
U.I.T.S

The Unit Investment Trusts

Packages of municipal bonds come in two main varieties—*unit investment trusts* and *managed funds*. We describe unit investment trusts—*U.I.T.s* for short—starting with this chapter. Section III deals with managed funds, beginning in Chapter 13.

Wall Street had been creating and selling many kinds of stock and corporate bond packages since way back in 1924 but was not allowed to do this with municipal bonds until 1961. Then, after Ira Haupt & Co. finally convinced the I.R.S. to permit trusts to pass through tax-exempt bond interest to potential buyers, they put together and sold the first municipal bond unit investment trust. Figure 5.1 shows the story of U.I.T.'s subsequent development. Unfortunately for them, Haupt isn't enjoying the fruits of their hybrid tree—their firm perished in the sorry salad oil scandal of 1963.

☞ *A DEFINITION*

Unit Investment Trust (U.I.T.)

A *fiduciary (trust) entity, closed end* in structure, which holds a *fixed portfolio* of municipal bonds from which it distributes *tax-exempt income*.

The Four Trust Elements

Unit investment trusts are standard items, all sharing one common form. They are formal fiduciaries (trusts), are closed end, their portfolios are fixed, and they stay strictly in tax-exempt municipal bonds.

1 - The Trust

U.I.T.s are *trusts*, a specialized financial vehicle formed by a contract, a *Trust Agreement*, between a sponsor (a bond dealer or other securities company), a trustee, and (usually) an evaluator. The *sponsor* creates the U.I.T.; the *trustee* holds the securities, guards unit holders' rights, and sends out the checks; and the *evaluator* prices the bond portfolio. A formal fiduciary, closed end, fixed portfolio and tax-exempt. You may wish to skip ahead to compare these features with managed funds as described in Chapter 14.

2 - Closed End

U.I.T.s are *closed end,* that is, each separate trust is offered and sold to the public just once. U.I.T. shares are called *units*, each standing for one fractional interest of the whole. Joe had bought fourteen parts of a 10,000 unit trust, and so owned 14/10,000 of its principal value. He also was due .14% of its $720,000 annual income, or $1,008 per year. For example, in Chapter 9 we will see an imaginary offering of Gamma New York Tax Exempt Trust #66 which came out with 10,000 units. This trust would remain at 10,000 units until its bonds are retired. Sponsors package U.I.T.s, one after another, each one belonging to a long series of separate but similar trusts. After sponsors sell out #66 they package and sell #67 as quickly as they can.

3 - Fixed Portfolio, Fixed Maturity

U.I.T.'s are composed of *fixed portfolios* of municipal securities. The sponsor assembles ten or more different lots of municipal bonds and deposits (transfers ownership of) them to a trustee, according to an irrevocable (unchanging) trust agreement. These bonds remain in this trust permanently. No new bonds are bought and none are sold, so the original securities stay fixed and put. As a result, the income they pay out is also fixed. Joe was getting $72 a year for each of his units, and will keep getting $72 until the trust's bonds are retired. What you see is what you get, and keep—sponsors don't trade trust portfolios in or out. You can buy a trust's initial offering, hold on to it for many years, and see its original bonds pay off at their exact principal worth.

With this fixed portfolio goes a *fixed maturity*, providing a certain amount of security—if all goes as planned you'll get your money back on the bonds' retirement dates. If you ever get confused by the difference between trusts and funds (as plenty of people, even bond dealers, do), if it has a *fixed* portfolio of bonds it *has* to be a U.I.T.—the only kind of municipal bond bundle that stays permanently put. U.I.T.s are *unmanaged*. The managed funds, as their name says, are *managed*, that is, their bonds are sold and replaced as conditions change. A package of fixed bonds? U.I.T. A package of traded bonds? Managed fund.

4 - Tax Free Income

U.I.T.s pay out income *exempt from Federal income tax*. As we have said, municipal bond interest is shielded by federal law from the I.R.S. This interest passes through to holders tax-free, according to the number of units owned. The advantage of earning tax free income is clear, and the many ads do their best to dramatize this to individual customers.

Convenience Features

There's no doubt that unit trusts provide investors with great convenience. The bond chores performed by their trustees include: 1.) Collecting interest and sending out income checks; 2.) Watching for bonds being called and maturing, and distributing these monies; 3.) Issuing annual reports; and 4.) Redeeming units

Figure 5.1
U.I.T. SALES AND SPONSORS

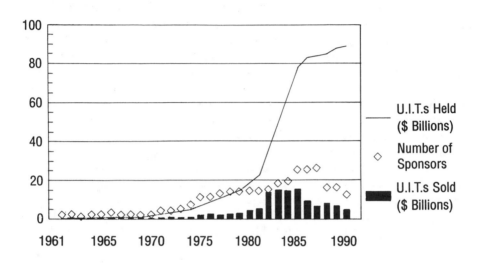

upon request. In addition, the prices investors pay for trusts are set by a reasonably fair method of evaluation. So to a certain extent U.I.T.s offer trouble-free investing, an attractive proposition to many individual buyers.

The Sponsor Creates a Trust Series

Now a word about our sponsors, the investment houses that manufacture these wonderful U.I.T. vehicles. Some are regular *dealers* like real life Merrill Lynch or John Nuveen, or our imaginary Gamma. Others are *independent investment managers*, such as Vanguard, T. Rowe Price, or Dreyfus. Sponsors first set up a trust series format using a single blanket indenture (legal authorizing document), such as for a series which invests only in insured bonds, or in bonds exempt from Ohio income tax, etc. The sponsor is the quarterback, calling the plays for the special teams that create the trust series, including lawyers, a trustee, and an evaluator.

Marketing a Trust

After a trust series type, such as Gamma Ohio Tax-Exempt, is completed, the sponsor forms a syndicate called an *underwriting group,* a cluster of dealers associated by contract for this special purpose. The lead sponsor's trust traders then assemble a group of bonds which fit its purposes, then hands off this packaged ball, perhaps Gamma Ohio #1, to the underwriting group to sell to customers. This process is called the *initial public offering,* or I.P.O..

Although trusts are officially formed for the benefit of their unit holders, their sponsors are the active element—first, last, and always. Sponsors accumulate bonds at their discretion, deposit them with a trustee, and its underwriting group sells the trust units. Afterward they supervise the evaluation process, re-register the trust with the S.E.C. every year, and (although they can't trade its bonds around) monitor the trust portfolio; if they discover approaching credit troubles they can liquidate bonds. For a nominal yearly fee sponsors perform these and other similar chores until the bonds are paid off and the trust eventually expires. Where do they make their serious money? During the bond assembly and selling phases, to which we will return later.

Where to Buy a U.I.T.

There's no problem finding a U.I.T. to buy—as Joe and Marci found, they're very likely to come and get you. Sponsors and other brokers spend millions to advertise in all the media. Many printed ads feature response coupons—send one in, as Joe did, and you'll soon get a call from a young and hungry trust pitcher. Most of the radio and television ads provide toll free, even twenty-four hour a day, telephone numbers. Sometimes registered salespeople pick up your call, but more often you'll get a trained phone answerer. If you seem serious enough, and meet their minimum dollar requirement, then you'll surely get a follow up sales call.

The various features of bond trusts add up to a sophisticated parcel of consumer goods carefully shaped for high-powered advertising and finally sold by persistent sales forces. U.I.T. benefits may be summarized like this:

1.) *Bond selection.* Trusts are assembled by professional sponsors, so you don't need to know a thing about the municipal bond market, or its specific securities.

2.) *Portfolio diversification.* Since the risk is spread among many issues, if anything happens to just one of the component bonds investors lose only on that fraction. A dozen eggs in twelve baskets. Protected by di-

Figure 5.2
U.I.T. FAMILIES AND THEIR SPONSORS

Trust Name	Lead Sponsor	Market Share	Location	Telephone
Nuveen, I.M.T.	John Nuveen	30.1%	Chicago	312-917-7810
M.I.T.	Merrill Lynch	25.8%	Princeton	800-282-8800
Van Kampen	Van Kampen Merritt	17.0%	Chicago	800-225-2222
First Trust	Clayton Brown	7.0%	Chicago	800-621-1675
Tax Exempt Securitites Trust	Smith Barney	5.0%	New York	800-223-2532
National Municipal	Prudential	*3.3%	New York	800-221-3088
Kemper	Kemper	2.9%	Chicago	800-422-2848
Empire State, M.I.N.T.	Glickenhaus	2.8%	New York	212-953-7532
Municipal Securities Trust	Bear Stearns	2.4%	New York	800-237-7020
Sears Municipal	Dean Witter	*2.1%	New York	800-The-Dean
Municipal Bond Trust	PaineWebber	*1.2%	New Jersey	201-902-3000

*Also underwriters of Municipal Investment Trusts (M.I.T)

versity, sponsors can securely buy medium quality, and thus higher yielding, bonds.

3.) *Tax-free return.* Free from Federal income tax, and often from state and local levies as well.

4.) *Convenience.* With a minimum of fuss you can lock in almost any investable amount and throw away the key, confident of receiving your income check twice a year, or even monthly. The securities are in safe-keeping, are professionally evaluated, and can be redeemed at any time, producing cash within a few days.

SUMMARY ** CHAPTER 5 ** SUMMARY

Introduction to U.I.T.s

* U.I.T.s are held in a closed end trust for the benefit of their owners.

* The bonds in a trust portfolio are permanently fixed and unmanaged. They are not traded around or added to.

* U.I.T.s offer professional bond selection, portfolio diversification, convenience, and tax-exempt income. They are readily available in any investable amount.

CHAPTER 6

AN INDIVIDUAL INVESTOR CASE EXAMPLE—PART 2

In the meanwhile, Marci and Joe, our imaginary example couple from Chapter 4, were referred by a friend to a municipal bond salesman, one Steve Haddock. Steve worked for Tower Securities in New York and was glad to offer them his financial services. Joe said that he and Marci were interested in learning more about tax-exempts, especially U.I.T.s, and Steve promised to explain everything to them, no problem. After being briefed on their income and investments, Steve informed them that Joe's Ohio trust was subject to New York's state and local income taxes. He mentioned that Tower was offering some U.I.T.s which were *triple exempt,* that is, free from all three income taxes, federal, state, and also New York City, at a 7% yield. Steve went on to point out the advantages of U.I.T.s' diversification, explain how they are evaluated daily, and introduced him to another feature that some trusts carry—insurance against loss of principal.

Salesman Steve painted quite a rosy picture, but the Zottis naturally had some doubts. Rightly so—a *salesman* is paid to *sell,* and it's a rare one who takes his customer's entire financial situation into account, or who fully and frankly describes his product. Although Wall Street salesmen aren't supposed to misrepresent the facts, they really can't be relied on to present a balanced investment system. It's up to you to dig out the whole story and how it applies to you and not to fall for a one-sided sales line.

In the following days, Joe noticed half a dozen ads for tax-free investments—plain unpackaged municipal bonds, something called no-load funds (some of which offered check writing privileges), as well as U.I.T.s. Meanwhile, Marci called or wrote four different bond advertisers, stopped in three book stores, went to the public library twice, and even looked at a college course catalogue. After weeks of trying, her results were poor. Neither the bookstores nor the library had anything about tax-exempts, and no courses on investing were offered until September. Several bond companies did send kits filled with booklets and prospectuses, but the booklets were too general and too simple, nothing but selling their product, really, and the prospectuses were impossible to understand. It was discouraging, because the only sources of information seemed to come from people trying to sell them bonds, or U.I.T.s, or whatever.

Going over the U.I.T. sales brochures Joe and Marci did find some bits of valuable information. Most of the trusts were priced at about $1,000 each, and every portfolio seemed to be composed of many bonds, with no mention about trading them around. They concluded, rightly, that a fixed income flows to U.I.T. holders to the end of its life. They saw that some trusts were insured, which sounded safe enough, but they figured that they could still lose money, in a way they didn't quite grasp.

A few days later, Joe phoned Steve wondering what his old U.I.T. was worth. Steve gave him that day's quote, $1,020 per unit. Joe divided his annual income of $72 per unit by this quote, and got a 7.05% current yield, still not a bad return. Steve agreed, but pointed out that the New York taxes would reduce that to about 6.50%. He explained that Tower was a New York Stock Exchange member firm, and belonged to SIPIC, a securities insurance corporation which protected $100,000 cash in any account, and also $500,000 worth of securities. Steve suggested that Joe send his trust certificate to Tower to get an account opened, which Joe agreed to do.

Joe then asked if the insurance on U.I.T.s would cover all losses, or only part. Steve replied that the insurance guaranteed the portfolio bonds against default, that is, failure to pay principal and interest, but not against a decline their market price. Insured trusts, especially those made of long term bonds, can go up or down, he said, but that they were certain to pay back their principal. Joe asked him if there was a U.I.T. that would lose less than others, and Steve said there was one kind, the short maturity type, but that he didn't recommend them because their yields were so low right then, only about 6%.

Then Joe brought up a more difficult question. If U.I.T.s fell in price, which kind would go down most, the plain ones, or the insured? Steve said it depended, things couldn't be foreseen exactly, and so on. Joe concluded that he really didn't know, but didn't have what it took to admit it. Zotti then asked how he could get a quote on his U.I.T., in *The Wall Street Journal*, for instance? Steve said no—there were too many U.I.T.s to make that practical—but anyone could call up the trust sponsor and get the latest market quote. Winding up his presentation, Steve suggested, considering their savings and their tax bracket, that they put $25,000 to work in 25 units of Gamma New York #66 yielding 7%, triple tax free. To equal this they would have to find a taxable bond at around 11%, which would mean junk, maybe a casino bond. He explained that Gamma was the highest yielding New York U.I.T. and that it was practically certain to pay off.

All in all this U.I.T. sounded pretty good to Joe, and he asked Steve if he had something to read about them? Steve replied that he would send a copy of a prospectus, ending the discussion for then.

SUMMARY ** CHAPTER 6 ** SUMMARY

An Individual Case Example—Part 2

- Do not rely on salespeople for information. Dig it out yourself or get it explained properly.

- Never buy anything you don't understand.

CHAPTER 7

THE U.I.T. MENU

Before we see how U.I.T.s are priced, let's acknowledge somehting I have been hinting about. Wall Street has developed U.I.T.s strictly for little fish—tasty little fish. This shows up most obviously when securities firms reach out for new buyers, often from lists of prospects they've bought, complete with telephone numbers. Bond dealers routinely assign their least experienced sales personnel to canvass this way, salespeople who don't yet have a thick 'book' of customers with whom they do business over and over again. If they did, they wouldn't be calling strangers. It takes a lot of profit to pay for this time-consuming technique, and so, of all municipal bond products, *U.I.T.s carry the highest sales commissions*, enabling dealers to pay for the high expenses of fishing for individual investors, especially new ones.

The other side of the coin is this: without U.I.T.s, many individuals wouldn't be getting tax-exempt income. You can't cover the small investor without charging a lot, and trusts certainly fill this bill. Their *loads*, the usual 4 to 6% markups, are fuel for the engines which propel the U.I.T. machine over rough terrain, year after year. Naturally, the sponsors soft-pedal the load factor, preferring to emphasized the customer benefits. One ad showed parents smiling at each other over their little girl tucked fast asleep in an insured U.I.T. bed. Expect to hear lots of fine sounding, heartwarming phrases from trust salespeople, with only a few figures sprinkled in here and there. I suggest you focus on the *numbers* and filter out those so heartfelt *words*.

HOW U.I.T.S ARE PRICED

Unit Denominations

A U.I.T.'s principal, or face, value is the amount of money the investor will be returned when the bonds in the trust's portfolio are paid off. U.I.T.s come in two sizes or *denominations* of principal value: the more common one is $1,000, and the less common, $100. $1,000 is the denomination used throughout this book—if you ever run into a $100 trust, just multiply by 10 to catch up. These small denominations can certainly be handy for individual investors—we saw that Joe had once bought exactly $14,000 worth, 14 units, which fitted his investment needs to a 'T'.

Unit Pricing

When sponsors design a trust portfolio they usually pack together a bundle of bonds they figure will be priced at just above their principal value, for instance at $1,002, or $1,004.34, etc., load included. They hope to sell the whole issue at that price before the market changes much. However, if the market does change before all the units are sold, the offering price is often adjusted, sometimes downward, and sometimes up. If the evaluation rises by 1% of principal value, then the sponsor has to raise the price by about the same amount, from $1,002 to $1,012, etc. If, instead, the market declines by 1%, then the units may be evaluated one point lower, and the sponsor has to reprice at $992, or whatever. After the issue is all sold the worth of the portfolio continues to fluctuate with the municipal bond market and the evaluation process tracks these movements. You can get this quotation from your broker, or directly from the sponsor, any business day of the year—quite an advantage over most unpackaged bonds which are often harder for individual investors to price.

The Redemption Price

U.I.T.s offer another feature which plain unpackaged bonds do not. Their sponsors stand ready to *redeem,* that is buy back units, at a price based on the current daily evaluation. Suppose you own 25 units of a certain trust and need $10,000 as part of a house down payment. You could get your money by simply selling some or all of the units back to the sponsor. The sponsor pays the evaluated market price, usually less a fee of about $10 per $1,000 unit. For instance, if their evaluated price is $923, the redemption price will be about $913. Selling 11 of the units would raise the $10,000. If the evaluation is down around $846, the redemption will be at $836 and you'd have to liquidate 12 units to realize $10,000. The sponsor assumes the risk of reselling these old 'redeemed' units to new investors. They typically offer them to other investors at their evaluated price plus a load, a handsome 6% markup. Trust sponsors are allowed to advertise "No Redemption Fee", even when their redemption price is $10 under the market valuation. They explain that this is a *price* and not a *fee*.

THE TRUST PORTFOLIO MENU

1 - Arranged by Maturity

Now that we're proficient at trust pricing, let's lay out the general U.I.T. bill of fare, like the booklets of local restaurant menus that you often see in resort towns. Our U.I.T. menu starts with their most significant factor—maturity range. Then we move on to credit quality—national, state, and lower grade trusts. You will find that many sponsors offer most, or even all, of these dishes. For a list of sponsors see Figure 5.2.

As covered in Chapter 3, volatility is a measure of how near a security will stay to cost; in good grade municipals volatility equates to maturity. Back in the early nineteen-sixties the financial world thought that long-term tax-exempts would stay forever in their fifty year trading range of about 2 to 4%. However, we were wrong. Interest rates rose dramatically and many long maturity bond investors, U.I.T. owners among them, experienced the severe losses of principal shown in Figure 3.2, sometimes exceeding 50% of the face amounts. These frightful experiences created demand for a product less vulnerable to market changes and U.I.T.s are now available in short, intermediate, and long maturities. Our example couple, fearing losses on long bonds, heard broker Steve mention the effect of maturity on volatility and we'll see what they decided to do about it in the next chapter.

Short Maturity Trusts

Short maturity U.I.T. portfolios are composed of bonds due within about five years. A short trust sold in 1991 is put together of bonds due in perhaps 1995, 96 and 97. A year later, in 1992, its bonds will have a four year average maturity. In 1993 it will average three years and will be paid off entirely by 1997, when the trust expires. Because 100% of principal will be returned within a relatively short period, this kind of U.I.T. provides high price stability and low volatility. Generally speaking, if five year maturity bond market interest rates go up 1% (as from 5% to 6%), their evaluated market worth drops only about $40, from

$1,000 to $960. Combining this $40 loss with its typical $50 per year income, means that after one year a holder would be about $10 ahead. This applies only to unitholders who do not cash in—for yields if trusts are redeemed see Chapter 10. Investors who hold onto short U.I.T.s get all their principal back in five years, plus the income, a sure total return. Naturally, you pay for this low volatility. Short-term trusts will typically return around 1% less than long term trusts, perhaps only about 6%, rather than 7%. See Figure 12.1

When interest rates rise, you are better off with a short term, rather than a long-term, investment. Not only do you lose less, but at maturity you will be able to invest all your principal at higher rates. But if interest rates fall short, term investors come out worse. When the trusts, or bonds, are paid off, your reinvestment decision comes in a lower interest rate environment. It's up to you to figure which length represents the right owning and risking element. You pays your money and you takes your choice. Chapter 3 had some ideas about choosing. The load on short term U.I.T.s is usually about $20 per $1,000, 2%, or about $4 per year if spread over their 5 year life.

Intermediate Maturity Trusts

Most sponsors offer U.I.T.s with portfolios of bonds neither short nor long, the so-called *intermediate trusts*. Some are called *short* intermediate trusts, about eight years in average original maturity; they provide investors with a medium level of price stability. For every 1% interest rates go up, they will fall in price about $60, or from $1,000 down to $940. This $60 approximates a typical intermediate U.I.T.'s return, so after one year a holder would be even. If rates continue to rise, holders may have to wait the full eight years to get 100% of their principal back. When short U.I.T.s yield 6% and long ones 7%, the short intermediates usually return about 6.25%. Their load averages about $30 per $1,000 principal amount, or $4 annually over a full 8 year life.

Long intermediate trusts are composed of portfolios of about fifteen years average maturity. A 1% rate rise on a twelve to fifteen year maturity will generally produce a decline of about $75 a unit, from $1,000 down to $925. Here again, you may have to wait a long time to get all your investment back. When short trusts are yielding 6% and long term national U.I.T.s 7%, longer intermediate trusts may yield 6.5%. The loads on long intermediate trusts average 4%— $40 per $1,000 unit, which is about $3 per year spread over 15 years.

Longest Maturity Trusts

Long term U.I.T.s are the most common kind offered. In fact when you see a trust advertised without maturity, dollars to doughnuts it's long-term. The reason they are most popular? Long bonds and packages of them provide the highest returns, appealing strongly to the individual investor. Long U.I.T.s are usually invested in twenty-five to thirty year bonds, exposing their holders to the greatest degree of volatility. A 1% rise in interest rates typically causes the price of a long U.I.T. to drop about 10%, or $100 per unit. This is from $1,000 down to $900, a serious fall, usually well over a year's income. Loads on longest maturity U.I.T.s average about 5%, or $50 per unit, which works out to about $2 per year.

THE TRUST PORTFOLIO MENU
2 - Arranged By Credit Type

National Trusts

The first municipal bond trusts featured portfolios of long term, medium quality bonds in, typically, five to ten different states. For just $1,000 you could lock in a nifty 3.50%, tax-exempt, for 30 years. *National* trusts we call them, and these generic U.I.T.s are still the bread and butter of every trust sponsor's restaurant.

State Trusts

The U.I.T. menu's special of the day is the appetizing state-tax exemption. You can buy trusts which are immune in some 25 states, including high-tax California, New Jersey, Connecticut, etc. Remember the rule from Chapter 2—multiply your top state tax bracket by 5 to get how many basis points you lose on a non-state-exempt investment. The top Missouri tax rate is now 6%. A Kansas City resident would multiply 6 by 5 to get 30 basis points, the advantage of owning a U.I.T. composed of Missouri bonds. A 7% exempt yield equals 30 basis points more than a non-exempt 7.30%. Because so many people wish to avoid local taxes on their income, about one third of all U.I.T.s are particular state tax-exempted. Their investment characteristics are similar to those of national trusts, but because they are less diversified they are somewhat more volatile. See Figure 12.1.

Insured Trusts

In the 1970's the next significant evolution in unit trusts occurred—*insurance*. A number of specialized insurance companies began selling strongly backed, non-cancellable policies against default on unpackaged municipals and also directly on trusts. The financial service agencies rank most insured bonds triple A, their highest rating. Sponsors have found that many customers will readily give up about .25% in yield for these ratings. Bond insurance does provide protection, but as Steve pointed out, it does not protect against losses caused by market changes.

The next step was logical—trusts which are both state-exempt and insured. For instance, in 1990 Van Kampen Merritt brought out a little $3.450 million Tennessee IM-IT Series 3 trust, all of whose bonds were covered by A.M.B.A.C. and other insurance companies. Insured triple A, state-exempt, and easy to sell.

You might think that insured bonds would fluctuate less than the uninsured, but that is not so. Similarly defined trusts, whether insured, or not, act almost identically in the marketplace, going up or down together.

THE LOWER GRADE TRUSTS

Higher Yield and Lower Quality

During the early 1980's municipal bond investors got a taste of wonderfully high rates of return, 12% and sometimes more. Then, when yields fell back to more normal levels, sponsors began to tempt buyers with gamier trusts, composed of lower quality, higher yielding bonds. There are two categories of these high yield U.I.T.s: lower medium, but still investment, grade; and junk. Most *lower medium grade* trusts invest in a diversified portfolio of long-term, basically sound but slightly chipped or tarnished bond situations (Baa or BBB rated, for instance). Since this type of U.I.T. sticks to bonds which, though not gilt edged, in all probability will pay off, their yields are usually only .50% or so higher than regular uninsured trusts. So far their volatility has roughly equalled comparable maturity national trusts, but it's hard to predict what will happen over a longer period of time.

Junk Trusts

Really *junk* trusts are a different story, entirely. This kind is made up of a portfolio of speculative, not lower medium grade bonds. How can you tell them apart? By the ratings of their bonds. As said, most bonds in a high yield trusts are investment grade, typically Baa or BBB by Moody's and Standard & Poor's. Most junk bond portfolios are not rated, the most dangerous category of all. (For a further explanation of the rating system see Chapter 25). Quite a number of these were issued in the late eighties with some extremely poor results. The bulk of them were sold to unsophisticated individuals riding the tide of Wall Street's junk bond wave. Find out what you are doing before buying low quality issues, no matter how attractively packaged. Investigate, then invest.

In the past three years a multitude of U.I.T. credit type mixtures have appeared—like the new combinations in nouvelle cuisine—crossbreeds of the national, state, and insured varieties. For example, intermediate term insured Minnesota exempt, etc., and no doubt other new kinds will be coming along soon. In Chapter 11 we'll return for some suggestions on choosing the best values and the most nourishing fare.

SUMMARY ** CHAPTER 7 ** SUMMARY

The U.I.T. Menu

- Most unit investment trusts come in $1,000 denominations.

- They are priced at the market by a professional evaluator.

- U.I.T.s carry the highest sales commissions of all municipal bond products.

- They are sold to investors at the evaluated price plus a sales charge, usually of about 5%.

- They may be redeemed back to their sponsor at the evaluated price minus a fee of about 1%.

- National U.I.T.s are composed of bonds of several states, all exempt from Federal income taxes.

- State U.I.T.s are composed of bonds exempt from both Federal and a single state's income tax.

- Combinations of national and state credit types, both uninsured and insured, are offered in short, intermediate, and long maturities.

AN INDIVIDUAL INVESTOR CASE EXAMPLE—PART 3

Back in Chapter 6 we left the Zottis waiting for a U.I.T. prospectus. When it arrived—it was a four part combination offering several different Gamma-sponsored U.I.T.s, all bound into one booklet—they looked it over carefully. They were interested in two of its trusts—Gamma Intermediate #22, and New York #66. Their yields, 6.55% for the Intermediate, and 6.93% for #66, told only a small part of the story. The prospectus consisted of over 50 pages of fine print, heavily laden with phrases such as 'to which reference is hereby made', and a caution that if they wanted the full story they'd have to go to Washington and look under the Securities Act of 1933.

Although not financial wizards, the couple did know something about investing, but this document did indeed seem formidable, a feeling that most individual securities buyers share. The cover's legend, 'THESE SECURITIES HAVE NOT BEEN APPROVED OR DISAPPROVED BY THE SECURITIES AND EXCHANGE COMMISSION OR ANY STATE SECURITIES COMMISSION NOR HAS THE COMMISSION OR ANY STATE SECURITIES COMMISSION PASSED UPON THE ACCURACY OR ADEQUACY OF THIS

PROSPECTUS. ANY REPRESENTATION TO THE CONTRARY IS A CRIMI-NAL OFFENSE', wasn't exactly a confidence-builder, either.

Joe and Marci persevered, but soon ran into a mass of figures which made little sense to them. (See Chapter 9 for deciphering a U.I.T. prospectus.) Then they saw about ten pages of dire warnings that practically anything could go wrong with all the bonds in the trust. They took these admonitions with a grain of salt—after all, the bonds looked pretty sound to them, with names such as New York State Power Authority and Metropolitan Transit Authority. Near the end they found a list of the eleven issues in Gamma 66's portfolio, enough, it seemed to them, for adequate diversification. The bonds were due out as far as 2025, and some of them were in Puerto Rico, which Marci remembered from one of the brochures were also exempt in New York. The Intermediate portfolio similarly consisted of a large variety of New York and Puerto Rico bonds, but none due later than 2006, fifteen years out. Everything did seem carefully and professionally designed.

We saw in Figure 4.2 that the Zottis had a number of investments, including a $45,000 bank certificate of deposit which was about to come due. The bank had tried to get them to roll this C.D. over into a new one at 8%, but Marci figured that this wasn't even 5% after their combined 39% federal, state and city income taxes. At 6.93% Gamma #66 would bring them about 2% more than the certificate. Even $20,000 at 2% would net them about $400 more income a year, tax paid. A ski week-end for free, Joe commented. Every year, Marci replied.

They thought it over some more and finally decided to buy 20 units of Gamma New York Insured #66 and keep the rest of the cash in a money market account. They also got to thinking about this money market account. At 7.50% it was returning only 4.50% after taxes. Steve's firm was running a tax-exempt money market paying 5.75%, offering them 1.25% more a year, and also the satisfaction of maximizing their return. They decided to put the rest of the cash from the C.D. into the tax-exempt money market fund, upping their annual income by $563, and achieving immediate liquidity. See Chapter 15 for more on tax-exempt money market accounts. They had also chosen to invest only part of their available funds, similar to the dollar cost averaging mentioned in Chapter 3, staying liquid while waiting for something better to come along.

Joe Zotti called broker Steve the next day and told him that they wanted 20 units of Gamma New York #66. Steve thanked him for the order, and said that the units were still available at about the same price, $1,010, and confirmed the transaction, going over the number of units, the exact price, the total including accrued interest and the returns, 6.93% current yield and 6.88% long term yield. Joe asked if that would be the total price—what about taxes and commissions? Steve explained correctly that there were no taxes and no commissions on U.I.T. sales. All prices were net.

Figure 8.1
MARCELLA AND JOSEPH ZOTTI, JR.
INVESTMENTS—JANUARY 1991

	Market Value	Before Taxes		After Taxes	
		Yield	Income	Yield	Income
Certificate of Deposit	$25,000	7.7%	$1,938	4.75%	$1,188*
Money market accounts	10,000	6.5%	650	3.97%	397*
Common stock mutual fund	36,000	3.6%	1,296	2.20%	791*
U.S. Treasury Bond	20,000	7.2%	1,440	4.97%	994**
Gamma Nat. Tax-Ex.#31	14,000	7.2%	1,008	6.62%	927***
Gamma New York Tax-Ex.#66	20,000	6.93%	1,386	6.93%	1,386****
Totals	$125,000	6.17%	$7,718	4.55%	$5,683

* Federal (31%), plus New York State (7.7%) and New York City (3.91%) income taxes (after their Federal deduction) leave about 61% to spend.

** Federal income tax leaves 69% to spend.

*** State and city income taxes leave 92% to spend.

**** 100% tax-free.

Reinvesting

Steve then asked if they wanted to reinvest their income, ploughing it back into New York Builder Tax-Exempt, automatically? Joe said that they'd prefer to get the checks themselves, and Steve put it down that way. Joe asked how re-investing was possible since U.I.T.s were closed end and couldn't issue any more units? Steve explained that New York Builder wasn't a trust, it was a *fund*, which expanded as new money from the U.I.T. came in for re-investment. Joe asked him what other differences there were between U.I.T.s and funds, and Steve said that funds were managed, that is their traders moved bonds in and out of the portfolio as things changed. He said that although he felt that U.I.T.s were better overall, the Builder was fine for reinvestment, and they could always reconsider.

Semi-annual or Monthly Checks?

Steve told him that they could take either monthly or semi-annual income payments, but that the cost of mailing twelve checks a year rather than two would reduce their return by .05 a year. Steve advised taking the semi-annual payment plan and they followed his suggestion.

A Larger Investment Question

Another investing challenge surfaced that month when a relative of Marci's passed away, leaving her mother a substantial amount, and naming Marci executrix. When Joe mentioned this to broker Steve he said he would prepare a proposal, naturally without charge. One evening after work the Zottis were looking at the headline in the evening paper which was screaming about stocks again. Down 55 points! Record volume!

MARCI: Good thing we don't have any.

JOE: What do you mean? The averages are *up* 15% in six weeks. It would take our U.I.T.'s two whole years to go up that much.

MARCI: I'm talking about how stocks went *down* today. You'd never see this happen to a U.I.T.

JOE: True. They say the stock market is off because long Government bonds are down. Guess that makes them around eight per cent.

MARCI: Taxable. What's that after taxes?

JOE: Well, knock off a third, only five percent. The U.I.T.'s are better. O.K. How about corporate bonds, or junk bonds? Everybody's talking about them these days. I heard of one at fourteen percent.

MARCI: No, thanks. There's no way I'd buy junk for Mother. Are you nuts?

JOE: Good corporates, you can get nine. Knock off a third ... that's only six percent. Still not as good as a U.I.T. at seven.

MARCI: Well, what's to be done with Rose's money?

JOE: I guess it wouldn't hurt to keep it in T-bills, but short ones, three months maybe. That would give you and the family time to think it out.

MARCI: Sounds reasonable.

Though they may seem to be just groping along, Joe and Marci are actually doing quite well. They considered the merits of stocks and also speculative bonds, but the risk seemed too great. They were right about their tax rates. They figured several after-tax yields correctly and compared them accurately to other returns. And they knew that the estate should act conservatively, for everybody's protection. Had they brought in one more factor, inflation, they'd be close to perfect.

One evening Steve came to visit, little expecting the newly acquired financial sophistication he would encounter.

STEVE: Aunt Rose was a Massachusetts resident, and she left about six hundred thousand, half to your mother, and the rest split among her three children. Right?

MARCI: Right, split as you said. And I'm the executrix, and also for my mother.

STEVE: I see, Marci. And your mother lives where?

MARCI: Florida.

STEVE: She's making out well? No money problems?

MARCI: Just fine, but not rich or anything. Here's a list of her investments. She has what she needs—about nine thousand a year from Social Security and maybe thirty from bank C.D.'s and other investments, and she also gets something from Dad's pension. The condo is all paid for, so she's set for life.

STEVE: That's a fair amount of money. Looks like your dad did well by her, and she's in the 28% bracket. Here's a preliminary plan for you to look at. Just try it on for size.

Steve took out a bunch of papers from his briefcase, including three prospectuses, for Gamma Insured #61, Munisured Discount, and Gamma Daily, a tax-exempt money market fund. He handed out copies of a proposal letter, along with what appeared to be a form-portfolio, in which he had pencilled some of the numbers Marci just gave him.

Figure 8.2.
MS. ANNE YOUNG
INVESTMENT PORTFOLIO–JANUARY 1991

	Market Value	Before Taxes		After Taxes*	
	Market Value	Yield	Income	Yield	Income
Money market accounts	$ 15,000	6.25%	$ 938	4.50%	$ 675
U.S. Treasury Bond	75,000	8.25%	6,188	5.94%	4,455
Certificate of Deposit	160,000	8.05%	12,880	5.76%	9,216
Massachusetts H.F.A.	25,000	6.75%	1,688	6.75%	1,688
Tampa, Florida Sewer Rev.	50,000	8.00%	4,000	8.00%	4,000
Totals	$325,000	7.91%	$25,694	6.16%	$20,034

PROPOSED ADDITIONAL INVESTMENTS

	Market Value	Before Taxes		After Taxes*	
	Market Value	Yield	Income	Yield	Income
Gamma Daily Tax-Ex. Fund	$ 100,000	5.75%	$ 5,750	5.75%	$ 5,750
Gamma Insured #61	100,000	7.00%	7,000	7.00%	7,000
Munisure National Discount	100,000	5.25%	5,250	5.25%	5,250
Totals	$300,000	6.00%	$ 18,000	6.00%	$18,000

* Using a Federal rate of 28% leaves 72% to spend. Florida has no income tax but levies a small personal property tax on the market value of out-of-state municipal bonds.

STEVE: With this new money she'll have almost seventy-five thousand a year. And she has plenty in her money market for emergencies. Of course, you have to think about your brothers and yourself some day. See that discount line? That's an estate builder. She buys at $700, and it pays off at $1,000. She gets the income, and eventually the principal goes to her estate.

MARCI [Turning to the Munisure Discount prospectus and looking at the bonds in the portfolio]: I'm worried about all those long bonds. Twenty-five or thirty years out. Mother is pushing seventy.

STEVE: Well, of course that's a consideration. But you can sell the units any time you want to, with no redemption fee. It's all paid for when you buy it, included in the sales charge. You're one hundred percent liquid.

JOE: You mean that we get our sales charge back if we have to sell in a year or so?

STEVE: No, Joe, I'm afraid it doesn't work like that. I wish it did. You pay the sales charge, up front, so you don't pay a redemption fee, not a penny. That's one thing I like about our U.I.T.'s.

MARCI: Suppose she bought a hundred units of Gamma #61. That's $100,000, right?

STEVE: Right, and the sales charge is included.

JOE: That's five percent. Is that five hundred dollars?

STEVE: It's four point nine percent.

JOE: Four hundred ninety dollars?

STEVE [Slightly uncomfortable]: Four thousand nine hundred, approximately. [Joe and Marci looked at each other, feeling the weight of this fee.]

STEVE [Quickly]: But you can figure it's only half of that, because you get to sell it free, if you ever have to. And besides, the sales charge is tax-deductible.

Joe didn't buy that explanation. Marci doubted that the tax law had such a deduction, and rightly.

MARCI: So let's suppose she wants to sell back, retire them, what do you call it?

STEVE: Redeem. Suppose you wanted to redeem ten years from now. Just let me know and you get your money. Simple. No hunting around that secondary market for a bid.

MARCI: O.K., but what if it were just a year later, what then?

STEVE [Frowning a bit]: Marci, and Joe, she's in units strictly for the long haul. We already said she has plenty of liquidity, so she'd never *have* to sell the units. They'd just keep on working for a long time.

JOE: O.K., but just suppose. We buy it today, Marci's mother buys it today, I mean. What's the price of that 61?

STEVE: $1,020 each.

JOE: A year from today, what would she get back if she redeemed it?

STEVE: It depends, Joe. If the market is down, you get less. If the market is up, you get more. And the way bonds have moved up lately, you might have a good profit. Who knows?

MARCI: How about even. What would she get back if the market doesn't move at all, up or down?

STEVE: Then you send in her units, and she just automatically gets the money in a few days.

JOE [Not pleased with this sudden evasiveness]: How much would she get back? Just *suppose.*

STEVE: Well, we don't usually figure it this way, since these units are meant for the long haul, but if the market were exactly the same, here's how it would work. She pays a thousand twenty now, take away forty-nine for the sales charge. That's nine hundred seventy-one. When you add in her income she'd still be ahead. Look, if you're planning to sell in a year, we'd better buy something else for her. Let me show you...

MARCI [Interrupting]: I thought I read there was a $10 a unit charge for selling. That means you'd have to subtract another $10—which means we'd only get $961 a unit back after a whole year. Forty-nine sales, ten bidding side, or whatever they call it, that's fifty-nine, so against seventy income that's only $11 a whole year, just 1%!

STEVE: It's true that when you sell it's on the *bid* side.

MARCI: Even if she holds it *two* years I don't think it's going to look too good.

JOE: Seventy times two is one forty. Take away the fifty-nine and that's eighty-one. Divided by two years, that's only 4.1% after two years. That's terrible! Do you have to wait until the bonds pay off until you get that 7%?

STEVE: Joe, when you consider the whole program you'll see you should never have to sell Gamma. It's definitely not meant to be traded in and out, like some of those wild stocks these days.

Steve went on to recommend that they put one-third of the money each in short, intermediate, and long trusts, and explained the advantages of the program: all bonds chosen by professionals, mostly insured, 100% exempt (no income taxes in Florida, he added, correctly) and no fuss with cutting coupons or storing bonds—the ultimate modern investment. He finished his pitch on an up note, explaining how concerned he was with the family's financial future, thus ending his presentation, and left them shortly.

JOE: He's a pretty good salesman, isn't he?

MARCI: He should be. Five percent of six hundred thousand, that's thirty grand. Do you think he's trying to cheat us, with that redemption line?

JOE: Of course not. It's just that U.I.T.'s are high profit items. Like some of the little gizmos we sell at the warehouse.

MARCI: It looks to me like U.I.T.'s are not so bad for a few thousand dollars, but for bigger amounts, maybe we should look at a tax-exempt fund.

JOE: Or we could just buy some bonds. I saw some in the Sunday paper. Seven and a half, I think.

MARCI: Well, let's look at a fund first, maybe a no-load, and then we'll see.

JOE: Sounds good.

As you see, J & M had made giant strides in their financial education. Steve was a convincing salesman, and presented a plan for Marci's family which had some merit, though it was certainly too heavily weighted in unit investment trusts. They were knowledgeable enough to challenge Steve about how much is lost if a U.I.T. is redeemed within a few years. Unhappily for him, he glossed over the fact that trusts are redeemed at about $10 per unit under the base price, and relied instead on the technically true, but misleading sponsors' statement that they charge no redemption fee. This proved a key mistake, since he lost credibility with the pair. In real life, and within my experience, this is only one of many ways investors can be misled when buying trusts.

M & J continued receiving received their monthly statements from Tower, and also the following January their yearly statement from Gamma's trustee, showing that this income was exempt from New York and federal income taxes. Marci filed away the statements and found them useful in preparing their tax forms at filing time. We shall see if they do as well with managed funds in the next section.

SUMMARY ** CHAPTER 8 ** SUMMARY

An Individual Investor Case Example—Part 3

- U.I.T s are the first and lowest tier in tax-exempts.

- They are handy for individual buyers with small amounts to invest.

- With more than a few thousand dollars, look elsewhere.

CHAPTER 9

UNDERSTANDING A U.I.T. PROSPECTUS

A U.I.T. prospectus is a Wall Street document which purports to describe the investment features of trust securities to potential customers. Although prospectuses may be gold mines of facts, they are so long and deep that they are practically unusable to an untrained investor. Some have been face-lifted with modern headings and titles, but all are written in profoundest lawyerese. As if these drawbacks weren't formidable enough singly, many U.I.T. prospectuses are now published in clumps, with several quite different trusts offered in one omnibus booklet. So, most investors understandably, if lazily, settle for learning about U.I.T.s through one or more sales pitches—ads and short brochures, or directly from brokers; only a few bother to dig out the facts themselves. What can you do about it? Learn before you buy. As Manager F. M. has said, "Don't buy anything you don't understand". Start mastering U.I.T.s by breaking one down into its pieces. It isn't all *that* hard, once you get used to it. With your brains and my experience, how can we fail?

The Form of the Prospectus

Most U.I.T. prospectuses have five sections, often presented in this order: a summary of essential financial information; a section describing the trust's objectives and features; a multitude of disclaimers of sponsor liability; a catalogue of unit holder rights; and a list of the bonds in each separate portfolio. As mentioned in Chapter 5, sponsors set up the framework for a series of trusts, such as Gamma National Tax-Exempt, or Fidelity Insured Massachusetts, etc., and then proceed to issue separately numbered packages of them. After one standardized prospectus is written for the whole series the variable items of each separate trust are filled in—the amount, price, yields, and so on. Then it is numbered and sold as Gamma National Tax-Exempt #1, 2, 31, 499, etc. For our example trust we are going to use the imaginary Gamma New York Tax Exempt #66, the sixty-sixth offering by Gamma Securities of its long-running New York State series. Our example tries to present an average state uninsured U.I.T. typical of the form being issued in the real market currently. Let's divide and conquer by taking a look at each of its five sections.

SECTION 1—ESSENTIAL FINANCIAL INFORMATION

The Offering Price

The cover page of most U.I.T.'s presents a fine print summary of the trust's features, ending with a warning about the S.E.C. Their second and third pages chart out their amounts of principal, income, expenses, etc., as illustrated in Figures 9.1 and 9.2. After we are introduced to the U.I.T.'s sponsors, trustee, and evaluators, and also told its birthday (Date of Deposit), Figure 9.1, Line 1 (Principal Amount of Securities) states the size of the trust. Gamma New York Tax Exempt Trust #66 started at $10 million with 10,000 units, each with a face value of $1,000, so each unit is 1/10,000 of the whole. Next comes the offering price calculation, starting with Line 5, 'Aggregate offering side evaluation'. As discussed, a professional prices each bond in the trust daily, on the offered side of the market, then adds up the total. This $9,605,178 total is divided by the 10,000 units to produce $960.51, Line 10, the *Sponsors' Initial Repurchase Price*. This is the price upon which buying and selling is based.

Line 8 shows the sales load, $49.49, and Line 9 is the *Public Offering Price*, the base price plus the load, $1,010.00. This was the price investors paid the first day #66 was offered. Each day thereafter the trust portfolio will be reevaluated and its price will go up or down with the municipal bond market. Clear so far? Begin with the total value of all the bonds, divide by the number of units, add in the load, and that's your buying price. $9.605 million divided by 10,000 units gives $961 per unit. Add on $49 to get $1,010. Note that the percentage markup from the evaluation price to the offering is actually 5.15%, but I

Figure 9.1
GAMMA NEW YORK TAX EXEMPT TRUST #66
SUMMARY OF ESSENTIAL FINANCIAL INFORMATION

SPONSORS:	Gamma Securities, Inc.
	The Fixed Income Corp.
	Hudson & West Securities, Inc.
	Tower & Co.
AGENT FOR SPONSORS:	Gamma Securities, Inc.
TRUSTEE:	Security Trust

Date of Deposit: February 1, 1991

1	Principal Amount of Securities in Trust	**$10,000,000**
2	Number of Units	**10,000**
3	Fractional Interest per Unit	**1/10,000**
4	Public Offering Price Calculation	
5	Aggregate offering side evaluation	
6	of Securities in the Portfolio	$9,605,177.87
7	Divided by 10,000 Units	960.51
8	Plus Sales Charge (4.9% of Offering Price)	49.49
9	Public Offering Price per Unit	**1,010.00**
10	Sponsors' Initial Repurchase Price per Unit	**960.51**
11	Excess of Public Offering Price over Repurchase Price	**49.49**
12	Redemption Price per Unit	**950.51**
13	Excess of Public Offering Price over Redemption Price	**54.49**

suppose 4.9% of the offering price sounds better. Some trusts add accrued interest at this point, some, like Gamma, do not. See Chapter 19 for accrued interest.

Where does the $50 load go? The sellers get the largest share, about 70%. Some sales are made by the sponsors' sales people, some by those of the other dealers listed in the underwriting account, some by salesmen who work for outside dealers. In each case there is a takedown system to pay the sellers about $35. Typically $15 goes directly to the selling salesperson, and the sales department keeps $20. The balance of approximately, $15 goes to the sponsors and other underwriters. Of this perhaps $10 pays the expenses of advertising, administering, and marketing, leaving a $5 per unit net profit.

The next lines show all these profit figures, fair warning. You can't fault trust sponsors for hiding how much they make. Line 11 shows the five percent load, and Line 13 the six percent spread between buying and selling. If you bought ten units on Monday at $10,100 and then changed your mind and redeemed them the same afternoon you would get back $9,605, or $495 less. If you redeemed them the following week, after the offering was closed, assuming no change in the market evaluation you'd get the bid side redemption price, $9,505, another $100 less.

The Redemption Price

So you *buy* units at the offered side of the market, plus about $50, or 5%. Line 12 'Redemption Price', shows how much you get when you 'redeem', that is, *sell* your units back to the sponsor. When you sell it's at the *bid* side of the market. How is the bid side figured? In this case by taking the same base, the bid side, or Repurchase Price, and then subtracting 1%, Line 10 minus Line 12. The six (up five plus down one) point spread is the cost to buy and then sell a U.I.T., or approximately $60 per $1,000. This is its marketability charge, about 6%, decidedly not cheap.

Sponsors' Profit

After these leading facts, U.I.T. prospectuses continue the financial part as shown in Figure 9.2. The sponsor doesn't buy a U.I.T.'s bonds the day the trust is publicly offered, they employ specialized traders to accumulate them in advance. When the sponsor comes to create a trust by depositing these accumulated bonds with the trustee, if their valued price is higher than cost (as it is over 90% of the time), then the sponsor shows a profit for their risks and skills. The sponsor then splits this profit or, occasionally, loss, with any co-sponsors, by pre-arrangement. Gamma #66's bonds were deposited into the trust at $9.605 million. Line 14 shows that Gamma made $60,000, $6 per unit—easy money on a captive transaction. What had happened between the time the bonds were bought and the time they were deposited? The municipal bond market might have risen by that amount, or the bonds might have been bought advantageously, perhaps on the bid side, then later evaluated at a higher, offered side price. There are other definite pluses for sponsors hidden in this process, the advantages substantial buyers command in a sophisticated marketplace.

Figure 9.2
SUMMARY OF ESSENTIAL FINANCIAL INFORMATION, (Continued)

			Monthly	Semi-annual
14	Sponsors' Profit on Deposit		$ 60,077.50	
15	First Settlement date: February 8, 1991			
16	Minimum capital Distribution per Unit			5.00
17	Minimum Termination Amount			2,000,000.00
18	Calculation of Estimated Annual Unit Income			
19			*Monthly*	*Semi-annual*
20	Estimated Annual Interest income		$71.74	$71.74
21	Evaluator's Fee		.30	.30
22	Sponsor's Fee		.25	.25
23	Trustee's Fee and Expenses		1.60	1.10
24		Expenses Total	2.15	1.65
25	Estimated Net Annual Income		69.59	70.09
26	Estimated Income Distributions		5.80	35.05
27	Estimated Current Return		**6.877%**	**6.927%**
28	Estimated Long-term Return		**6.826%**	**6.876%**
29	Daily Rate of Estimated Income Accrual		**.1933**	**.1947**
30	Record Date: Fifteenth of the month of distribution			
31	Distribution Date: Twenty-fifth of the month			
32	Daily evaluation hour: 3:30 P.M. New York time			

Other Principal Matters

The *settlement date* is when you're supposed to pay for any securities pur-chases—U.I.T.s, managed funds, or individual bonds. This is normally five busi-ness days after the sale, seven on the calendar, counting weekends. So if you say yes on a Tuesday, your money is due on the following Tuesday, etc., unless a holiday, or some special arrangement, has changed the normal routine. On the day of deposit, February 1, 1991, the settlement date was February 8, five busi-ness, and seven calendar, days later.

Line 16, *Minimum capital distribution:* When any bonds in a U.I.T. are called in by the issuer, or (rarely) sold out by the sponsors, the cash received is used to reduce the principal value of the trust. If only a few bonds are retired the trustee sensibly doesn't send out less than $5 per unit at a time. I've been warned that many investors fail to recognize these separate checks as a return of their capital and treat them as income. U.I.T. annual reports spell this out, so you can check there if in doubt.

    Termination amount: When a trust is down to tag ends, when most of its bonds etired, it's time to disband. Thus, when in twenty years or so Gamma #66 has only one or two million left in its portfolio, those last bonds will be sold and the proceeds distributed to unit holders. That's it for the principal numbers, now on to the investors' payoff—when and how income is earned and distributed.

Income and Expenses

Line 20, *Estimated Annual Interest Income,* displays the total amount of per unit gross income the trust should receive every year, $71.74. The expense items of the evaluator, sponsor and trustee are then deducted. The *Evaluator's Fee* is about $3,000 a year. After a U.I.T.'s initial distribution the sponsor makes most of its profit by buying back units and then reselling them to new investors. Their *Sponsors' Annual Fee,* here $2,500, pays just for monitoring the trust portfolio and other maintenance work. The *Trustee's Fee,* usually about 60 cents per unit annually, covers the work of keeping records, and supposedly representing unit holders' interests. Other expenses arise from such items as the processing and mailing of checks to the unitholders. In this case the monthly plan expenses were 50 cents greater than for the semis, resulting in lower income.

    These routine expenses add up to about $2 per year per $1,000 on an uninsured portfolio, but there's no help for it. This amount is deducted from the yearly interest earned by the bonds in the portfolio. So the semi expense of $1.65 a year reduced the unit income from $71.74 down to $70.09, or about 2%, Line 25. Line 26 divides that by twelve and by two. Buy one unit of this trust and you'll get $5.80 every month, or $35.05 twice a year.

    Had we chosen an insured example trust, there might have appeared a line here for the annual charges that insurance companies charge for this form of credit enhancing. Such as "BIGBAC annual premium per unit $1.46". So the unit holders might pay the same routine expenses, and also for their insurance, perhaps a total of about $3.00 per year.

Current Yield and Official Dates

Line 28 shows the *Current Return* of the units, 6.92% on the semis, their $70 income divided by the $1,010 offering price. Formerly this was the only yield price tag U.I.T.s carried, but the regulators now make sponsors calculate a somewhat fairer figure, here called *Estimated Long Term Return*. This is a *hybrid* yield, similar to yield to maturity, and which weights income, maturity, call features and market value. Line 29 shows the results, a 6.87% for the semi-annual return, .05% lower than the current yield.

I like the next line, the *Daily Rate of Interest Accrual*. In our example you earn almost 20 cents a day. At 7%, every $1,000 well invested earns 20 cents a day. $10,000 gets you $2, and $100,000 brings in $20, every day of the year.

Whoever is officially recorded with the trustee on the *Record Date*, Line 30, gets the income for the preceding period on the *Distribution Date*. If you buy into a trust, make sure your broker gets you recorded properly; if you miss an income check you'll eventually get a credit, however, straightening things out can be quite a nuisance.

Orders to buy or redeem units received before 3:30 P.M. are all executed at that one daily fixing price. Orders received afterward are executed at the following day's price, so you can't take advantage of short term fluctuations in the bond market. Either way you won't know exactly what the price is until after the fixing. Similarly, the trust's date of deposit was February 1, and so its initial valuation was made the day before, January 31, 1991. As you can see, there's a lot of information packed into three pages. Now on to some pretty thick boiler plate.

SECTION 2—DESCRIPTION AND OBJECTIVES

The second section of most U.I.T. prospectuses usually begins on the third or fourth page with a description of the trust series and its objectives. You often see a statement like "This trust is one of a series of investment companies created by the Sponsor, all of which are similar, but each of which is separate, and designated by a different series number." Then follows its legal basis, such as "Gamma New York Tax Exempt #66 was created under the laws of the State of New York pursuant to a Trust Indenture and Agreement between Gamma Securities, Inc. (the Sponsor), Security Trust, Inc. (the Trustee), and QuoteCo (the Evaluator)". A minority of trusts do not use an outside, supposedly objective evaluator, but instead do it themselves, usually through a subsidiary, and so disclose in this section.

Next may come a brief description of the type of trust, whether insured or not, state-exempt or national, and so on. Each trust also declares its objectives, such as "formed for the purposes of obtaining high tax-exempt income while maintaining safety of principal", followed by the trust's maturity and other limitations (approximately 3 to 5 years, insured, etc.). Finally, to prepare for the remote contingency that the trust does not actually receive some of the bonds it has contracted to buy there is a notice that "Replacement Bonds" might have to be substituted.

SECTION 3—WARNINGS ABOUT THE BOND PORTFOLIO

The third section of U.I.T. prospectuses is attorneys' happy hunting ground, where they attempt to ward off your future lawsuits. In the old days municipal bond prospectuses emphasized the strong points of their issues and they made generally cheerful reading. Around 1970, the liability picture frosted over, and the sponsors' lawyers started monitoring the prospectuses closely. They saw to it that investors were warned in writing about everything that might conceivably go wrong, figuring that if something did then the sponsors' liability for it would be lessened. Now as many as fifteen pages may be devoted to possible calamities. Dozens of potential weaknesses may be described at length, perhaps ending with "All such issuers have been experiencing some of these problems in varying degree". *Taxes, bond insurance,* and *portfolio concentration* are the main disclaimer topics.

Naturally, a U.I.T.'s chief selling point is the holders's ability to exclude income from federal, and also some state and local, income taxation. However, this is not an absolute right. As detailed back in Chapter 2, other levies have to be paid, including capital gains taxes, non-exempted state and local taxes, the alternative minimum tax, and the inclusion of tax-exempt income for Social Security calculations. In addition, the tax lawyers often dig up a few other tax hazards which rarely affect individual investors and also waffle around by stating that this particular tax-exemption is based only on the opinion of another lawyer.

Insured portfolios are especially filled with disclaimers—even sometimes mentioning certain circumstances where defaults are not covered. Particularly emphasized is the valid point that bond insurance provides protection only against default and not against market losses caused by interest rate changes or other factors. The insurer's financial statement is often included in this section, which ends with the sponsor stating that if the insurer doesn't pay, it's not their fault and that they told you so all along.

The last major disclaimer concerns diversification. One of the benefits of buying U.I.T. packages is that they avoid concentration in any one kind of bond. Sometimes, however, a trust is overweighted in one type of holding and this part of the prospectus tries to explain that away, thus ducking future complaints. I've seen some trusts where this disclaimer certainly came in handy, so take a look at the portfolio yourself, and see if it appears sufficiently diversified.

As distinguished lawyer T. E. says, "The investor who takes all these warnings literally would be nuts to buy anything at all." You'd think that New York in particular was composed solely of deadbeat state agencies, leaky nuclear plants, and litigious Indian tribes. Although, goodness knows, it has more than its share of such elements, that's not quite the whole Empire State picture. Where can you find the real credit story? Listen to your salesperson, read the prospectus, look at the ratings, and make up your own mind. For more on credits, see Chapter 25.

Some miscellaneous features are put in this part, including an explanation of the rating agencies' systems, how the portfolio is valued, a table of broker discounts, and also some bare bones information about the trustee, the evaluator, the lawyers and the auditors. These are largely self-explanatory and not terribly fascinating. One interesting point here—how bonds may be liquidated from the portfolio. Sponsors can't add bonds to a U.I.T., but bonds under threat of default may be sold from the trust if the sponsor catches the problem in time. In my experience this process has seldom benefited the unit holders.

SECTION 4—OWNERS' RIGHTS

After the disclaimers we get to the so-called *rights* of the owners. In fact, as in tenants' leases, the interests of the customers are not well represented by these provisions—most of the "rights" are actually only additional sales pitches. Sponsors offer *quantity discounts*, that is, reduced sales charges for larger purchases. This is an inducement for people investing over $100,000 worth, sometimes over $500,000, to join the fun. Sensibly, fewer than 1% of U.I.T. buyers accept the invitation.

Exchange Option and Re-investment Plans

Most U.I.T. sponsors offer their holders the "right" to reinvest their trust income automatically. This encourages holders to plough their income back into tax-free, or other, investments. The most common vehicle attached to U.I.T.s for this purpose is a separate municipal bond managed fund, with its own load firmly attached. Take a close look before signing up. The income on *these* may also be reinvested, compounding merrily at the current rate. If re-investment no longer fits your plans just call up the salesman or the trustee and the next distribution will come to you in cash, with no extra fee involved.

Most trusts also offer a switching option should holders' goals or conditions change. If, for instance, you move from one state to another, or if you get nervous about a certain U.I.T., some sponsors let you switch into another of their offerings at a reduced sales charge.

Lost and Found

In this section the prospectus usually tells how the trustee will replace lost, destroyed, damaged or stolen trust certificates. This process normally takes quite a bit of paper work, a month or longer, and a small fee. If you want to transfer certificates to another person, it's easy—just get a form from your broker or the trustee.

Yearly reports. One of the Trustee's chores is to provide annual statements for their unit holders (sometimes called certificate holders). These are usually mailed every January and are handy for income tax purposes. They show the annual trust financial results, interest, expenses, and income, any capital distributions, and what part of the income is exempt in which states. Also, bonds sold from the portfolio, a list of which ones remain, and the units' year end valuation.
PART 5—THE BONDS AND THE UNDERWRITERS
Somewhere in the prospectus is a list of the bonds in the original trust portfolio. Ten to twenty different holdings are the rule, described as to principal amounts, name, call features, ratings, and their cost to the trust. As noted, several different portfolios are often combined in one single trust. If one of the omnibuses comes your way, just track the trust that concerns you.

Most U.I.T.s are underwritten (bought and distributed) by a group of from five to twenty dealers. The fancy new name for a dealer is an 'investment bank', but believe you me, a dealer is a dealer. Their names and the amounts they underwrote are listed. Naturally, there are dozens of other, less significant, items in these wonderful prospectus documents but that covers the essentials.

Figure 9.3
PORTFOLIO OF GAMMA NEW YORK TAX-EXEMPT TRUST #66

Principal Amount	Issuer	Refunding Features	Rating*	Price to Gamma #66	Yield to Trust
1. $ 1,000,000	Municipal Assistance Corp. for New York City Series 68 7.40% due 7/1/08	7/1/99 @102	AA-	$1,000,000	7.30%
2. 1,000,000	Metropolitan Transit Authority Contract Fac. Series 3 7.50% due 7/1/16	7/1/00 @102*	A*	980,000	7.67%
3. 1,000,000	Nassau County, New York General Obligation MBIA Insured 8% due 11/01/85	Non-Callable	Aaa	1,086,000	7.24%
4. 1,000,000	New York State General Obligation 6% due 6/1/14	Non-Callable	A	855,000	7.29%
5. 1,000,000	New York State Dorm. Authority State University Series T 7.375% due 7/1/19	7/1/00 @102	A*	990,000	7.45%
6. 1,000,000	New York State Energy Dev. Auth. Con. Edison Inc. Subject to A.M.T. 7.50% due 7/1/25	7/1/99 @101	AA-	980,000	7.66%
7. 1,000,000	New York State Housing Fin. Agency Health Facilities—New York City 8% due 11/1/08	11/1/00 @102	A-	1,015,000	7.80%

*All ratings are by Standard & Poor's Corporation unless indicated by * for a Moody's Investor's Service rating.

Figure 9.3
PORTFOLIO OF GAMMA NEW YORK TAX-EXEMPT TRUST #66 (Continued)

	Principal Amount	Issuer	Refunding Features	Rating*	Price to Gamma #66	Yield to Trust
8.	1,000,000	Port of New York and New Jersey Cons. Series 60. Subject to A.M.T. 8.25% due 4/1/23	4/1/95 @102	AA-	$1,070,00	6.82/7.66
9.	1,000,000	Puerto Rico Elec. Power Auth. Refunding 6% O.I.D. @89.094	7/1/99 @100	A-	850,000	7.45
10.	250,000	Puerto Rico Elec. Power Auth. Series O Capital Appreciation 0% due 7/1/17	Non-Callable	A-	35,625	7.39
11.	750,000	Triborough Bridge & Tunnel Auth. General Purpose Series I 7.625% due 1/1/14	1/1/96 @102	A+	761,250	7.39
	$10,000,000				9,622,875	

*All ratings are by Standard & Poor's Corporation unless indicated by * for a Moody's Investor's Service rating.

SUMMARY ** CHAPTER 9 ** SUMMARY

Understanding a U.I.T. Prospectus

- U.I.T. prospectuses are long, dense collections of financial and other information.

- One generic form defines one whole series of trusts, then a specific prospectus describes each individual U.I.T. when it is offered for sale.

- Prospectuses are designed to shield their creators from potential liability suits. However, they are the best source of definitive U.I.T. facts. Their most nourishing kernel—*The Summary of Essential Financial Information.*

CHAPTER 10

WHAT TO DO WITH YOUR OLD U.I.T.S

If you own a U.I.T., you need help. They are often the first investment that people make, and I've seen many substantial individual portfolios still holding a sprinkling of decades-old trusts. If you are holding any U.I.T.s, it's time to see if they suit your present needs. Where do you start? By examining your old trusts to see exactly what they are today. Next? Determine if they are helping you to meet your present investment goals. If they still work well for you, stay put. But if not, get ready to switch to a more suitable security—another U.I.T., a managed fund, or whatever.

Time Marches On

In one respect U.I.T.s change continually as their fixed maturity grows closer with the passage of time. Maybe you have moved and now need a different state exemption. Municipal bond credit quality also changes as the years go by, mostly positively, as bonds grow in credit strength, or acquire enhanced security. These and other factors affect your real, after-tax return. What do you do? First the diagnosis, then the prescription. Bring a list of your U.I.T. holdings to your broker to uncover these facts:

1.) The present maturity of each bond in the trust portfolio.
2.) Their credit quality.
3.) Your real yield.
4.) The present unit redemption price.

If you can turn in your old lemons for new oranges, you will come out way ahead. One caution: showing a securities salesman what you own is an open invitation for a serious pitch to do something, anything, that will bring *him* a profit. Later on I have a few suggestions, but *you* have to be in charge, and *you* have to make the decisions. See Chapter 19 for some lists of securities dealers who are ready to provide the information needed to evaluate existing U.I.T.s. They won't charge you for this evaluation, but naturally hope that some day it will lead to a trade or two.

All things equal, I suggest that you forget about switching tax-exempts around unless you can improve your true yield by at least 1% a year, preferably 2%. (Longer maturity, lower credit quality, or higher commissioned securities are *not* equivalent, so watch out for propositions which downgrade your holdings without good reason.)

One piece of advice about these calculations. Base your rate of return on *today's* market, and not on what you paid for something years ago. You can't cancel a bad purchase, any more than your broker can cancel a good one. To find your real income rate divide income by today's value, not that of yesteryear. If you are going to improve your asset's power, adjust to today's market, up, down, or sideways.

Compare and Improve

That's the system in a nutshell—first figure out what you really own, what you can really expect to receive, and then compare your alternatives, staying put, or reinvesting. If you can find a better deal, sell the trusts, and replace with something that returns you more, all things considered. On $50,000 you may be able to increase your income by $1,000 a year, tax-free, enough to buy some very nice things. Sound investing *does* make a difference.

How to Switch

Once you decide to sell, STOP. Don't just docilely stand in line in front of the sponsor's redemption window. You have two other options. 1.) Many trusts run in families which permit switching from one of their products to another at reduced sales charges. Investigate, then decide. 2.) Try to find a redemption price for your units that's higher than your sponsor's quoted number. First ask your broker to negotiate a higher price with the sponsor—they may need your units for their own purposes. Also, it's perfectly legal for outside dealers to compete against sponsors in trying to buy investors' units. Direct your broker to get a competing quote from one of these. The savings can be worthwhile. Then what? Take your cash for your old trusts, and go on to choose your new investment, perhaps following the suggestion in the next two sections.

SUMMARY ** CHAPTER 10 ** SUMMARY

What to Do with Your Old U.I.T.s

- Ask your broker or the sponsor for the current information on your old U.I.T.s.

- Determine their present principal amount, maturity, quality, and return.

- Measure these against your present investment goals.

- Make changes where appropriate.

CHAPTER 11

HOW TO CHOOSE A U.I.T.

Now let's see if we can put all this wonderful information about trusts together. Unless you have your heart set on buying a U.I.T. I'd suggest that you first take a look at the sections on managed funds and unpackaged bonds. Then, if you still like the looks of U.I.T.s, come on back here. I see tax-exempt investing as a five-step process: a prerequisite step; a market step; a step each for maturity and credit; and a shopping for yield step. Few Wall Street sales people advocate long term views for their customers, and most will try to force you to take a different set of steps. So prepare to say no and to make some lonely decisions—there's no help for it.

The Prerequisite Step

The first step is to review the qualifications we started with in the Introduction to make sure you're heading in the right direction. Things do change, so start by asking yourself the *three prerequisite questions*. Do you have a sufficient cash reserve—at least half a year's living expenses in readily available form? Is your current income bracket high enough to benefit from the naturally lower tax-free yields? Better private investments unavailable? If it's yes to all three, then you're cleared for takeoff.

The Market Step

We saw in Chapter 3 how to look carefully before you go onto the long term investing highway. Are the buy signals right, the highway traffic moving well? Are long, good quality tax-frees at 8%? Are long yields 3% higher than inflation? Do long municipals yield more than 83% of Treasuries? If these signals seem favorable, then proceed. If not, keep your savings liquid, using money market or similar funds until the road is clear.

The Maturity Step

As detailed earlier, *maturity length* is the chief factor governing how much a fixed income security will yield, and also how much it will go up or down. The shorter the maturity, the lower the risk and yield. The longer the maturity, the higher the risk and the yield. The first step in picking the right type of trust is to pick the maturity—short, intermediate, or long—that matches your needs and expectations. Take a look at Figure 11.1 which tries to show how much of your

Fig. 11.1
EFFECT ON BOND PRINCIPAL OF 1% A YEAR RISE IN INTEREST RATES FOR BONDS OF 5, 15 AND 30 YEAR MATURITIES

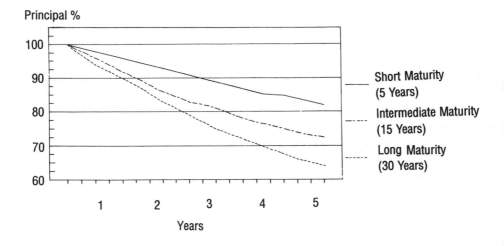

principal on a bond or trust would remain if interest rates rose by 100 basis points (1%) annually for five years in a row. Look at the three lines and see how they strike you. Then compare these to the relative yield price tags in Figure 12.1. How does a loss down to 94% on the five year investment feel? If that's all the risk you can take, then a short term trust may be for you. Compare this to the 15 year line. Can you accept that much possible decline in principal value, but no more? If so, the extra yield may make that the one for you. How about the 30 year, which could lose one third of its value, all in five years time? Remember, of course, that in each of these cases the units will eventually pay off, 100 cents on the dollar. If these potential market losses don't worry you too much, and the extra yield seems worth the risk, then by all means take the higher income. You have the information, do your own choosing.

The Credit Step

The second step is to find the trust in your maturity range whose *credit quality* you like, remembering that the safer you go the less you get paid. One question often pops up here—whether or not to buy an insured trust. Insured U.I.T.s typically sell at about .25% less yield than uninsured ones (7.25% versus 7.50%, for example). This .25 divided by 7.50 means that insurance costs about 3% a year. If the trust runs for twenty years, then taking the insurance means you are betting that there's a 60% (3% x 20 years) chance that the *whole portfolio* is going to hopelessly default. Is it worth it? Look at the bonds in the portfolio and see if they are that bad. If so, then by all means take M.B.I.A., or A.M.B.A.C., or whatever company's wager. In plain fact, these sharp outfits don't operate like life insurers, expecting to pay a certain number of claims each year. They approve sound credits only and rarely experience losses. In effect, the sponsors do little more than buy a triple A rating and it's expensive. Unless you find something unusual, I'd recommend that you skip the insurance and take the extra income. Again, insurance is only against default, and not against the more significant loss factors—inflation and interest rate changes. See Figure 25.1. Buying insurance against bicycle collisions won't protect you against cars and trucks, the municipal bond roadway's big threats.

Overall, on U.I.T.s I suggest that you loosen up on quality, since credit risk is slight in all investment grade trusts. Look at the lower grade, but still investment quality trusts, as covered in Chapter 7.

Current Return or Total Return?

Before you take the plunge, think back a moment to what we discussed in Chapter 3. Are you looking for the highest possible *current* income or the highest *total* income? *Current income* investors (who typically depend on investment income to help meet everyday expenses) should look at several U.I.T.s whose units cost close to $1,000. Among these, pick the one that carries the very fattest current yield. The combination of a price near par and the highest long term yield should indicate the best deal.

Investors who can afford to let income accumulate and wish to maximize their *total return* should look around for the unit trust that offers the highest long term yield, regardless of unit price. Ask the sales person which trust has the highest. In any case, avoid any trusts with zero percent coupons in their portfolio—they usually distort the yield picture.

Diversification

Let's see om practice what we discussed earlier about *diversification*. In the 1970's investors lost confidence in the bonds of many states, causing mass liquidations and severe price declines. Diversify, diversify. Don't put too much money in any one place. What if you're in a particularly high-tax state? Still diversify. Especially after you have bought $100,000 or more in tax-exempts, give up part of your local tax-exemption to achieve greater real safety. One rule I use: no more than one-quarter of your uninsured tax-exempts in any one state; no more than another one-quarter if insured; and the rest elsewhere. If for some reason you have a large amount of money to invest at one time, as from life insurance proceeds, or the sale of substantial property, refer to the dollar cost averaging techniques also back in Chapter 3.

The Shopping for Yield Step

The highway looks good, you have picked your maturity and quality, you've decided to maximize either current or total return and you are well diversified. *Now* you're ready to do some yield comparing. Joe and Marci did it by feeling their way along, but let's see if we can organize things better. If you're like me, you shop at the supermarket with a sharp eye out for the best buys, even on the littlest things. It feels better to get good deals. Why not be at least as smart in the financial supermarket where you can save a thousand times more? The last step is to calculate what yield you will get after all taxes. It's easy to be persuaded that a state-exempt trust will be better for you, but test the numbers before you buy. I've seen many people pay so much for bonds of their own state

Figure 11.2
1991 STATE AND LOCAL TAX LEVIES ON OUT-OF-STATE MUNICIPAL BONDS
COMBINED INCOME AND PERSONAL PROPERTY TAXES IN MAXIMUM BRACKETS

NONE 0%	LOW 1 - 4%	AVERAGE 5 - 7%	HIGH 8 - 9%	HIGHEST 10 - 14%
DEDUCT 0%	DEDUCT .05 - .20%	DEDUCT .25 - .35%	DEDUCT .40 - .45%	DEDUCT .50 - .70%
Alaska	Florida	Alabama	Arizona	Connecticut
Nevada	*Illinois	Arkansas	California	Hawaii
New Mexico	Indiana	*Colorado	Delaware	*Iowa
South Dakota	North Dakota	Georgia	D.C.	Massachusetts
Texas		Kentucky	Idaho	Montana
Utah		Louisiana	*Kansas	N.Y.C. & N.Y.
Washington		Maryland	Maine	
Wyoming		Mississippi	Michigan	
		Missouri	Minnesota	
		Nebraska	New York	
		New Hampshire	North Carolina	
		New Jersey	Oregon	
		Ohio	Vermont	
		*Oklahoma		
		Pennsylvania		
		Rhode Island		
		South Carolina		
		Tennessee		
		Virginia		
		West Virginia		
		*Wisconsin		

* These states also tax some of their own bonds.

Source: *Guide to State and Local Taxation*, Merrill Lynch & Co., 1991.

that they would have been better off buying higher yielding out-of-state bonds. Let's say that you're a resident of San Francisco, and that you have located an offering of a national trust at 8%, at the same time that someone is trying to sell you a similar quality long-term, California U.I.T. yielding a 7.25%. Figure 11.2 shows that an out-of-state yield of 8% reduces about .40%. to 7.60% after California state tax. Which one do you buy? The national, because you keep more even after state tax. So, before you buy, shop around. Most of the sponsors listed in Chapter 5 offer many state and national exempt U.I.T.s, so pick the one that gives the highest after-all-tax yield.

Choosing Among Sponsors

Which sponsor should you use? It doesn't make much difference. That's why they advertise so heavily. Far more important is that you pick the one that suits you best.

As we have pointed out, unit investment trusts are only one way to earn tax-exempt income. They have their flaws, but since so many individuals buy trusts I thought we should spend a fair amount of time on them. Unit holders tend to be the smallest investors, the little guys. But the little guys have a way of growing bigger.

SUMMARY ** CHAPTER 11 ** SUMMARY

How to Choose a U.I.T.

- Check the prerequisites—income, savings, other opportunities.

- Inspect the bond market signals—8, 3, 83.

- Pick the maturity that matches your needs.

- Select your credit quality, preferably not too high.

- Find the trust with the highest after-all-taxes yield.

CHAPTER 12

RATING THE U.I.T.S

WHITE'S INVESTMENT RATING FOR U.I.T.S: *

The Plus Side

As you may have gathered, I don't greatly admire unit investment trusts. One star says it all. Easy shopping for the customers, great money for the sellers. Most trusts are composed of well diversified bond portfolios, have experienced few major credit troubles, and certainly distribute tax-exempt income; there's no denying the convenience. If municipal bond investing were like eating out, U.I.T.s would be the fast food restaurants. However, convenience adds substantially to cost. The few extra dollars spent on take-out food may seem worthwhile, but with securities the expense is more serious. Joe and Marci encountered one of these expenses when they found that the cost of buying and selling trust units almost equalled an entire year's payout. Let's look at some of their other drawbacks.

The Minus Side

1.) *Immobility*. Unit investment trust portfolios stay fixed permanently, a significant fault, because during a U.I.T.'s life some of their bonds will inevitably weaken, some will grow stronger, and other dislocations come to pass. In any of these cases unit holders miss an opportunity because the portfolio is frozen shut.

101

2.) *The Load Loss.* U.I.T.s carry high sales charges, averaging about 5%. Even worse, if units are *ever* redeemed, not only is the sales charge lost, there is, also a redemption cost. As a result, unless unit holders retain the trust until its maturity, they *never* receive their promised rate of return.

3.) *Portfolio Composition.* Most sponsors pick their U.I.T. portfolios partly in response to sales considerations, resulting in inferior bond composition. The fastest selling U.I.T.s are those offering total tax-exemption, a selling price near $1,000, and big commissions—high powered, simple, and rich. Sponsors get the point, and design trusts which sacrifice longer term investment considerations to gain these quick and profitable sales. Their usual construction works against the U.I.T. customer in two respects: the relentless pursuit of complete tax-exemption over-concentrates portfolios in bonds of one state; and choosing offering prices near $1,000 deliberately sacrifices true return.

4.) *Yield.* U.I.T.s compete against unpackaged bonds and so they have to show about the same yields. Unpackaged bonds are usually marked up about 2% to individual buyers, but U.I.T.s are marked up 5%, which would naturally decrease their yield. The trust sponsors have no magic—they pay the same as other dealers for their bonds. The 3% differential is manufactured, by a synthetic process of combining shorter, higher coupon bonds with longer, lower coupon ones, resulting in a yield overstated by at least the 3% extra profit margin.

I estimate that the combined effect of these flaws adds up to something like 1.00% in yield each and every year. Here is my breakdown, although I'll be the first to admit that these are difficult numbers to calculate with precision.

Loss of Income from U.I.T. Flaws

1.	Immobility	.50%
2.	Load factor	.25
3.	Portfolio Composition	.25
	Total	1.00%

A trust advertised and sold at, for instance, 7.50%, will only return a true, actual 6.50% or so. Think how you would react if you subtracted 1% from the income on all your investments and see how you'd feel about the shortfall. Untrue at any yield. Many investors agree with these conclusions and are now buying fewer trusts and more funds and bonds.

The Worst U.I.T.s

So there's the picture—advantages and drawbacks combine to make a one star, fairly decent parcel of tax-exempt goods. Let's review the four principal drawbacks—immobility, the load factor, faulty bond composition, and the yield game, to see how to avoid the worst U.I.T.s. First, immobility. Trusts cannot respond to either favorable or unfavorable developments, so if you buy one you're stuck. Secondly, the load loss factor. If there's anything but the *remotest* chance you'll want to take the money out within a few years avoid any U.I.T. like the plague. Better to spend and enjoy your savings than to see them eaten up. Third, bond composition. The selection of U.I.T. portfolios is strongly affected by their marketing elements to the detriment of investors. Beware of over-concentration of

Figure 12.1
U.I.T. INVESTMENT CHARACTERISTICS

	Price Stability	Principal Safety	Typical Relative Yield
Shorter Term			
5 Year National	High	Extremely High	6.00%
10 Year National	Moderate	Very High	6.50%
12-15 Year National	Moderate	Very High	6.75%
Long Term			
State Insured	Low	Extremely High	6.50%
State	Low	Very High	6.75%
National Insured	Low	Extremely High	6.75%
National	Low	Very High	7.00%
Lower Grade	Poor	Moderate	?%
Junk	Very Poor	Very Low	?%

bonds in any one state—it's risky business. Particularly shun trusts containing any zero coupon bonds. At maturity just guess what you'll be stuck with. Also watch any trust containing many premium bonds. The higher the premiums, the more likely they will be called in early. Fourth, yield calculations are tricky work, and U.I.T.s usually overstate return. In any case, use the procedures detailed in Chapter 11.

However, despite all their faults, unit trusts do have their place. After all, investors have bought $100 billion worth, so there have to be some reasons. If you want a certain income, don't want to put your money where it's traded around all the time, and can't chose a bond yourself, then maybe a U.I.T. is for you. Trusts are easy-to-understand tax-exempt vehicles, and will get you where you want to go. However, like some of our flashiest older cars, they guzzle fuel, grow shabby fast, and are primarily designed to bring sponsors big profits. Fortunately, there are plenty of other choices.

SUMMARY ** CHAPTER 12 ** SUMMARY

Rating the U.I.T.s

- U.I.T.s offer one star tax-exempt income.

    For investors with a few thousand dollars they do provide substantial convenience.

- Their drawbacks are substantial:

    Their original composition is inherently faulty.

    Their high sales charge impairs total return.

    Their immobile portfolios prevent replacing and improvement.

- Their yield is overstated.

- Look elsewhere before buying a U.I.T.

Section III
The Managed Funds

WHITE'S INVESTMENT RATING: **

CHAPTER 13

AN INDIVIDUAL INVESTOR CASE EXAMPLE—PART 4

We left our Zotti example couple with an investment problem—what to do with a significant family bequest. In my experience, receiving substantial proceeds from insurance or from inheritances, both of which are apt to occur unexpectedly, can cause people a lot of trouble. All of a sudden there's a lot of money and no one knows how to invest it. Buying a few U.I.T. units was not an investment disaster for Marci and Joe. However, they are now beyond the category of small investors. They correctly intuit that they should leave U.I.T.'s behind and proceed to other fields. Appropriately, an ad for a growth stock fund, the Leif Ericsson Adventure, caught Joe's eye one day. In a low-keyed, self-assured way, its manager, Olde Yankee Financial listed its fine record, and boasted that it never charged any sales fees. Joe, recalling the hefty U.I.T. load, showed the ad to Marci.

> MARCI: Yes, I was reading about this kind of fund, a managed stock fund I think they called it. Some of them have stocks and others have bonds. Funds don't charge when they sell to you, like U.I.T.'s. It said they charge just a little every year, like half a percent. I think it said they're called open end.

JOE: What happens when you want to redeem them?

MARCI: I'm not sure. How should I know? Why don't you ask Steve?

When Joe called Steve he was surprised to find that he was no longer with Tower & Co., and soon heard a new "account executive" throwing a hard sales pitch straight at him. He didn't like it and quickly said good-bye. Joe and Marci talked it over that night, resolving to forget about Steve and Tower entirely.

One evening Marci called Olde Yankee, using the toll-free number in the ad, and asked about their tax-exempt bond managed funds. Olde Yankee was offering three municipal bond funds—intermediate maturity, long term, and high yield. When she asked about their yield, she got three quotes—one each for three different funds, in both price and yield—but there were so many numbers she didn't catch which was which. When Marci asked what the return would probably be for the next year, she was told that that was all the yield they could mention. Marci guessed that they were being careful not to violate some security regulations, and she was right—you have to be careful how you sell or represent securities to the public in any detail. The representative gave her some more bond fund quotes, took Marci's name and address, promising to send some material, which arrived promptly.

One night Joe picked up Olde Yankee's material and peered at its seven or eight pieces of literature ranging all the way from a little bright blue square describing a taxable Ginnie Mae fund, to yellow and green fold-outs with lions and pyramids describing Olde Yankee Aggressive, to a long IRA application. He pointed out to Marci a graph of Aggressive's record of growth. Except for a little dip in the early nineteen eighties, it had gone straight up from $50 million to over $300 million. They looked at it and wondered whether this increase represented profits for the investors or something else.

JOE: It looks as though they *manage* the bonds, not like U.I.T.s, where they stay put forever. And here's the part about a fund's being open-ended. They issue more shares when money comes into the fund, and then retire them when people redeem—that's why funds grow so much.

The couple saw that the money from Marci's mother's bequest was sitting in U. S. Treasury bills, and when Joe looked up the bill rates in *The New York Times* he saw that they were around 7%, which he figured would leave her only four and change after tax.

JOE: O.K. How about a stock fund?

MARCI: No, thanks. There's no way I'd buy stocks for mother. I know nothing about them. I'm definitely keeping the money safe.

JOE: A good corporate mutual fund, I think you can get ten percent. Knock off a third ... that's only six something. Still not as good as seven tax-exempt. Maybe we'd better look at the bond fund stuff again, to see what's what.

Questions about Funds

Joe knew that the income on a U.I.T. is fixed for its life at so many dollars a year and he looked for a corresponding figure in the Olde Yankee fund material. The covering two-color letter asserted that Olde Yankee never imposed a sales charge and that you could write checks on the account for free. But it said nothing about the funds' income rates. He saw a sheet describing the ratings of the bonds in the various fund portfolios and their geographical distribution, a handy application return envelope, and also a prospectus for a money market fund. They certainly make things easy, he thought, maybe too easy. He looked at the 16-page prospectus titled 'Olde Yankee Tax Free Fund', but aside from income figures for the past 8 years, there was no yield information and nothing in the little brochure, either. Very cagey, he thought.

He puzzled his way through thirteen vertical columns and ten horizontal rows of per share data until he thought he saw the column he wanted—the price history of the shares (the net asset value). They had come out at exactly $10.00, hit a low of $5.30, and were currently worth $8.45. At one point the shares had lost almost half their value and after ten years were still lower than their original price. Not too impressive, thought Joe.

MARCI: Look how badly Olde Yankee Aggressive did. They lost almost half their money. Some managing!

JOE: That's because the yields went up. You know, back in the early eighties, when interest rates went sky high. Right there, next to the share price, you can see how the yields went up. Twelve percent tax-free! Wish we could get that now.

MARCI: Yes, but look at the loss, half their investment. That's more than all the income—a loss counting everything.

JOE: But they made a pretty good comeback. From the bottom there, at $5.30, it went up as high as $9.45. Almost doubled their money.

MARCI: But this is supposed to be a *managed* fund. Maybe they didn't watch very well, or bought some of those WHOOPS bonds I've read about, which didn't pay back at all.

JOE: Maybe. Let's take a look at the income.

MARCI: I started that. Aggressive was paying sixty cents to start. Now if this was a U.I.T. it would stay at sixty cents, even if the price went up or down. Where is its dividend—that's what they call fund payout—dividends, right?

JOE: Right. Income on trusts, dividends on funds. It's flat. Sixty, sixty, sixty-one, fifty-nine, back to sixty last year. No change. Let's figure the whole thing. Say ten years at sixty cents, or six dollars income. Take away the dollar fifty-five loss, that's up about four and a half. Ten dollars invested, and only four and a half back, that's forty-five percent in ten years. That's only four and a half percent. That's terrible! After inflation it's nothing!

In the meanwhile, Marci had called Hy Allman, her mother's broker. Hy was with Hudson & West Securities, a large full service securities house, and she asked him if he could recommend a municipal bond fund. Hy told her that he talked to her mother every few months, reporting to her about the investments he watched over for her. All was well, he said. Hy asked Marci a few questions about the purpose of the investments, and also about her own financial situation, but in a general way, low pressure. Allman said he would be glad to send some material describing the Hudson & West family of funds, and suggested she look especially at Hudson Higher Yield Fund. Within a few days three sets of their literature arrived, all green and yellow, pretty slick, with folders and brochures and four-color inserts. Once you start calling investment firms these days your mailbox is soon stuffed fuller than usual. These enclosures were similar to Olde Yankee's, again with no hint of the future rate of return. The material appeared much the same, except that instead of boasting about no sales charge, this pack included a schedule of fees, ranging up to 4%. One fund also started operations at $10 a share, hit a low in 1982, at $7.31, or off 27%, and she saw that it now was at $10.70, 70 cents, or 7% in ten years.

MARCI: That Olde Yankee stinks, compared to this one. Look at this Hudson fund's income. From 65 cents to 75, and now 78 cents. Much better. I wonder why the big difference?

JOE: Beats me. Maybe Hy will know.

So Marci called broker Hy Allman, who suggested some unpackaged New York Power Authority bonds, not in a fund, but she was negative. She said she had seen an ad for an Olde Yankee high-yield fund at 7.25%—better than the six something most of the other ads were pushing. Hy said that he liked the high yield funds right then, but that Hudson Higher Yield had the best record of this kind, better than any no-loads, and he would be glad to show her why some day. Marci asked him what the difference was between U.I.T.s and funds, and Hy replied that there were two big differences. Trusts stay the same size and their bonds are not traded around. Open end funds grow larger or smaller according to how much money is in them and their bonds are switched around all the time. Marci rather liked Hy's matter-of-fact tone and an appointment was arranged. A few days later Joe and Marci both went up to Hy's office and they soon got down to business.

Hy handed her the prospectuses for four different funds—Hudson Daily, Hudson Munisured, Hudson Discount Insured, and a lower grade fund, Hudson Aggressive. He showed them the proposal in Figure 13.1.

MARCI: I don't want to invest it all right away, I like the idea of keeping some in the money market account. I'm worried about all those twenty or thirty year bonds, insured or not.

HY: That's something to consider, absolutely. I know your mother relies on you and naturally you'll want to talk it over with your brothers as well.

Figure 13.1
MS. ANNE YOUNG
PROPOSED ADDITIONAL INVESTMENTS

	Market Value	Before Taxes		After Taxes	
		Yield	Income	Yield	Income
Hudson Daily T-X Fund	$150,000	5.75%	$ 8,625	5.75%	8,625
Hudson Short T-X Fund	75,000	6.65%	4,988	6.65%	4,988
Hudson Insured T-X Fund	75,000	7.35%	5,513	7.35%	5,513
	$300,000	6.38%	$19,126	6.38%	$19,126

MARCI'S INVESTMENT

HY: Now about *your* part of the money. What ideas do you have there? Stocks, bonds, funds, what?

She told him she didn't like stocks, but asked more about tax-exempt managed funds. Hy questioned her to make sure she had an adequate cash reserve, was in the 28% bracket, and said he'd be glad to open an account for her. Joe and Marci liked his approach, and these questions and answers soon followed.

Q: Should we worry about managed fund prices going up and down?

A: Yes, definitely. Market action tells you a lot about an investment. The higher the price goes the better.

Q: Was their analysis of Olde Yankee's and Hudson's results correct?

A: A little simplified, but essentially correct.

Q: Were these funds' results typical?

A: Yes.

Q: Why the big disparity between the two funds' market performances?

A: Olde Yankee probably loaded up with long bonds when the market was high, suffered big losses, then switched out near the bottom, underperforming both down and up.

Q: Why the difference in income growth?

A: Hudson traded all the way down, and also on the way back up, increasing its income substantially.

Q: Can past fund results predict future results?

A: That's hard to prove. Funds change management strategies, and also their personnel, all the time.

Q: Why don't they include a total return figure in the ads, showing yield after losses, or profits?

A: If it looks good, they brag. If it looks bad, they don't have to show it.

Q: Doesn't the S.E.C. really care about the truth in advertising part?

A: Yes, but they don't know what they're doing. Mostly hungry young lawyers dying to get onto Wall Street themselves.

Q: Who can we rely on—just ourselves?

A: Who else? I can help, but it's really up to you.

Q: Are funds better than U.I.T.'s?

A: Some funds have had better results than trusts, some worse, but overall funds have performed about 1% better in total annual return. 1% of 8% yield is plenty big.

Q: Which is better, load or no-load?

A: The one that goes up and increases income. If they perform the same, a no-load is better.

Q: What load does Hudson Munisured charge?

A: 4%.

Q: With so many no-load funds out there, how can your load funds compete?

A: Because we have to work harder to outperform the no-loaders, and we have.

Q: Which ones would you recommend for me?

A: Hudson New York Munisured and New York Aggressive.

Q: Who should I buy from?

A: I'm doing the work and I should get the order. It looks as though tax-exempts are definitely for you. Would you like me to work up an investment sheet?

Hy pointed out that only half of Anne's money would be invested then, following our ideas on dollar cost averaging. They liked that idea, and continued with a discussion of Hudson & West's tax-exempt product line, Hy finally half-convincing them about his load funds' superiority. He also said that funds provide 100% liquidity at all times, echoing the assertion of one of the sales pamphlets.

How accurate was Hy's information? Excellent, right on the beam, until he veered toward his products, where the salesman in him took over. They promised to take another look at the literature and thanked Hy for all the answers as they left.

JOE: Why do they charge a big load with all the no-loads around? That's a lot of money.

MARCI: O.K., but you'll have to admit their record isn't bad. However, I don't like Aggressive or Higher Yield. They're too ... aggressive.

Within a few days the couple received a copy of Hy's proposal, as in Figure 13.2.

Marci thought it all over and after consulting with her mother and the family gave him the order to go ahead with Anne's legacy. She figured that she could stand more risk with her own money in return for more income. We will see how she made out in Chapter 17.

Figure 13.2
MARCELLA AND JOSEPH ZOTTI, JR.
PROPOSED ADDITIONAL INVESTMENTS

Plan A	Market Value	Before Taxes		After Taxes	
		Yield	Income	Yield	Income
Hudson Daily N.Y. T-X Fund	$ 20,000	5.25%	$1,050	5.25%	1,050
Hudson Aggressive T-X Fund	40,000	8.30%	3,320	7.64%	3,056*
Hudson N.Y. T-X Fund	40,000	7.55%	3,020	7.55%	3,020
	$100,000	7.39%	$7,390	7.13%	$7,126

Plan B	Market Value	Before Taxes		After Taxes	
		Yield	Income	Yield	Income
Hudson Daily N.Y. T-X Fund	$ 50,000	5.25%	$2,625	5.25%	2,625
Hudson National T-X Fund	25,000	8.00%	2,000	7.36%	1,840*
Hudson N.Y. Insured T-X Fund	25,000	7.55%	1,888	7.55%	1,888
	$100,000	6.51%	$6,513	6.35%	$6,353

*New York State and New York City only

SUMMARY ** CHAPTER 13 ** SUMMARY

An Individual Investor Case Example—Part 4

- Municipal bond mutual funds consist of packages of tax-exempt securities.

- Fund portfolios are actively traded by their managers.

- They come in no-load and load varieties.

CHAPTER 14

INTRODUCTION TO MANAGED FUNDS

History of Managed Funds

Back in Chapter 1 we talked about one of Wall Street's principal functions—helping the government sector, federal, and state and local, to raise money by placing its bonds with private investors. One mechanism in this process is the relatively new apparatus of tax-exempt *managed funds*. Although many other kinds of bond and stock funds have been around since 1924, unenlightened Federal regulations long prevented them from passing tax-exempt interest through to investors. The rules finally flexed in 1976, when the first municipal bond managed fund appeared. By year-end 1990, investors had placed $136 billion of their savings in a great variety of tax-exempt funds and were outselling U.I.T.'s by over four to one. At this rate I estimate that by 1995 they will hold one-quarter of all outstanding municipal bonds.

Managed Funds Defined

What are these amazingly powerful municipal bond vehicles? They are specialized financial entities, designed and sold by an investment firm, managed by securities companies, and owned by their shareholders. One company, such as Dreyfus, creates a fund. The same, or a related company, such as Dreyfus Services, sells it, initially perhaps to a thousand or more investors who put their

117

Figure 14.1
MUNICIPAL BOND MANAGED FUNDS (OPEN AND CLOSED),
GROWTH

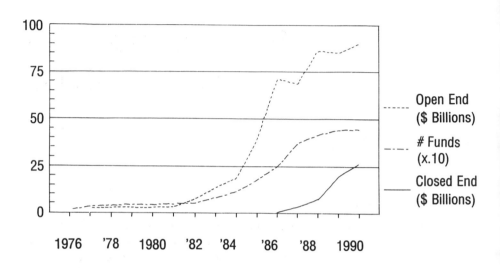

money into one big pool. Dreyfus as manager then buys and continually moni-
tors a portfolio of tax-exempt bonds within a defined set: nationwide or in one
state; short maturity or long; insured or not, etc. Each investor owns his proportionate part and everyone in the pool gets the same regular treatment, tax-free
and clear. How do fund managers make a profit? By charging an annual fee,
usually about three-quarters of one percent of principal. In addition, some funds
charge sales fees.

☞ *A DEFINITION*

Municipal Bond Fund

A *shareholder owned investment company* which holds a *managed portfolio* of
floating maturity municipal bonds from which it distributes *variable amounts* of
tax-exempt income.
There are two subtypes, open end and closed end.

The Four Fund Elements

Shareholder owned; managed portfolio; floating maturity; and *variable income.* These I call the four *general* features—they apply to all municipal bond funds. Later we will concentrate on the *special* features which distinguish their two subtypes, open end and closed end.

1- Shareholder Owned

Municipal bond funds are *owned by their shareholders,* the people who have pooled their savings together for a common investing purpose. Shares are issued and if an emergency ever occurred their owners would have the final say. However, since the business is run entirely by the managers, and so far smoothly, most funds dispense with the formalities of annual meetings and take no shareholder votes.

2 - Managed Portfolio

Fund portfolios are *managed.* When you put your money into one of them you delegate buying and selling control to the fund and its advisors, who within their defined investment limits—maturity, quality, or whatever—trade bonds as they see fit. What is the secret of their success? They buy bonds at wholesale, monitor and trade the portfolio, taking a reasonable annual fee for their services. The accent is on efficiency. The purpose of managing is to shelter the portfolio from losses, and to increase its value and income. This managing angle particularly appeals to investors who figure that the pros rarely make any really dumb moves. Everyone who drives a car makes a wrong turn once in a while, but investors figure that fund managers are more like bus drivers—they can get stuck in traffic like anyone else, but they don't get lost too often.

3 - Floating Maturity

Most bond funds *have no fixed maturity.* They are meant to be perpetual, not to go out of business when their bond portfolios mature. If, for example, you buy shares in a ten year intermediate fund, your money will not be returned in ten years. When the bonds grow shorter with the passage of time, the managers will sell them and re-invest the proceeds in longer intermediate term bonds. A U.I.T. will return $1,000 at a certain date, but fund runners roll their bonds over indefinitely. *Managed funds live forever.*

4 - Variable Income

Fund traders try to enhance the value of their portfolios by selling some of their bonds and replacing them with others as they see opportunities arise. Suppose a buyer is willing to pay a particularly high price for some California exempt bonds, to take advantage of exemption from that state's high income tax structure. If a nationally diversified fund can sell some San Diego 7% bonds and at the same time buy equal quality state of Illinois 7 1/4% at the same price, it may well decide to do just that. They maintain quality, equal out on price, and increase income by 1/4%. Trading like this results in a change in interest income to the fund, and thus in the rate of the fund's income distribution to shareholders. Naturally the managers try to increase income, but some trades may result in lowering it, or in changing the fund's face amount of bonds.

As you see, some of these features resemble those of the U.I.T.s. However, four differences sharply distinguish funds from trusts. 1.) Funds are owned directly by their shareholders. U.I.T.s are held in a trust. 2.) The bonds in fund portfolios are actively managed, that is traded in and out, almost continuously. U.I.T.s' bonds stay fixed in the trust. 3.) Fund managers gradually float the length of the portfolio longer, extending its life indefinitely. When U.I.T. bonds come due the trust expires. 4.) As fund portfolios are traded around their interest earned, and also face amount, fluctuates. U.I.T. income and principal does not change.

To repeat, with a U.I.T., the bonds stay put—what you see is what you get. Contrastingly, with funds you pool your money with other investors, receiving your share of the interest income and trading results, with no set date when your money is returned. Think of U.I.T.'s as *bonds*—fixed, closed-end packages of municipal bonds. Think of managed funds as *stocks*—in a company whose business is to manage your tax-exempt portfolio.

Managed funds come in two forms—*open end* and *closed end*. Both ends share the four general tax-exempt fund features—shareholder owned, managed portfolio, floating maturity, and varying return. First we look at the *special* qualities of the open end funds.

OPEN END FUNDS

Open End

A *mutual* investment company that issues a *variable number of shares* which are *priced by evaluation.* Their distributors offer *many* auxiliary *financial services.*

---

1 - Mutual and Expandable

When people mention *mutual funds* they usually mean the huge common stock funds, such as Magellan or Oppenheimer. *Open end* municipal bond funds are a specialized form of mutual fund. Mutual funds are officially known as open end, diversified, investment management companies and operate under the Investment Companies Act of 1940. All mutual funds are open ended, that is they are expandable, so that the number of their shares *varies* as money moves in or out of their pool. Investors, new or existing, are welcome to buy at any time. New shares are issued when investors buy shares, and shares are bought back when holders sell.

This feature, open-endedness, enables their managers to issue as many shares as they please. For instance, Fidelity advertises liberally, trying to attract more money into their various funds, tax-exempts included. If they succeed in attracting $3 million to a municipal bond fund selling at $10 on a certain day they issue 300,000 new shares, adding perhaps to the already issued 300 million. If, on the same day, other shareholders also chose to cash in 100,000 shares this produces a net change of plus 200,000 shares, or $2 million worth. With this added money Fidelity's managers will soon buy another $2 million dollars of tax-free bonds and add them to the portfolio. Each additional share sold means more profit for a distributor, and as Joe and Marci saw, fund salesmen aren't a bit shy about pushing their products.

2 - The Net Asset Value

Mutual fund portfolios are priced daily by professional evaluators. This appraisal is divided by the number of shares outstanding, to produce that day's *net asset value*. All investors who buy on the same day do so at this single price, *based* on the N.A.V. This price appears in the mutual fund sections of financially tuned newspapers. Shareholders who wish to sell simply turn their shares back to the distributor at that day's net asset value.

3 - Auxiliary Services

Most kinds of investments are more or less solitary, but not mutual funds. They are part of an outgoing family, and swing wide their doors to greet you with a hearty shout and open arms, eager to display their financial wares, stock, municipal bond, and many others. It's no ordinary doorman stationed there, either—it's a wise old lion, or even Ben Franklin himself at the height of his powers. Consider some of their personal services: watchful managing, monthly allowances, easy retirement income, no redemption fees, and even, magically, no taxes. Tax-exempts are only the beginning. Their operators offer taxable bond funds, stock funds of multiple market sectors, all suitable for I.R.A.s, Keoghs, 401(k)s, and other retirement plans. They will integrate your checking and savings accounts, safeguard your securities, and make it simple to switch assets around freely. You

Figure 14.2
NO-LOAD FUND DISTRIBUTORS–1990

	Tax-Ex Funds Managed	N.A.V. ($ Billions)	No-Load Market Share	Info Phone
Dreyfus	7	9.0	22.5%	800-645-6561
Fidelity	18	7.4	18.6%	800-544-6666
T. R. Price	4	2.2	5.5%	800-638-5660
Scudder	4	1.2	3.0%	800-225-2470
U.S.A.A.	3	2.2	5.5%	800-531-8000
Vanguard	9	6.3	15.8%	800-662-7447
		28.3	71.1%	

Source: Lipper Analytical Services, Inc.

can write a check, arrange for your regular bills to be paid, receive one unified statement, and get answers to your questions at toll free numbers twenty-four hours a day. We'll cover some of the their drawbacks in Chapter 18.

Open End No-load Funds

These families of open end funds come in two branches. They look almost alike, sound alike, advertise alike, practically identical twins. But these is one major difference. When you buy shares from a *no-load* fund distributor, such as Dreyfus, Fidelity, or Vanguard, you pay the N.A.V., the net asset value, and not a penny more. Their ads invariably trumpet this great advantage and it is indeed an appealing one. Who are these distributors? They are not registered broker-dealers; they are independent investment companies who run tax-exempt funds, among many other financial services. For instance, Scudder, Stevens and Clark manages 10 tax-exempt no-load funds totaling $1.5 billion. If you need information, just pick up the telephone, and they'll be delighted to oblige. At year end

Figure 14.3
LOAD FUND DISTRIBUTORS 1990.

	Tax-Ex Funds Managed	N.A.V. ($ Billions)	Load Market Share	Info Phone
Colonial	3	2.2	2.7%	800-248-2828
Franklin	11	22.8	27.8%	800-632-2180
I.D.S.	4	6.2	7.6%	800-328-8300
Kemper	1	2.2	2.7%	800-621-1048
Merrill Lynch	7	5.8	7.1%	800-637-3863
M.F.S.	5	2.8	3.4%	800-343-2829
Nuveen	2	1.5	1.8%	800-621-7210
Prudential	4	2.6	3.2%	800-648-7637
Putnam	5	4.5	5.5%	800-354-5487
Shearson	2	2.1	2.6%	212-528-7000
		52.7	64.2%	

Source: Lipper Analytical Services, Inc.

1990 over 70 no-load municipal bond funds were in business with total assets of $44 billion, for about a 35% tax-exempt fund market share.

Open End Load Funds

Open end municipal bond *load* funds function internally just like no-loads. But where no-load funds sell right at the N.A.V., load funds add on a sales charges, a substantial one, typically 4 percent. The load funds are distributed by dealers, like Oppenheimer and Shearson, and also by the independents, like M.F.S. and N.E.L. If something like 'No commissions' doesn't leap out at you from a fund ad, you can bet you'll pay a sales fee, since their no-load competition never misses a chance to emphasize its sturdiest selling point. The loaders claim that they work harder and get better results. We will take a look at the performance records in Chapter 17. Loaders comprise about 50% of all managed funds, running $65 billion in total money.

To recapitulate, *all* municipal bond managed funds (open end no-load, open end load, and closed end) share four general characteristics—shareholder owned, managed, floating maturity, and varying dividends. *Open end* mutual funds, both no-load and load, share three special characteristics—expandable, priced by evaluation, and full of service.

CLOSED END FUNDS

Now that we understand open end funds, we move on to the *closed end* kind. Closed end corporate stock and bond funds have been around Wall Street for a long time, but the first one composed of municipals appeared in 1985. Closed ends share the *general* characteristics of all managed municipal bond funds—shareholder owned, managed, floating maturity, and variable dividend payments. However, closed ends are *not* mutual. They do not share the three *special* characteristics of open end mutual funds (expandable, evaluated, and other services). Closed end funds issue a *fixed number of shares*. They are *priced by the market*. They provide few *other financial services*.

One language slippery place: Closed end funds sometimes calls themselves *trusts*, perhaps to satisfy regulatory or legal demands. If Einstein Tax-Free *Trust* is a *fund*, it's an un*trust*worthy name.

☞ *A DEFINITION*

Closed End

An ivestment company that issues a *fixed number of shares* which are *priced by market action,* and offer *few* auxiliary *financial services.*

Fixed Number of Shares

Closed end trusts begin life when a *fixed number of shares* is sold in a large public underwriting. After a public offering is sold no more shares are issued, it's closed. You either have to wait until another new deal comes along, or you can buy shares of an existing fund. In 1986, the first sizeable one, $350 million from Massachusetts Financial, was offered successfully. In the following year Nuveen started its $1.5 billion Municipal Value-Fund. At year end 1990 over fifty closed end tax-exempt funds were outstanding, with about $25 billion in total assets.

Traded on an Exchange

Closed end funds shares are transferable—owners buy and sell to one another, through brokers. Shares trade like any other stock, and prices are set by current supply and demand on either the New York or American Stock Exchange. Take a look at the regular stock tables, and you'll see 'KmpMu' 'NuvCal' right along with 'GenEl' and 'CocaCl', etc. How do you invest in one? By placing an order with your broker just like buying any other listed security and paying a regular commission. If you need information, ask your broker or contact the fund distributors directly. There are usually two or three different prices per day, such as 10 1/2, 10 5/8 and 10 3/4, as their market swings up and down. When you want to cash in closed end shares you simply sell them on the exchange, again paying your broker's commission.

Closed end shares also have a N.A.V., bond portfolio value divided by number of shares. Supply and demand dictates that closed end shares will trade differently from their underlying value, sometimes higher, sometimes lower. Recently they have been trading higher than their portfolio value, that is, above the fund's N.A.V, indicating a rising market or a shortage of tax-exempt bonds. See the following chapters for more on this.

Figure 14.4
CLOSED END MUNICIPAL BOND FUND ORIGINATORS

	Funds Managed	T.N.A. ($ Billions)	Closed End Market Share	Info Phone
Allstate/Witter	7	1.539	11.5%	800-841-8000
Colonial	3	.621	4.6%	800-248-2828
Dreyfus	5	1.115	8.3%	800-645-6561
Kemper	2	.506	3.8%	800-442-2848
M.F.S.	1	.329	2.5%	800-343-2829
Merrill Lynch	4	1.231	9.2%	800-637-3863
Nuveen	17	6.371	47.5%	800-351-4100
Putnam	3	.768	5.7%	800-354-5487
VanKampen	3	.327	2.4%	800-225-2222
Other	5	.614	4.6%	
		13.415	100.0%	

Sources: Llipper Analytical Services, Inc., 12/31/90.

Closed end funds do not imitate their brother open ends, they provide few other *financial services*.

Don't worry too much if fund structural differences seem puzzling at first—even experienced financial people mix them up all the time, with little harm done. To simplify, just remember that all funds have a managed portfolio. Open ends trade only through their sponsors, while closed ends trade on an exchange.

SUMMARY ** CHAPTER 14 ** SUMMARY

Introduction to Managed Funds

Municipal bond funds have:
- Managed portfolios.

- Floating maturities.

- Variable returns.

- There are two types, open end and closed end.

- *Open end* funds are mutual—their number of shares expands and contracts as money moves in and out of them.

- They are priced theoretically, by daily evaluation, and trade only through their sponsors.

- Some, the *no-loads*, carry no sales charge. Others, the *loads,* carry substantial sales charges.

- *Closed end* funds issue a fixed number of shares.

- They are priced by supply and demand, as investors buy and sell them on a stock exchange.

- Commissions are paid as with other listed stocks.

CHAPTER 15

THE MANAGED FUND MENU

Funds represent one step up from U.I.T.s in the tax-exempt world—sometimes I think of fund buyers as on the second tier of municipal bond investing. Fund investors tend to hold larger amounts, often adding on to existing positions. Fund distributors advertise their wares energetically and push a formidable assortment. However, before you succumb to their sales pitches, hold off a while, and see what's what. I like to go over a restaurant's bill of fare carefully, and don't mind asking the captain for explanations; all the more important with investing. First let's discuss the basics of how funds are priced and then organize a menu of the products their distributors are so anxious to sell.

Open End Denominations

We saw that U.I.T.s come in handy $1,000 denominations, but open end funds make it even easier to invest. Their denominations are *shares*, and above a minimum as low as $100 you can buy exactly the amount you wish, right down to thousandths of a share. Suppose that an open end is selling for $10. If you happen to have exactly $25,500.51 in a money market account you can switch all of it into 2,550.051 shares of a fund and every penny is invested, passbook savings style.

Net Asset Value

Openend funds are born in an I.P.O., an *initial public offering*. A typical offering comes out at $10 per share. Distributors may offer 25 million shares to the public, each at $10, thus raising $250 million, a worthwhile amount to manage. After the money is raised and invested the fund's portfolio is evaluated daily. This value divided by the number of shares produces the *net asset value* per share. So if the portfolio of the same fund is later evaluated at $225 million, the new N.A.V. would be $9 per share. All subsequent share sales, and also all redemptions, are *based* on the prevailing N.A.V. (Some distinctions follow shortly.) Many financial newspapers carry fund quotes under 'Mutual Funds' headings, as in Figure 15.1, so you can see their current value and also the price changes from the previous day.

Figure 15.1
A NO-LOAD FUND QUOTATION LIST

Fidelity Spartan:

CAHY	9.85	NL	+ .01
Govt	10.27	NL	+ .04
MunInc	9.88	NL	+ .01
NY HY	9.79	NL	...
PAHY	9.63	NL	...

The New York Times, 10/2/90.

No-load Fund Pricing

A translation of Figure 15.1: Fidelity Spartan is operating four tax-exempt managed funds—a short-term, an intermediate maturity, and also long-term insured and (Aggressive) lower grade funds, all no-load. The second column shows the price at which investors can sell their shares, the N.A.V., $10. The next column indicates the price at which investors can buy. If Joe and Marci had decided to buy $25,000 worth of Spartan Short Term, they would have bought exactly 2,500 shares. In this case it reads "no-load", meaning that the buy price is also the N.A.V. You can buy or sell from a no-load fund at the same price, like magic. The last column shows the changes from the prior day. Their short fund fell one cent a share, the intermediate three cents, etc.

Load Fund Pricing

Load funds can be redeemed (sold back to the distributor) right at the N.A.V., but when you *buy* they add on a sales fee, usually about 4% on long-term funds.

Figure 15.2
A LOAD FUND QUOTATION LIST

```
Dreyfus Premier:
  CAMu  p  12.00  12.57  + .01
  CTMu  p  10.93  11.45  + .02
  FLMu  p  13.51  14.15  + .02
  Gnma  p  14.09  14.75  + .04
  MDMu  p  11.66  12.21  + .01
  MIMu  p  13.82  14.47  + .02
  MAMu  p  10.70  11.20  + .01
  MNMu  p  13.87  14.52  + .02
  NYMu  p  12.61  13.20  + .01
  OHMu  p  11.67  12.22  + .01
  PAMu  p  14.79  15.49  + .02
  MuBd  p  12.83  13.43  + .01
```

The New York Times, 10/2/90.

Where the no-load fund newspaper quotes have only one price, the load funds carry two—the N.A.V. and also the selling price, usually about 4% higher.

No-load Fund Sales

No-load and load funds advertise almost identically—you have to look hard to see which is which. The tip-off is that the no-loaders invariably brag "NO COMMISSIONS" or "Never a sales or redemption fee!", while the load funds stress other points, such as their high yields and easy marketability. If no-loads buy or sell at the same price, how can they make money? From the fees they charge for managing the portfolio, averaging around 3/4% a year, 7 or 8 cents on a $10 share. This may not sound like much, out on 250 million shares it adds up to $18 million every year. What is their marketing strategy? Heavy advertising, customer response, and low cost handling. The Zottis responded to an Olde Yankee ad, received a lot of literature, and are seriously considering buying. No-loads resemble a take-out-only Chinese restaurant. They advertise, you choose, and pay little for service or atmosphere.

Load Fund Sales

Load fund distributors operate almost identically. They also charge for managing, but, more importantly, they also take a mark-up when selling to investors. Most of the load funds are autonomous corporations, but affiliated with general securities dealers. The load funds run by advisory companies owned by Shearson, Dean Witter, and Prudential are prominent examples. They also publicly advertise for sales, but they rely heavily on their own brokers' contacts with customers. The other loaders, like Franklin, M.F.S. and Putnam, are independent distributors, not owned by dealers. The independents advertise liberally and employ their own sales forces to contact customers. In addition, some have contracts with dealers with whom they split their 4 or 5% loads. Merrill Lynch will gladly sell you their own regular funds; however, if you want a high yield fund, you'll probably be piloted (*steered,* even) toward the Eaton Vance Fund. Eaton Vance builds in a profit, gives up most of it to Merrill, so they—and the herd—are content.

Many people wonder how load funds can exist in the same investment universe as no-loads, since they provide an apparently identical product at a significantly higher price. We'll make some recommendations in Chapter 17, but it's well to understand that they are not identical in one significant respect—service. Buying takeout food can be a perfectly good deal, but sometimes I like to sit down to a Chinese meal, be served, read the fortune cookie message, and

walk out leaving the clean-up behind. Most dealer fund sales stem from an established relationship between brokers and their customers. The broker supplies
information, responds to questions, finds the best fund for the customer, and
suggests changes when appropriate. At least that's the aim. A broker who provides you with such services deserves to be paid. If not, not, and maybe a no-
load is for you.

The Redemption Price

Shareholders *can redeem* most open end funds, both no-load and load, right at
the N.A.V. What does redeem mean? It's just a fancy term for *sell*. You or your
broker can sell mutual, open end funds directly back to their distributor at that
day's evaluated price. Any amount, no questions asked.

Closed End Funds

The introduction of the *closed end funds* was the most radical innovation in the
packaged municipal bond market in recent years. They are now selling at almost
one-third the rate of their older brothers the open ends and over half a million
U.S. households own shares in them. We discussed the similarities and distinctions between the two kinds in Chapter 14, and how closed end funds are priced
by investors. How can individual investors set the price of a bond fund?
Through supply and demand for their shares, sort of a financial democracy, one
share, one vote. Closed ends trade publicly on either the New York or the American Stock Exchange, and their price goes up and down as people buy and sell.
You buy shares on an exchange, paying a commission to your broker just as you
would on any other stock transaction. Instead of *redeeming* shares, you just sell
them in the same market, where they trade in price steps of eighths of a point,
like other listed securities.

Fund Commisions

On a continuum between the 0% no-loads and the 4% loads, closed end funds
represent a mid-way point. Stock Exchange Brokers usually charge 1 or 2% in
and the same out, in effect a low-load. Except for the way they're priced, closed
end funds act much like open ends. We return to discuss some other distinctions
in Chapter 17.
     Now let's go on to the menu proper, listing the funds, both open and closed
end, by portfolio composition. First we discuss bond *maturity*, the most signifi-

---

Figure 15.3
CLOSED END BOND FUNDS ON THE NEW YORK STOCK EXCHANGE

			Div	Yld	PE	Vol	High	Low	Close	Net Chg
81¾	48¼	Nucor	.48	.7	27	1229	73¾	69¾	73¾	— 4
10⅛	7	NuevE n		...	...	231	9⅞	9⅝	9⅞	— ⅛
12⅝	11½	NvCMI	.80	6.6	...	180	12½	12⅛	12⅛	— ⅜
15¼	13⅝	NvCPP n	1.02	6.9	...	51	14⅞	14¾	14¾	— ⅛
15⅛	13⅝	NvMAd n	1.06	7.2	...	566	14⅞	14⅝	14⅝	— ⅛
15⅛	13⅝	NvMO n	.18e	1.2	...	417	14⅝	14½	14½	...
15⅛	14⅝	NCMM n		...	...	31	15⅛	14⅞	14⅞	— ⅛
10⅝	9¾	NuvCal	.67a	6.6	...	105	10⅜	10⅛	10⅛	— ⅛
15⅛	14⅝	NvIQI n		...	...	168	14¾	14⅝	14¾	...
15¼	14⅜	NNMM n		...	...	81	15¼	15	15	— ¼
11	9⅞	NuvNY	.68a	6.6	...	130	10½	10¼	10¼	— ¼
15¼	14⅛	NvNYP n	1.05	6.9	...	63	15¼	15	15⅛	+ ⅛
12⅜	11¼	NvMul	.84	7.1	...	84	12	11⅞	11⅞	...
10⅝	9⅞	NuvMu	.71a	6.8	...	1828	10⅜	10¼	10⅜	+ ⅛
14⅞	13¾	NuvPP	1.05	7.2	...	373	14¾	14½	14½	— ¼
15⅜	14⅜	NuvPI	1.08	7.2	...	797	15	14⅞	15	— ⅛
92	73½	Nynex	4.56	6.1	18	3375	75⅛	73½	74¾	— ½

The New York Times, 8/4/90.

---

cant factor in determining fund performance. Then on to portfolio *quality* and its special types.

THE FUND PORTFOLIO MENU
1 - Arranged by Maturity

Back to the Yield Curve

We started talking about the yield curve in Chapter 3 and saw how shorter maturity dates mean lower volatility, and longer ones higher. In the U.S. economy, demand for short-dated, *highly liquid, low volatility* investments is usually greater than for long ones, resulting in *higher* prices and therefore lower interest rates. Does this make sense to you? Don't you sometimes *have* to settle for any available interest rate in order to have quick, 100 cents on the dollar, access to part of your money? If so, you see one factor that produces the yield curve, the desire for liquidity. Since 1971, the yields on unpackaged municipal bonds due in one year has averaged about 5%, on those due in five years about 6%, and on long bonds about 7.25%. Now let's see how this applies to fund yields, short, intermediate, and out long.

The Money Market Funds

The first tax-exempt money market funds appeared in 1980, and now some 225 of them manage over a million separate accounts totalling $75 billion. They are mutual, open end, and no-load. Everybody seems to be running one these days—independents such as Scudder, Stevens and Clark, and also dealers, for instance Butcher and Singer, who keep odd bits of my money busy between other investments. Money market funds are priced at $1 each and are designed to stay right there. Buy at $1, sell at $1, no fluctuations and no fees. In return for maximum liquidity investors accept whatever short term yields are available.

This breed of fund invests in municipal notes and other obligations which come due within a few weeks or months, thus avoiding fluctuations from their $1 value. You have to rely on the managers' credit choices, but so far none have disappointed. Some stay ultra-liquid, owning only high grade, shortest term securities, while others may go out a little longer, and richer, on the yield curve. In late 1990, you could get a 5.75% tax-exempt, a little better than a taxable money market rate of 7.50%, which was equivalent to 5.25% after tax.

Short Funds

Now we move from virtually risk-free parking places to our main subject, permanent investing in tax-exempts, and out a few years on the yield curve. (At this point the reader may wish to review my ideas about investment strategies in Chapter 3.) The tax-exempt money market funds provide *maximum liquidity*, and as we will see, the long-term funds offer *maximum income*. In between lie the *short* and *intermediate* maturity funds, which offer moderate liquidity and moderate income. *Short* funds, such as U.S.A.A.'s, emphasize the liquidity aspect by investing in portfolios due in about five years. If interest rates rise by 1% for five consecutive years, you can expect that short managed funds will lose about 20% of their principal value. See Figure 17.1. In late 1990 short uninsured funds were paying about 6%.

Intermediate Funds

Intermediate funds, such as Vanguard's Municipal Intermediate, emphasize the income aspect more strongly. They typically invest in bonds due in ten to fifteen years. See Figure 18.1 for my ideas on some fund investment qualities. In addition, a few funds take a different approach, limiting their purchases to an exact maturity. Their bonds are traded around some, but will all gradually come due, thus acting almost like trusts or unpackaged bonds due in that year. In any of these cases you can ask your salesperson to determine the exact length of any fund, and thus its safety/volatility factor. Or you can look at the most recent portfolio yourself—it's in the back of the prospectus. Five years of interest rates rising by 1% will probably bring a loss of about 30% to a 15 year maturity fund. In 1990 intermediate term national funds were paying about 6.75%.

Long Maturity Funds

The most common maturity fund type is the long term, composed of bonds due from about 25 to 40 years out. This is natural, since the majority of tax-exempt holders are in for long pull, and this is where the highest yields are found. The safety of principal ranges from high to extremely high. Once again, the market prices of long term bond funds depend on the level of competing interest rates. *Total return*, your income plus any profits or minus any losses, is what you should be seeking, and will depend on how you manage your own money. The N.A.V. of long funds will probably decline by about 35 to 40% in a five year period of rising rates. Long term funds were returning about 7.25% in 1990.

Funds Live Forever

I'd like to repeat that the maturity of U.I.T.s and unbundled bonds grows shorter with the passage of time. Not so with managed funds. They remain around a constant 5, or 10, or 35, years out, as their traders sell and replace their bonds, rarely allowing them to mature. Therefore, *the market value of managed funds, even shorter term ones, does not necessarily return to 100 cents on the dollar at any specific time*. Therefore, if you pay $8 a share for a fund originally issued at $10, its value may never return to $10. Indeed, many a fund started when rates were lower still sits at $7 or $8, even after a prolonged period of falling rates. As time passes, fund managers almost always sell out any bonds that have shortened maturities and replace them with longer, higher yielding, more volatile ones, thus keeping the fund alive. It's a rare fund manager that outperforms the market as a whole, so don't presume they will keep your bonds out of trouble. Watch your positions like a hawk, remembering 8, 3, 83. If you buy any maturity fund, think of it as a vehicle to help reach goals you set, and remember that it is your job, not the managers, or anyone else's, to maintain it properly.

THE FUND PORTFOLIO MENU
2 - Arranged by Credit Type

National Funds

The first municipal bond funds, the generic, no frills line, were composed of portfolios of investment grade, nationally diversified bonds. We call them *national funds*, and they are still the largest selling single variety with about a 30% share of the market. Their portfolios are composed mainly of average quality, 'A' rated bonds. Gilt edge, triple A bonds, and the low yields they pay, do not usually appeal to uninsured funds. National funds limit *credit* risk by diversifying, spreading their investment over many different bond issues, both as to location and to sources of payment. For example, in August, 1990, the largest single holding within any state in the $598 million Shearson Managed Municipals portfolio was $49 million of various bonds within Texas, only 8% of the total. Funds also watch out for over-concentration on one security type, usually avoiding owning too many housing, or health care bonds, for example.

State Funds

We discussed state and local taxes, which can run as high as 14% on municipal bond interest. In an effort to avoid these burdensome rates, higher income investors have long been buying unpackaged blocks of state and local tax-exempt bonds. A logical development was in the state-exempt direction and about 40% of all funds are now composed of bonds exempt within a single state. Some are free-standing, with their very own prospectuses. Others are issued under a combined title, a manager's umbrella entity under which many different funds are distributed. What kind of yield do state funds carry? Usually something like 1/4 to 1/2% lower than national funds. In late 1990 when the largest national funds were offered at a 7.25%, ten New York-exempt funds were yielding only 6.85%.

The Insured Funds

Municipal bond funds with portfolios protected against default began to appear in the early 1980's. Although over 99% of all municipals issued in recent years have met their obligations in full and on time, a few have not. During less stable economic cycles, notably during the early 1930's, a sizeable number of issuers defaulted on their debt service contracts. In addition, the various urban bond crises of 1974-76 still echo, if faintly. The specially designed insuring groups active in this business, with such names as M.B.I.A., A.M.B.A.C., B.I.G.I., and F.I.G.I.C., and also their triple A ratings, have made a great impression on investors.

Fund ads correctly point out that it's the portfolio that's insured and not the shareholders' market value. During 1986-90 35% of all managed funds were sold as insured. In most markets, insured funds can be bought at about .25% lower yield than comparable uninsured funds. In October 1990, one of Merrill's insured national funds was offered at 6.90%, while its comparable uninsured fund was at 7.20%. That's the price you pay for anti-default pills. We return to discuss the merits of insured funds in Chapter 17.

Lower Grade Funds

The wonderfully fat interest rates of the early eighties lured a great number of individual investors into our markets. Some fund operators, calling themselves 'High Yield', 'Aggressive', or 'High Income', have tried to recreate the returns of the good old days by putting together funds of higher yielding, but lower grade, municipal bonds. Since 1983 they have grown at an annual rate of 17%, and now comprise 7% of all tax-exempt funds. We sometimes call them "junk" funds, but not to their faces, and in fact this highly charged word doesn't entirely fit them. Many of their managers assemble maximum return portfolios through two devices by buying premium bonds, and buying bonds just under regular investment quality. These high yield funds are definitely worth looking at, but through a magnifying glass.

The Fund Hybrids

In the past five years managed funds have grown enormously. As I was walking along Park Avenue the other day, I passed one of their 'investment centers', a casually decorated office where you can sit down and invest on the spot. Individuals were being fitted for short, medium, and long maturities, like shoe lengths, and also for insured, state, and high yield widths. What happens if your investment requirements are both short and insured, or New York and an intermediate maturity? No problem, just order up one of the new hybrids, New York Intermediate Insured, at a 6.40% yield, like a black loafer, Size 9B, for $140. Many distributors have fashioned funds to fit the variety of customer needs, and at this writing you can buy a multitude of sorts, with more sure to come. You may wish to look at Figure 28.1 to see how funds fit into the whole municipal bond picture.

SUMMARY ** CHAPTER 15 ** SUMMARY

The Managed Fund Menu

- A fund's net asset value is produced by dividing the portfolio worth by the number of shares outstanding.

- The N.A.V. is the base for buying or selling.

- *No-load* funds can be bought or redeemed at the same price, the N.A.V.

- *Load* funds can be redeemed at the N.A.V., but investors pay a sales charge of about 4% when buying.

- Open end funds trade only with their distributors.

- Closed end funds trade on stock exchanges according to supply and demand.

- Managed funds come in short, intermediate, and long-term maturities. However, they do not mature, their sponsors keep on trading them. The longer the maturity the greater the yield and the greater the risk.

- Managed funds come in many combinations of national and state exempt, uninsured and insured, portolio type—in a variety of maturity ranges.

- Lower quality, higher yielding funds are also available.

CHAPTER 16

UNDERSTANDING A FUND PROSPECTUS

Fund Information Sources

When I tell my fellow dealers that I am writing a book for individual investors they often say, only half-jokingly, 'Don't tell them everything. We don't want our customers to get too smart.' I see their point, but disagree. Every product, financial or other, has both strengths and weaknesses and it's insulting to assume that the customer investor won't know that. When salespeople show only the positive side, high after-tax yield for instance, they're trying to override this understanding. The fact that an unbalanced presentation works in enough cases to make it profitable is not sufficient justification. The notoriously short term of the relationships between customers and Wall Street salespeople is enough proof. I'm trying to show the buyer both sides of the equation, quantifying risk versus reward, liquidity versus yield. The truth shall set you free.

We saw that investors like Marci and Joe learn about U.I.T.s through ads, brochures, sales presentations and prospectuses. Much the same system prevails with managed funds. In one respect managed fund information improves upon that of the U.I.T.s—their prospectuses have a first part that tends to be shorter, perhaps 20 pages rather than 56, and easier to read, though still filled with patches of densest legalese. However, they more than make up for it with the 40 or so page second part that's virtually undecipherable. No doubt saving on expenses, up to six or more managed funds are often described in one omnibus prospectus—the Managed Fund Sixplex Theater. At each step the information flows from the sellers, but presumably you are reading this book to develop the tools to interpret these facts yourself. And now that we've mastered the U.I.T. prospectus, maybe it'll be easier to decode the funds'. We start with an open end prospectus, moving on to a closed end one later.

The Form of the Prospectus

Fund prospectuses come in many sizes and formats. Most common these days are those written in two parts, called A and B, uninspiredly. The first pages of Part A usually list: some *essential financial information;* a statement of the fund's *investment objectives;* a part dealing with various *options* offered to shareholders; and finally, a *general information* section. Part B (or a *Statement of Additional Information*) usually appears in a separate folder which contains some of the fund's technical details and describes its latest portfolio. No matter how large a fund grows to be, all of its shares are issued under just one prospectus, amended periodically. As our example we'll be using Scudder, Stevens and Clark's Scudder Managed Municipal Bonds, a good sized open end no-load fund reporting results from 1980 through 1989.

SECTION 1—ESSENTIAL FINANCIAL INFORMATION

Page 1 of a typical tax-exempt managed fund prospectus provides a quick gloss of its most important features. Some, Fidelity's, for instance, are quite restrainedly traditional, while others, like Dreyfus', use the opportunity to make a sales pitch like

    * NO SALES CHARGE
    * NO REDEMPTION FEES
    * FREE CHECK WRITING*

The essential financial information usually begins on page 2 with a chart similar to Figure 16.1. The numbers come in three divisions: *income and expenses; capital changes*; and various *performance ratios*. Some of the charts read chronologically from the right, some from the left, and a few read down to up, like the position of car controls on different makes but you get used to it. Everything is calculated in per share amounts and on an annual basis.

Figure 16.1

Financial information

Scudder Managed Municipal Bonds

Selected data (for a share outstanding throughout each period) and ratios are as follows (audited):

	For the Years Ended December 31,									
	1989	1988	1987	1986	1985	1984	1983	1982	1981	1980
Income and Expenses										
Income	$ .64	$ .65	$ .66	$ .66	$ .64	$ .74	$ .75	$ .78	$ .76	$ .73
Operating expenses	(.05)	(.05)	(.05)	(.05)	(.05)	(.04)	(.05)	(.05)	(.05)	(.06)
Net investment income .	.59	.60	.61	.61	.59	.70	.70	.73	.71	.67
Dividends from net investment income...	(.59)	(.60)	(.61)	(.61)	(.59)	(.70)	(.70)	(.73)	(.70)	(.65)
Capital Changes										
Net realized and unrealized gain (loss) on investments and futures contracts.....	.33	.38	(.58)	.77	.71	.02	(.02)	1.72	(1.46)	(1.72)
Distributions from net realized gains on investments and futures contracts.....	(.39)	(.02)	(.11)	(.24)	—	—	—	—	—	—
Net increase (decrease) in net asset value	(.06)	.36	(.69)	.53	.71	.02	(.02)	1.72	(1.45)	(1.70)
Net Asset Value:										
Beginning of year	8.60	8.24	8.93	8.40	7.69	7.67	7.69	5.97	7.42	9.12
End of year	$ 8.54	$ 8.60	$ 8.24	$ 8.93	$ 8.40	$ 7.69	$ 7.67	$ 7.69	$ 5.97	$ 7.42
Ratio of operating expenses to average daily net assets (%) ...	.62	.61	.63	.58	.58	.61	.65	.65	.69	.75
Ratio of net investment income to average daily net assets (%) ...	6.78	7.13	7.20	6.88	7.27	9.52	9.10	10.40	10.69	8.20
Portfolio turnover rate (%)	89.8	75.5	73.5	78.0	98.2	120.0	82.7	146.2	213.5	169.6
Number of shares outstanding at end of year (000 omitted) ...	80,909	73,897	71,817	74,173	68,401	70,883	62,482	38,080	18,261	14,514

Fund Income and Expenses

The first part of the essential financial information, Lines 1 through 3, presents figures on *income* and *expenses*. Line 1, *Investment income*, shows that this fund collected interest of 64 cents per share during 1989. $49 million in tax-exempt interest on 77 (average outstanding) million shares. Funds incur the same sorts of routine expenses as do U.I.T.s.—for evaluating bonds, mailing out checks, audit fees, etc., which in this example amounted to 1 cent a share. They also have a more substantial bill to pay—the fee for running the fund and its portfolio—in this case 4 cents, which of course U.I.T.s do not incur, not being managed. Line 2 totals these to 5 cents a share. Only a nickel a share, but that's not chicken feed. On 77 million shares it's close to $4 million every year the fund lives. These expenses reduce the income from 64 cents down to 59 cents, *Net investment income*, Line 3. At this point you may wish to glance at the income and expense numbers for the prior four years. Income of 65, 66, 66 and 64 cents. Expenses 5 cents plain and 98 cents per share. *Net investment income*, 60, 61, 61 and 59 cents. What is the picture? One of steady income and stable expenses. Next comes Line 4, *Dividends from net income*, again 59 cents for 1989, showing that 100% of the fund's coupon income was distributed.

Capital Changes

The second part (Lines 5 - 9) records the fund's *Capital changes*, that is, what happened to the N.A.V. that year, gain or loss. *Net realized and unrealized gain* shows a 33 cent profit and Line 6 prints the 39 cents the fund distributed to shareholders. Why the difference? Probably a combination of past year carryover and tax considerations. Line 7 posts the difference between the two prior lines.

This fund's initial public offering back in 1978 was priced at $10 a share. Thereafter, at the beginning and end of every fiscal year (Lines 8 and 9), the fund's portfolio of bonds is re-evaluated and the asset value calculated. At the beginning of 1989 it was $8.60, and at the year end, $8.54. Line 7 shows the change.

Fund Yield

Municipal bond funds don't project their future returns at all—the S.E.C. won't allow it. Trust and bond yields can be predicted with accuracy but who knows what a fund will do next? So, they just report past returns, usually the prior year and the latest 30 days. They calculate the yield to maturity or call of every bond in the portfolio for the year or 30 days, then average it out to produce these two yields. The 30 day yield is the moral equivalent and tolerable substitute for current yield, excluding any load. For more on fund yield, see Chapter 17.

If a fund is paying at the rate of 75 cents a year and the (after load, if any) share price is $10, its net yield is 7.50% ($.75 divided by $10.00 = .075, or 7.50%). However, at $11, the yield is 6.82% ($.75 divided by $11.00 = .0682), etc.

But you can't count on it for the future as you can for U.I.T.s or bonds where what you see is what you get, indefinitely. Funds are meant to switch their portfolios around so that the principal amount, interest income and also maturity length of their bonds is constantly changing. In addition, the open end fund shareholder base is always in flux, so they can't and don't guarantee the level of their dividends. That's why they appeal to many people, they are managed and therefore change all the time. For other people that's a drawback, because fund income and risk levels are hard to predict.

Financial Ratios

Ratios form the last part of this section. Line 10, *Ratio of operating expenses*, at .62%, is useful in comparing one fund's expense levels with another's. *Ratio of net investment income to assets* presents one measure of annual return, here a respectable tax-exempt 6.78% for 1989. The *Portfolio turnover rate*, Line 12, comes next, showing what proportion of the fund's bonds have been sold and replaced during the year. The industry turnover average for short, intermediate, and long funds has been about 75, 60 and 80%, respectively. Last comes a most important line to the fund runners, Line 13, *Shares outstanding*. The operators' fees are a percentage of the total fund value, so the more shares they sell, and also the higher their worth, the more money they make.

SECTION 2—THE FUND AND ITS OBJECTIVES

Page 3 usually brings us to the second part of the prospectus, where the fund is defined as *open end investment company*, that is, a mutual fund owned by its shareholders. If the fund is national the word *diversified* is added, meaning that its portfolio consists of a wide variety of securities; if the portfolio is narrowly composed, such as all Ohio-exempt and insured, it's *non-diversified*. The legal jurisdiction under whose laws the fund operates, the date of incorporation, and the par value of the shares (a purely technical item) are often mentioned here. Then comes the fund's *strategy*, or its investment aim, such as 'To provide as high a level of interest income exempt from Federal taxes, as is consistent with prudent investing, while seeking preservation of shareholders' capital'. Next, a brief summary of the fund's *bond portfolio character* such as 'The Fund will seek to achieve this objective by investing primarily in long term, high and upper medium quality municipal bonds'. Or, 'primarily in a portfolio of long term municipal bonds covered by insurance guaranteeing the timely payment of principal and interest', etc. Often the lawyers insist on sticking in some emergency provisions—the fund's right to buy taxable obligations (though no tax-exempt fund I've ever seen has), etc. If a fund is limited to bonds of a specified credit quality it says so here. A typical line is '80% of investments will be in municipal securities within the four highest ratings of either Moody's Investor Service, or Standard & Poor's Corporation, or in unrated securities of comparable quality'. Specialized funds add in the restrictions which define their particular goals—insured, high yield, short term, etc. Sometimes other governing restrictions will be included, for instance, a limit of 5% in any one issuer's bonds, a pledge not to borrow money, or a 20% maximum of non-rated bonds.

SECTION 3—SERVICES AND WARNINGS

After wading through this dense sort of material your attention might perk up at seeing 'Municipal Securities', or 'Special Consideration', perhaps in hopes of learning a few things about funds. Unfortunately for the reader these paragraphs amount to nothing more than warnings about the horrendous risks of owning municipal bonds. Here we can observe one kind of Wall Street schizophrenia—our ads paint a cheerful, yield-full picture, while our prospectuses of the same product harp on possible disasters. A brief definition of G.O.s and revenues soon leads to the pitfalls of both, with sample catastrophes. New York state funds make particularly frightful reading. I can picture the lawyers going over all this material and imagine them fretting that they'd left out something awful, causing them to add 'There are, of course, numerous variations in the security of municipal bonds (general obligation, revenue, and other), within particular classifications and between classifications, depending on multiple factors'. What is the effect of all these disclaimers? To make the prospectus so unrealistically alarming that the buyers return to the ads, fitting right into the distributors' marketing plan. The same approach holds for the prospectuses' witless warnings about changes in interest rates. 'The market values of municipal bonds may in certain circumstances decline in response to rising interest rates,' gives you the idea. My advice is to steer the middle course. Neither to be overly affrighted nor lulled to unwatchful dozing. Learn to understand the figures.

SECTION 3, CONTINUED

A few pages later the prospectus describes the distributor and its relationship to the fund. Some, such as Franklin New York Tax-Free Income Fund, are separately incorporated; others, as many of Fidelity's, are organized as business trusts. Each one has a board of directors (or trustees) which supervises the fund and selects its investment advisor, administrator, and distributor. In practice, Scudder, Stevens and Clark manages all the Scudder funds, Vanguard all the Vanguard funds, and so on, routinely. However, if trouble arose the boards' duty is to protect the share owner and defend the fund's assets. After one small fund ran aground a few years ago the board took charge, found a new manager, and its share owners emerged intact.

Two or more divisions of a single distributor may be employed to handle different aspects of a fund's business. So, parent Merrill Lynch and Co., Inc. (MUURRH!) has a subsidiary, Merrill Lynch Asset Management (MLAM), which in turn has a subsidiary, Fund Asset Management, Inc. (FAMI) which manages their large California Municipal Bond Fund (Calamity?), among many others. Still another division may perform the clerical work, all billings included in the expense figures.

SECTION 4—SHAREHOLDER OPTIONS

At this point the prospectus turns toward sales, with no load funds listing their own offices and numbers and loaders either the same or suggesting that you buy through your own broker. The sales price is defined, based on the N.A.V. Here some special charges may also crop up, such as 12b-1, and delayed load, which we comment upon in Chapter 17. No loaders may again emphasize the fact that they add nothing on and loaders list their sales charges. These generally start at 4.00% and decline after you have bought $100,000 worth. Next come several so-called shareholder 'rights', which in fact are various options owners may exercise. There may be a number of ways to get a discount on purchases, to reinvest income, or to get a regular monthly check in an amount different from the income distributions. Most operators permit you to switch from one of their funds to another, which may result in lower charges than would selling out and buying from another fund. If check writing is available its terms may be spelled out here. The redemption procedure is described, as is the share valuation method. Finally, at the very end of the main prospectus you may see a handy application form, presumably for impulse buyers.

SECTION 5—PART B

Late in Part B appears a list of the bonds in the latest available portfolio. These are usually arranged by state, with percentages of various kinds, to give an idea about the bond diversification. Naturally the managers shift their bonds around fairly often, so this list gives only a general idea about the holdings. Also a list of the fund's underwriters appears, along with their share of the deal.

Closed End Prospectuses

As described, closed end funds differ from the more common open end variety in one main respect—their fixed numbers of shares trade on a stock exchange according to current supply and demand, not at a price based on the N.A.V. Except for these differences, their prospectuses read practically identically to those of the open end kind. The *essential financial information* section is shorter, since share price isn't strictly determined by asset values; the *general information section* describes how its shares trade; and there is no mention of redemption procedures, since you just sell your shares on the open market. Closed end shareholders have fewer options than do owners of families of funds, but what they have, including their re-investment deals, are described near the end of the document.

This brings us to the end of the prospectus. Now on to how to choose the best managed fund for you.

SUMMARY ** CHAPTER 16 ** SUMMARY

Understanding a Fund Prospectus

- Managed fund prospectuses, both open and closed end, are mines of information but it takes a lot of digging to get the gold.

- They come in two parts.

- Part A contains: essential financial facts; fund objectives; shareholder options; and general information. Particularly interesting are the figures on fund performance, since these can be used to compare one fund's market record against others.

- Part B contains a long technical section and a list of the latest portfolio.

CHAPTER 17

HOW TO CHOOSE A MANAGED FUND

Before the Plunge

Now that we have all that information about managed funds down pat, let's take the steps toward choosing the one that's right for you. You may first want to take a peek at the next section, on unpackaged bonds. Then, if you still like the looks of managed funds, come on back to fund country. As to listening to sales people, understand that there is a basic conflict of interest between you and them. As we have said, timing is everything for the individual investor. But Wall Streeters are always under pressure to produce, and according to our sales people the time is always *right now*, today's the day, not tomorrow. How often have you heard something like "Better buy now, this special offer won't last long", compared to, "Why don't you wait until bonds get cheaper?".

We covered choosing a U.I.T. in Chapter 11. Choosing a fund involves a similar three part process: a maturity step; a credit step; and a shopping for yield step. In addition, since there are three types of managed funds, rather than U.I.T.s single kind, there is another step, selecting the one type of structure you prefer.

☞ *WILSON SAYS*

First, make sure of your timing.
   Check the prerequisites: savings, income, other opportunities.
   Inspect the bond market signals - 8, 3, 83.

To find the type of fund that's best for you.
   1.) Select your maturity range.

   2.) Pick the lowest credit quality fund you can accept.

   3.) Choose between: no-load, load, and closed end.

Then
   4.) Look for the fund that provides the highest after-all-taxes return.

☞ *WILSON SAYS*

Make sure of your timing.
   Check the prerequisites: savings, income, other opportunities.
   Inspect the bond market signals - 8, 3, 83.

To find the type of U.I.T. that's best for you.
   1.) Select your maturity range.

   2.) Pick the lowest credit quality fund you can accept.

Then
   3.) Look high and low for the trust providing the highest   after-all-taxes return.

Reviewing Old Fund Holdings

This might be a good time to review any existing funds you own. Are you happy with them? If not, figure out why, using a zero-position stance. Would you buy them today or are you just sitting with them unhappily? Start fresh and fire those that don't do the work you are paying for.

Before you begin, either reviewing old holdings or looking for new, check once again the three *prerequisite questions.* Do you have a sufficient liquid cash reserve—at least six months' living expenses? Is your income bracket high enough to benefit from tax-free yields? No private investments with a higher return available? If so, onward. We'll soon be getting back to Joe and Marci who have already met these prerequisites. Then, before zooming onto the high speed thruway of long term investing, look carefully to make sure the buy signals are right. Are long average quality municipal bonds at 8%? Are tax-exempt yields 3% higher than inflation? Do long maturities yield at least 83% of Governments? 8, 3, 83? If not, avoid congestion—take a slow but steady short term road, in tax-exempt money markets, for instance, until the highway clears. Figure 17.1 shows some interesting results achievable from 8, 3, 83. However, that's in the sitting duck past, a far easier shot than the moving target of the future.

Figure 17.1
ADVISOR, FUND, AND BOND PRICES 1977-1990
% PRINCIPAL VALUE

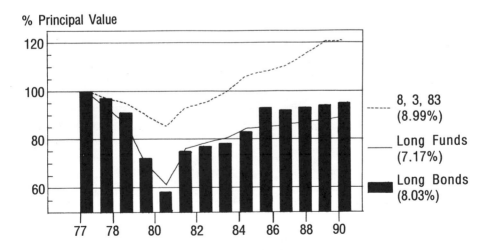

Step 1 - Picking the Maturity

As we have harped upon a number of times, maturity length is by far the most powerful determinant of municipal bond risk. Figure 17.2 illustrates the inherent maturity risk levels for short, intermediate and long maturity managed funds. The top line shows that if interest rates keep rising by 1% a year for five years, a typical short fund will lose one fifth of its value, declining from $10 down to $8 a share. The middle line shows that in the same period a typical intermediate fund will lose over a third of its starting value, from $10 down to something like $6.50. A long fund will lose the most, perhaps half of its face value, from $10 down to $5.

You may wonder how a fund that's managed loses so much money, but in fact that's what does happen. After their expenses few funds succeed in protecting invested dollars any more than do unpackaged bonds and often not as well. The difficult period 1979-82 saw these declines in managed funds occur left and right. Compare with Figure 11.1, which showed how trusts and bonds fare in the

---

Figure 17.2
TYPICAL FUND ASSET VALUES AS INTEREST RATES RISE 1% PER YEAR FOR 5 CONSECUTIVE YEARS

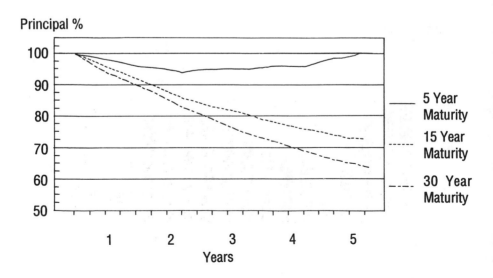

---

same rising rate scenario. If the market did decline this steadily during a five year period, intermediate and long funds show negative total returns. Their losses are greater than their income. In the same environment a short fund may break even, while a tax-exempt money market fund would be earning its steady, if unspectacular return. Figure 17.5 shows the comparative returns in the recent past.

There is also the other side to consider—the up side potential. Naturally investors in tax-exempts are more concerned with possible losses of principal than with making speculative profits. However, people who risk deserve to make money sometimes. If rates fall by similar amounts, money market funds earn no profits at all, they stay at $1 a share. Short, intermediate and long funds will show profits, although usually not so great as their corresponding losses. Why are potential profits smaller? Chapter 18 goes into details.

Which maturity range offers to best match your needs and expectations? Always assuming that the signals are right, if you are a super-cautious investor, averse to almost any risk, among funds perhaps you'd be best off buying one with a short maturity. Those who can tolerate moderate risk might well consider an intermediate maturity fund. If you're comfortable with maximum risk for maximum return, then you might profitably lean to the long maturities. We saw Joe and Marci looking at long term funds for themselves.

☞ WILSON SAYS

By far the most critical decision in fund selecting is picking the maturity. Buy the longest maturity you can tolerate.

Step 2 - Picking the Credit

Step two—look at the types of fund credit in your maturity range and choose the one you prefer, knowing that the safer you go the less you get paid. The usual first decision to make is whether to buy an uninsured fund or an insured. Figure 25.1 illustrates my views on credit risk, which I see as less of a threat to your capital than maturity risk, four times as great. Since funds are even more diversified than trusts you already have a natural insurance policy, so I'd recommend that you skip the insurance and take the extra income. When I rent a car I decline the insurance, figuring that the cost is too high to justify the extra protection. This is an especially strong indication on shorter funds. They are already in the low risk category, so why pay twice? However, if the insurance premium (in the form of lower yield) on a long fund costs you only a few basis points, it may be a good deal. Again, insurance protects only against default, not against the more significant inflation and interest rate changes.

☞ WILSON SAYS

Buy the fund with the lowest grade credit you can tolerate.
If you buy a short maturity fund buy the uninsured kind.
If you buy a long term insured fund pay only a small yield premium.

Your next decision may be between a state fund or a more diversified, national fund. State funds are inherently riskier than national funds, and despite the exemption from local taxes, I' advise, as with U.I.T.s and bonds, against putting more than one-quarter of your savings into any one state, perhaps adding another quarter of insured shares of the same state. I've seen too many state problems to ignore the probability that they will return some day, maybe soon. When that does happen, insured funds, no matter if their insurers will pay for any defaults, will certainly experience some market losses. Insured bonds of credits that come under threat trade at substantial discounts from other insured bonds. Investors perceive that instead of a municipality plus an insurer, that their only resource is the insurance company, and so these bonds become less desirable. Also, several apparently fine insurers have come upon hard times and have lost their gilt edge credit standing and their triple A's. Buy state funds, and buy more insured state funds, but don't go overboard. This particularly applies to New York. Although the Empire State doesn't have a monopoly on municipal bond trouble it sure is the odds-on favorite in the Doomsday Derby.

☞ WILSON SAYS

Put a limit of one-quarter of your savings in municipals of any one state.
Maybe half, if insured.
Beware of New York.

These days about 20% of fund investors are moving into those with lower grade portfolios. I cautioned about buying junky U.I.T.s, but higher yield funds are different, since their managers have the ability to switch in and out when the time is right. Most managers choose among medium and lower quality bonds with great care and monitor them vigilantly. At least take a look at the portfolios of the higher yielding funds to see if you can stomach their selections. Joe did just that and mentioned that Olde Yankee Aggressive portfolio didn't look so bad. See Figure 17.5 for the past return results. Despite the statistics, I'm used to getting lots of frowns when I urge investors to buy lower grade bonds. As a class, bond buyers instinctively equate safety with high credit quality, which is definitely wrong. To a certain extent this bias against medium quality bonds is built into our financial system. We in Wall Street are much more apt to be criticized if our customers lose $20,000 on a default than if they lose $50,000 when the market goes down. To me that's silly—a dollar is a dollar and the fewer lost from any cause the better.

☞ *WILSON ADVISES*

Look closely at the lower grade funds. If the extra yield seems worth it, invest as large a fraction of your savings as you can tolerate.

Step 3 - Picking the Fund Type

We discussed open and closed end funds in Chapter 14 and saw how alike they are. What factors should individual investors consider when choosing one over the other?

Open End Funds

Commissions apart, as a class open end funds hold a number of *advantages* over closed.

1.) Their managers guarantee a market in their shares and so far they have delivered on this promise. Investors can buy or sell virtually any amount based on the current market worth of the bond portfolio.

2.) Their price is set by an evaluation of the market for their underlying bonds. So even though there is an imbalance of buying or selling in the fund the share price theoretically stays steady.

Open ends carry these *disadvantages*:

1.) The orderly continuation of their market making would be threatened if their managers run into financial or legal trouble.

2.) The evaluation process is not perfectly objective, and the relationship between evaluator and manager cannot help being influenced by its mechanism.

3.) In a changing market, or during a portfolio switch, large amounts of money entering or leaving the fund can dilute the worth of existing shareholders' bonds.

4.) Most importantly, when a heavy wave of redemptions hits them open end managers may have to raise cash by dumping bonds into upset markets. When several funds are simultaneously forced to liquidate the markets can sink rapidly, resulting in more redemptions, more dumping, and poor prices for shareholders. This happened in the spring of 1986, climactically.

Closed End Funds

The closed ends have their own set of *advantages*:

1.) A buying opportunity for new investors may appear when market forces push share prices below the current worth of the bond portfolio.

2.) The share price is not subject to the distortions of the evaluating mechanism.

3.) Fixed fund size means no dilution of future worth by an influx of new money.

4.) Closed end funds do not redeem shares, so they are never forced to dump bonds onto an unwilling marketplace.

And their *disadvantages*:

1.) If the general equity market deteriorates, these largely unrelated fund shares can suffer. When the stock market almost crashed in October 1987, regular unpackaged bonds rose in value, as the Federal Reserve pumped in emergency money. But the shares of the giant Nuveen closed end fund dropped sharply in the general confusion.

2.) In markets where fund shares trade at a discount from bond worth sellers often get a poor deal. When they sell at a premium buyers may receive poor value.

Figure 17.3
NO-LOAD FUND PERFORMANCE RESULTS
ANNUAL COMPOUND PERCENTAGE RETURN

	1978-90	1986-90	1989	1990
Short Maturity				
*Average	6.13%	6.31%	7.01%	6.39%
Limited Term	—	7.46	7.80	6.48
T.R.Price	—	5.96	6.89	6.04
U.S.A.A.	—	6.15	7.40	5.87
Vanguard	6.13	6.15	7.08	6.57
Intermediate Maturity				
Average	6.25%	7.22%	8.07%	6.48%
Dreyfus	—	7.94	8.72	6.75
Fidelity	6.59%	7.77	7.82	6.96
Vanguard	6.06	8.90	9.99	7.19
National				
Average	7.02%	8.79%	9.51%	5.93%
Dreyfus	6.37	8.41	9.40	6.43
Fidelity	5.86	9.02	9.57	6.91
Keystone	—	8.79	9.12	6.67
T.R. Price	6.82	7.45	9.19	5.86
Scudder	7.10	9.30	11.15	6.77
Stein Roe	8.04	9.89	10.70	6.97
U.S.A.A.	—	8.79	10.62	6.56
Vanguard	6.05	9.55	11.51	6.80
Insured				
Average	—	8.51%	9.53%	6.49%
A.A.R.P.	—	8.60	10.84	6.33
Vanguard	—	9.43	10.58	7.03

*Averages are for all open end funds reporting, no-load, including others not in this or the
  following figure.

Figure 17.3 (Continued)
OPEN END *NO-LOAD* FUND PERFORMANCE RESULTS
ANNUAL COMPOUND PERCENTAGE RETURN

	1978-90	*1986-90*	*1989*	*1990*
Lower Grade				
Average	7.81%	8.71%	9.64%	5.05%
Fidelity	7.81	9.37	11.38	8.47
T.R. Price	—	9.69	10.51	7.11
Stein Roe	—	10.09	11.45	7.64
Vanguard	—	9.54	11.05	5.90
California				
Average	—	8.55%	9.62%	6.55%
Dreyfus	—	8.01	9.67	6.72
Fidelity	—	8.24	8.56	6.96
New York				
Average	—	7.98%	9.16%	5.25%
Dreyfus	—	7.60	8.93	5.50
Fidelity	—	7.94	9.28	5.10

3.) Investors may figure bond worth less accurately than do open end fund evaluators.

So, which are better, open end or closed? Closed end funds have only a few years record so we can't validly compare the performance of both kinds. The side features of the open ends seem to me to balance out the one great closed end advantage—their immunity from liquidation because of excess redemptions. On the one hand I'd lean toward the open ends, including the no-load expense advantage. On the other hand I'd recommend looking at closed ends when they can be bought at a discount to their market value. As mentioned, closed end funds are too new to validly chart. See Figure 14.4 for a list of them.

☞ *WILSON SAYS*

Favor open ends if you like their services.
Favor closed ends if you can buy them at a discount.

Figure 17.4
OPEN END LOAD FUND PERFORMANCE RESULTS
ANNUAL COMPOUND PERCENTAGE RETURN

	1978-90	*1986-90*	*1989*	*1990*
National				
*Average	7.02%	8.79%	9.51%	5.93%
Colonial	—	8.14	8.08	6.44
Franklin	—	8.72	9.00	5.52
I.D.S.	6.55	9.16	11.73	6.62
Kemper	7.38	9.62	11.30	6.66
Merrill Lynch	—	8.87	9.11	5.85
M.F.S.	9.44	9.34	9.71	6.28
Nuveen	7.22	9.59	10.87	6.29
Prudential	—	7.63	7.35	5.92
Putnam	8.62	9.44	10.86	4.93
Shearson	—	8.93	10.24	5.18
Witter	—	9.38	10.60	5.85
Insured				
Average	—	8.51%	9.53%	6.49%
Franklin	—	8.70	9.98	6.54
Merrill Lynch	—	8.98	8.96	7.04
Prudential	—	—	9.57	6.09
First Investors	—	8.56	9.53	6.02
Lower Grade				
Average	7.81	8.71%	9.64%	5.05%
Eaton Vance	—	6.33	8.22	3.42
Franklin	—	—	9.69	5.11
I.D.S.	—	9.22	11.39	5.20
M.F.S.	—	—	10.67	3.16
Prudential	—	—	10.76	4.68
Putnam	—	—	8.68	6.62

*Averages are for all open end funds reporting, no-load and load, including others not in-cluded in this or the preceding figure.

Figure 17.4 (Continued)
OPEN END LOAD FUND PERFORMANCE RESULTS
ANNUAL COMPOUND PERCENTAGE RETURN

		1978-90	*1986-90*	*1989*	*1990*
California					
	Average	—	8.55%	9.62%	6.55%
Colonial		—	8.19	9.68	6.14
Franklin		5.83%	8.49	8.63	6.60
Putnam		—	9.44	10.00	6.85
Witter		—	8.19	9.53	5.70
New York					
	Average	—	7.98%	9.16%	5.25%
Franklin		—	8.30	9.55	4.74
Merrill Lynch		—	7.90	8.87	4.93
Prudential		—	6.56	7.95	4.16
Putnam		—	—	9.45	3.32
Shearson		—	8.48	9.08	5.35

No-loads Vs. Loads

Suppose you have decided to buy an open end fund and are faced with choosing between a no-load and a load. Which is the one to go for? Why pay a hefty 4% load when you can get apparently the same product with no mark up? One reason is to maintain an ongoing relationship with a trusted professional. Joe and Marci started to develop one with Steve, and later with Hy, who provided them with valuable advice and information. They gave orders to both of them though they knew that no-load Olde Yankee was available. It's only natural to develop a source of counsel and to pay for it. If that's your aim then a load fund may be for you.

What about performance? Do load funds, as Hy said, because of higher profit incentive, actually outperform no-loads? It's one of Wall Streets' favorite pastimes to chart the past performances of managed funds and many people take it seriously. However, it's the future that counts, isn't it? Since managed funds have only been operating for fifteen years and since much has changed in the bond markets, I'm skeptical about the validity of extending old results into the future. It's like the incumbent politicians who claim credit for the favorable events that happened in their administration, no matter what their role had been in advancing them. However, after inspecting the data at great length, my conclusion is that on the better quality funds, no-loads have performed slightly better than have loads, overall by about 1/8% a year. On lower grades they have also outperformed, by about 3/8% a year. This doesn't count the effect of the load itself, just the portfolio performance over a varying number of the past fifteen years.

If commission cost is your primary consideration, then no-loads (or closed ends bought through discount brokers) may be logical choices. My recommendation is to buy a no-load unless you have a good reason, such as a valuable relationship with a broker, to pay the extra fee. But if full service is what you're after, then you may lean toward broker serviced funds—open end load or closed end. You may be interested in Figures 17.3 and 4, which present a list of the largest open end funds and their performance results. Mike Lipper and company have been invaluable sources of this information. Many funds add in one or both of two almost-hidden charges. 1.) 12b-1 fees, an unconscionable way of charging you with their advertising costs. 2.) Redemption fees, paid at the time you sell out. Watch out for these, they can reduce your yields substantially.

☞ WILSON ADVISES

Choose a no-load fund if you are particularly sensitive to fees and commissions. Choose a load fund if you want to pay the price for fine personal service, an established relationship, etc.

Let's survey the ground we've covered so far. You have the prerequisites to invest in municipals. The market is favorable. You have decided on a maturity range. You have picked the credit you prefer. You have selected among: open end, no-load; open end, load; and closed end. Now you are ready to take the yield step by choosing just one fund among the many.

Let's pretend you have decided on a long term, uninsured national open end no-load fund. This means that you will be acting without the advice of a broker, since no-loads are sold directly by their distributors, leaving no room for broker commissions. You might look at Figure 17.3 to check on past performance. Here we see that Stein Row has led the national pack for thirteen years and also for the past five- and one-year periods. This might be one factor to consider.

How about right now? What are these funds returning currently? If you use Figure 14.2, you could reach the largest no-loaders and ask them what their yields are. I just (4/15/91) called Dreyfus (after being put on hold too long at one of the others), at 800-645-6561 and after pushing various of my phone buttons to get to the right desk asked a Mr. Dolan for the yield on their tax-exempt long maturity uninsured funds. He quoted a 7.70% and explained that for all of 1990 it would have been a 7.85%. I know that right now it's hard to get more than a 7.25% on average quality municipals and asked him why it was so high. He replied crisply that this fund is absorbing .83% of annual expenses, and that it was 6.75% invested in BBB or higher rated bonds. I mentioned junk, but he patiently explained that BBB wasn't junk, that junk was two categories lower.

I asked him what the yield was on regular tax-exempts and he said that another fund of theirs, with 75% A or better bonds had a 30 day yield of 6.77%, that it had been 7.24% for 1990, and that they were not absorbing any expenses on that one. I asked him what a '30 day yield' meant, and he said that this was an S.E.C. daily yield, the average of the last 30 days' yield to maturity of all the bonds in the portfolio. He went on to say that the daily yield as of Friday was 6.94% and when I commented that if the daily, or current, yield was higher than the yield to maturity this must mean that the bonds must be premiums, he agreed. I later talked to his supervisor, Lisa Marayes, who confirmed these facts.

What is the meaning of them for a customer? First, after getting around the junk fund, Dreyfus was offering an average quality nationally diversified fund, just the kind we were talking about. That its current yield was 6.94% and its yield to maturity was 6.77%. And this is just the kind of experience you might have as a real investor in a no-load, except that they would also be glad to send you written information, prospectuses, etc., and also to be interested in signing you up as a customer. Get the picture? You call them, saving them all the expenses of beating the bushes for buyers. They have a variety of products to sell, all presented in a neatly wrapped package presented by trained and pleasant salespeople. The modern way to invest in tax-exempts.

You would find yourself heading toward a load fund in a far different way—most probably by your broker, as Joe and Marci were with Hy. Another game, more old-fashioned. Fast food drive through versus leisurely neighborhood restaurant. These are the facts and the approaches, yours is the choice. Both ways have much to recommend themselves.

We left Joe and Marci back in Chapter 13, looking at managed funds. Eventually Marci, with Joe's help, worked out a complete plan. She decided to put her share of the legacy into Hy's money market fund, and take the plunge, but not off the deep end, by putting $25,000 into the Hudson New York Munisured Fund. She and Joe had also looked at the past results on this one, finding that it had done pretty well. As for her mother's share, Marci decided to leave half of it in highly liquid form, postponing investing the rest, the dollar cost averaging method. She brought inflation into this calculation—after all,

Figure 17.5
PERFORMANCE OF OPEN END TAX-EXEMPT FUNDS
% AVERAGE ANNUAL TOTAL RETURN

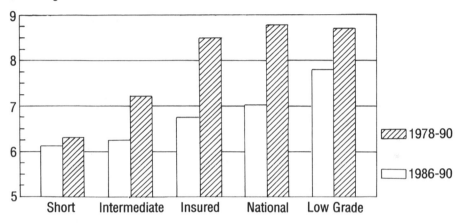

% Average Annual Total Return

Source: Lipper Analytical Services, Inc.

Anne would have her fixed income to live on for a long time to come. The price indexes were rising at about 4% and the long funds' rates of about 7.25% figured to keep her ahead of prices. After Marci had talked to her mother and her brothers, and to the lawyer at length, she came to her decisions. 50% of the legacy would go into a tax-exempt money market fund. Since Florida had no income tax she chose to put the balance into Hudson's National Tax-Free, a many-state fund. Aggressive sounded too risky for their blood. Marci called Hy, found that he was out of town, but gave these orders to his assistant:

What comment can we make on their decisions? Overall, they did well. The family got quite conservative and properly. Anne's first need was income, which was well provided for. Her tax bracket was correctly considered and her portion was appropriately invested. As for Marci's own investment, she couldn't quite bring herself to buy into the high-yield fund, and with the New York tax ready to take its toll of any success she had a good point. They considered no-loads, but eventually Marci bought Hy's load fund, along with his largely

Figure 17.6
MARCELLA AND JOSEPH ZOTTI, JR.
INVESTMENTS–1990

	Market Value	Before Taxes		Taxed By	After Taxes		Income Retained
		Yield	Income		Yield	Income	
Certificate of Deposit	$25,000	7.75%	$ 1,938	U.S. & N.Y.	4.75%	$ 1,182	61%
Money market accounts	10,000	6.50%	650	U.S. & N.Y.	3.97%	397	61%
Common stock mutual fund	36,000	3.60%	1,296	U.S. & N.Y.	2.20%	791	61%
Hudson National T-X Fund	25,000	8.00%	2,000	N.Y.	7.36%	1,840	92%
Gamma Nat. T-X U.I.T. #31	14,000	7.20%	1,008	N.Y.	6.62%	927	92%
Gamma New York Tax-Exempt #66	20,000	6.93%	1,383	None	6.93%	1,386	100%
Hudson Daily N.Y. T-X Fund	50,000	5.25%	2,625	None	5.25%	2,625	100%
Hudson N.Y. Insured T-X Fund	25,000	7.55%	1,888	None	7.55%	1,888	100%
Total	$205,000	6.33%	$12,788		4.90%	$11,036	85%

sound information and advice. I wouldn't quarrel with either decision. To their further credit, Joe and Marci did think about inflation, and their calculation that the current tax-exempt return beat inflation was well judged. Perhaps most importantly, both Joe and Marci had learned a lot and we can hope this experience will stand them, your proxies, in good stead.

SUMMARY ** CHAPTER 17 ** SUMMARY

How to Choose a Managed Fund

- Check the tax-exempt bond market for timing. 8, 3, 83.

- Pick the most suitable maturity range, remembering that long funds carry higher risk and higher return.

- Select the lowest quality credit you can accept.

- Choose between open end (no-load or load), and closed end funds.

- Look for the fund with the after-all-taxes yield satisfying your requirements.

CHAPTER 18

RATING THE FUNDS

WHITE'S INVESTMENT RATING: **

Giving just a single rating to the whole complex of managed municipal bond funds may seem presumptuous, but I ask your indulgence on the ground that I'm generalizing from the investor's point of view, not presenting a new financial measuring tool. You might also take into consideration my own bias which no doubt you have perceived to be against any packages and in favor of separately bought bonds. Overall I give U.I.T.s two stars. My ratings address the comparative value of managed funds versus the other tax-exempt products. I certainly don't attempt to predict future results of any kind and I take no responsibility for any investment outcome. Now let's go over my criteria.

1.) *Marketability.*
You can buy and then sell an open end no-load fund with little or no marketing cost. This is especially valuable to investors who switch around frequently. However, the marketing cost of the otherwise similar load funds is decidedly higher than the cost of selling unbundled bonds. The continuum runs like this, from highest to lowest *total* charges: U.I.T.s, load funds, closed end funds, no-load funds, unpackaged bonds. These charges include original mark-ups, loads, commissions and annual advisory fees.

2.) *Portfolio selection*.
Both the credit quality and the market value of the bonds which go into managed funds appear to be almost universally sound. This is a good thing, because about a third of all bonds in a typical managed fund portfolio stay there indefinitely. Funds buy portfolio bonds at their managers' cost, not at a marked up price, as in U.I.T.s.

3.) *Portfolio credit surveillance*.
After bonds come into a fund portfolio their managers try to identify holdings headed for credit or market deterioration, so that they can bail out before the bonds fall in price. Figures on their surveillance success rate are unavailable but I suspect that only a few troubled situations are diagnosed correctly.

4.) *Portfolio trading*.
Fund managers also swap bonds in order to increase yield and performance. Their prospectuses are quite vague about this aim, but in practice managers rarely dare to trade bonds that result in a lower current yield—it looks bad, even though it might be the correct move to make. They also try to upgrade the portfolio's quality and to outguess the direction of interest rates.

How can a professional upgrade holdings? By taking advantage of temporary imbalances within the municipal bond market. At this writing there is a demand for New Jersey bonds out of proportion to their tax advantages, and so a national fund might do well to sell its Hobokens or Trentons if it could find better names at higher yields. If a fund could sell these bonds at, say a 7.00% yield, and with the proceeds buy equivalent San Antonio, Texas bonds at a 7.50%, it would be improving its performance. Then, when Texas has regained its luster, it might be time to sell the San Antonios and replace them with other bonds with better value. Sometimes they can re-acquire the same bonds, perhaps selling the San Antonios at a 7.00% and buying the Trentons back at a 7.50%. We call this "reversing the swap" and it certainly helps improve fund results.

Since interest rates are practically impossible to foretell and experience has shown that bad guesses hurt funds more than good ones profit, most managers are quite reluctant to try to outfox the market. No fund that I know has ever stayed even in a down market or gone up much more than a rising one. They just aren't built that way. Why? Or how? Their primary concern is to stay in business, and they will stay in business if they don't make too many big mistakes. This precludes dramatic and inspired shifting around of the portfolio. So don't expect funds to do as well as unpackaged bonds. It won't happen. Stock mutual funds are different. They gamble. Their shareholders will switch out of them and into another fund at the drop of an article in *The Wall Street Journal*. If they take a chance and way outperform their competitors they will benefit as the investor sheep move over into their pasture. Not so municipal bond mutual funds. Their owners are more like contented cows chewing their tax-free cud. It takes a lot more to make them stampede. Don't do anything rash and they'll probably hang around. But if their cowherd manager makes a hasty wrong move they might all panic out together. It just doesn't pay municipal bond fund managers to take many chances and that's where performance is born. When they are convinced that rates are on the rise, they can *sell, switch* into more defensive bonds, or *hedge*.

Managed funds holdings can theoretically be dumped before rates go up and then bought back later, and in the meanwhile they can be put into very short term securities. Since this results in immediate loss of fund yields, traders and directors are usually reluctant to stick their necks out so far. We call this open end trading and managed funds use this technique sparingly.

A manager anxious to limit a fund's losses may switch the bonds likely to fall most, ordinarily the longer maturities, and replace them with shorter, more defensive bonds. This also tends to minimize the fund's income, a dangerous side effect, making the product harder to sell and decreasing the manager's revenue. How frequently this is done is unknown, but it appears to be more common than outright selling.

The third technique is the newest—a managed fund operator can hedge his bonds by selling futures in an abstract package of similarly constituted bonds. If the market does go down, then the value of his futures should go up an equivalent amount, and he suffers no overall loss on the protected part of the portfolio. If, instead, the market goes up, then the reverse happens, and he will be rewarded with a loss. Indications are that managed funds are hedging perhaps as much as 10% of their portfolios, but I have my doubts that it helps them a great deal.

5.) *Security handling*.
Although it's a problem a lot of people would like to have, there is a certain amount of nuisance, and some expense, involved in running your own portfolio. Bond chores include storage, coupon clipping and collecting, record keeping, and tax preparation. In addition, keeping track of calls, tenders and refundings, any of which could affect portfolio strategies, can be a lot of trouble even for professionals. These are eliminated or at least simplified and organized by owning a managed fund (or a U.I.T. or using a financial advisor), rather than buying unbundled bonds individually.

6.) *Tie-ins with auxiliary financial features*.
We discussed the many options that managed funds offer their shareholders. These are not available at present from other tax-free income sources.

7.) *Sales relationships.*
Some bond customers need advice or want the personal touch. Others really prefer dealing with anonymous phone answerers—it's cleaner, simpler, less sticky. Just call them up, tell them what to do, and that's that. Both approaches are available in managed funds, so take your pick.

8.) *Income.*
Here is the weak point of managed funds. Year in and year out the yields on packaged pools of municipals are lower than those easily obtainable on individual bonds. You can normally get a 7.50% to maturity on good bonds when the yield on managed funds is 7.00% (and on the U.I.T.'s only 6.50%). They have to charge expenses, they operate under sets of constraints, and at time of extreme stress in their market open end funds may be forced to liquidate part of the portfolio in order to meet redemptions. Back in April 1986 when the municipal bond market cracked badly and individual investors crowded into their redemption doors, a number of managed funds, even the insured, started to dump their portfolios out at almost any price, thus further depressing the market they usually support. At the very time when great bargains suddenly appeared the open ends were forced to cash in their chips at 20 or more point losses. These disadvantages add up—you can usually get more yield on similar quality bonds if you buy them yourself, but you have to know how. See Section Four.

In summary, it's my opinion that the managed funds offer good, two-star, value. They are honestly run, their managers select their portfolios professionally and monitor their bonds competently, although perhaps not as actively as they imply. They provide maximum convenience. Funds' weakest points concern performance. Most do badly in down markets and rise slowly in up markets. Yields are consistently lower than those available on similar individual bonds.

MONEY MARKET FUNDS: ***

Here convenience pays. Idle funds have no place in today's world, and a system which automatically sweeps money out of a non-interest bearing account and into a tax-exempt money market can increase income substantially. Their popularity has proven their worth.

SHORT FUNDS: **

Average managed fund convenience and performance. Easy to beat with plain bonds. Avoid load funds here—their take decreases yield significantly.

Figure 18.1
MANAGED FUND INVESTMENT CHARACTERISTICS

	Price Stability	Principal Safety	Typical Relative Yield
Shorter Term			
5 Year National	High	Extremely High	6.75%
10 Year National	Moderate	Very High	7.25%
Long Term			
State Insured	Low	Extremely High	7.00%
State	Low	Very High	7.25%
National Insured	Low	Extremely High	7.25%
National	Low	Very High	7.50%
Lower Grade	Low	High	8.00%

INTERMEDIATE MATURITY FUNDS: **

Aiming at a balance between liquidity and income, they sometimes miss both. However, they can work out reasonably well.

NATIONAL FUNDS: **

The generic managed fund.

INSURED NATIONAL FUNDS: **

In my opinion there's a good case for insured bonds but not in funds. You've already paid for diversification, which is the best credit insurance money can buy, so why pay again? In some cases, as with state of Washington bonds, the insured are certainly stronger than their insurers, so it's just a matter of their having bought a triple 'A' rating.

STATE FUNDS **

Lower diversity and lower yields add up to a dubious bargain. Insurance helps with the diversification, but it costs.

LOWER GRADE FUNDS **

Many junky sounding funds are actually invested in perfectly respectable, if currently unfashionable, bonds. However, look before you leap. Inspect the portfolio before you buy.

Before jumping into any pool, one big, fat, caution—all funds are not created alike. There's no substitute for examining each one individually, both the fund itself and its manager. Some managers have done better than others in down bond markets and also have fared handsomely in falling interest rate climates. I particularly favor those which have succeeded in increasing their dividends over the years. I wish you the best of good fortune in finding a satisfactory managed fund.

SUMMARY ** CHAPTER 18 ** SUMMARY

Rating the Funds

- The managed funds offer individual investors a two star product. Their bond portfolios are generally well chosen and monitored and some of their managers have had success at increasing their value.

- Open end funds are convenient and tie in with many auxiliary financial services. The no-loads carry a zero sales charge which makes them particularly useful for investors who may switch their holdings frequently.

- The load funds operate similarly to no-loads, except they charge a sales commission of about 4%. You can buy them from a broker you know, thus maintaining a valuable sales relationship.

- The chief drawback of managed funds is their cost. Compared to plain unpackaged bonds you pay about 1/2% per year on uninsured funds, and perhaps 3/4% a year on insured.

Section IV
Direct Investing

WHITE'S INVESTMENT RATING: ***

CHAPTER 19

INTRODUCTION TO INDEPENDENT INVESTING

I've read and listened to quite a number of financial writers and other experts who recommend a single best way to buy tax-exempts. Some favor U.I.T.s, emphasizing the advantages of their fixed portfolios. Others prefer the funds, admiring their managing feature and swearing by the no-loads. Still others push their idea of some hot unpackaged bargain, while the private money managers claim that only their expertise will save you from double tribulation. Which way is right? The one that's right for you. U.I.T.s do have a certain value and managed funds a good deal more; their one and two stars aren't terrible ratings. If these satisfy, then relax and enjoy convenience and tax-free income. However, some investors aren't content with average values and insist on hunting for better results. If that's your case, then direct investing is the three star way to superior performance, the brightest in my galaxy.

Compare the different ways of investing in municipal bonds to the various ways tourists can travel abroad. U.I.T.s are like packaged tours, managed funds are like chartered groups and direct investing is like independent travel. Direct investors have more choices, as do those who tour on their own. However, independence also carries more risks, especially if you don't understand the language.

If you decide to buy unbundled bonds, then using professionals—the dealers who operate the markets—is inevitable. It's a rare person who knows someone who wants to buy or sell securities he is interested in, and besides, it's illegal to deal commercially unless you're registered. So, trading municipal bonds means using a dealer, even more so than in the antique, coin and stamp markets. Some tax-exempt dealers focus on the primary market, buying bonds from communities that need to borrow and then distributing them to investors. Later, in the secondary market, the same and other dealers stand ready to buy and re-distribute already issued bonds, providing the original investors with liquidity and new investors with a variety of offerings. Both kinds of market makers are tax-exempt income sources for you, their customers, always with a profit as their goal. As you see, it's dealers, dealers, dealers, and direct bond investors need a good contact among them.

Fear of Markups

There is one question that often bothers me whenever I'm about to buy something that costs more than a few dollars—how much profit is the seller making and how can I reduce it? With U.I.T.s or managed funds you can see the exact profit the sellers make but you may rightly feel suspicious about the markups on unbundled bonds. If funds load on 4%, how much are you paying on plain bonds. How can you get comfortable with dealer prices? Not by shopping around for the cheapest offering every time you buy—take my word for it, dealers will soon figure you out. Not by asking a salesperson, because they don't really know, and besides, there are many ways to answer the question, depending. How then? By finding and keeping a conscientious dealer. Read on about how to accomplish this.

Bond Denominations

Now, while we're still early in the chapter, a few technical terms. Back before 1960 municipal bonds were usually printed in $1,000 *denominations*. Bond business jargon developed around this unit, and when we say "a bond", or "one bond", we mean $1,000 principal amount. "Ten bonds" refers to $10,000 principal value, "one hundred bonds" means $100,000 and so forth, all in terms of principal amount. So when I write twenty-five bonds, it means $25,000 par *maturity* amount, with the present market value unspecified. Now, since inflation has reduced the value of the dollar so, most bonds come in $5,000 denominations, but our jargon hasn't changed. It's easier to change the numbers on the printing presses than it is in a Wall Streeter's vocabulary. In any case, the minimum investment you can make in most unpackaged municipals is $5,000, and many dealers prefer to sell no less than $10,000 worth, perhaps saying, "Remember, you salesmen, on this offering it's a ten bond minimum".

Dollar Prices

Using thousand dollar denominations would be awkward all day long, so we use percentages of principal *per bond*. 100 stands for 100% of the face $1,000, no matter how many bonds are involved. 99 is down 1% from that, $990 per $1,000 principal amount. So 25 bonds at 100 is $25,000 and at 99 is $24,750. And 96 means $960 a bond and so on, all as percentages of $1,000. These percents we call *dollar prices*.

Pop quiz: How much is 85 on one bond? Answer: $850.
Q: What's 85 on ten bonds? A: $8,500.

Points and Fractions

Each of these bond 1%s we call one *point*. So it goes 100 (always pronounced "par"), 101, 102, 103, etc., up in gradations of one point each. In between points we use fractions, so when I write 101 1/2, that's half way between 101 and 102, or $1,015 per $1,000 bond.

Q: What is 100 1/4 in dollars?
A: $1,002.50.

Q: How much on ten bonds?
A: $10,025.

That's dollar pricing, where if you paid $25,000 for twenty-five bonds and later see them quoted at 104, you would have a profit of $1,000.

Q: Is 104 on 25 bonds $26,000?
A: Yes. Up 4 points, or up 4% from 100 (par).

Accrued Interest

As mentioned in passing in Chapter 8 when you buy a fixed income security, in addition to the dollar price, another amount, the *accrued interest,* is added on. Most municipal bonds pay interest twice a year, often on January 1 and its twin, July 1. But some tax-exempt interest comes due every month of the year, usually on the first day. If you buy a bond for settlement on its interest payment date then you start fresh and pay zero accrued interest. However, if you buy a bond (or U.I.T. or fund) on any other date, then the selling investor who has held it x number of days since the last paying date deserves the interest proportionate to that period. Here, time is literally money. Interest accrues (accumulates) every day after the last coupon date and is paid by the buyer to the seller, thus splitting it fairly. So a confirmation on 25 bonds sold at 102 might read $25,500 principal plus $333.33 accrued interest, for a total of $25,833.33.

The municipal bond interest year has the usual twelve months, but with one neat twist. Every municipal month, even February, is assigned exactly thirty days, and interest accrues on a uniform 360 day calendar, leap years and common years alike. A 7.20% bond pays $72 per $1,000 per year, which is $6 every month. $6 a month divided by 30 days is 20 cents a day. So if you have been holding fifty 7.20% bonds and sell them 10 days after you were paid a coupon, in addition to the principal amount, your dealer pays you ten days times 20 cents a day, or $2 per bond. If a new investor buys them on the same day, she pays the same $2, dividing the coupon fairly between seller and buyer. 50 bonds at 98 amount to $49,000 principal, $100 accrued interest, and a total of $49,100.

Wire Houses

Getting back to municipal bond dealers, I think of them in three broad categories—the *wire houses,* the *tax-exempt specialists,* and the *institutional* firms. The *nationwide wire houses* are full range dealers, distributing all kinds of financial products through hundreds of offices across the country. Currently there are six—Merrill, Shearson, Paine Webber, Prudential, Smith Barney and Witter. My creation, Hudson and West Securities, where Marci and her mother bought managed funds is one example of this breed. Most national wire houses are now also classified as institutional houses, running both retail and wholesale departments under separate management, and using different pricing systems. In this they resemble the chains of retailers who operate stores all over the country, buying and pricing the same products disparately in different stores. Together they sell about one-quarter of all the unbundled bonds done with individual investors.

In addition to the national chains, about 25 *regional wire houses* maintain dozens of offices in one or more sets of states, the smaller chain stores of the financial industry. They also do about one quarter of all the retail plain bond business. The reliable houses listed in Figure 19.1 maintain markets in both national and local securities, including tax-exempts, and have told me they would be glad to hear from individuals who have money to invest.

Figure 19.1
REGIONAL WIRE HOUSES

Dealer	Year Founded	Main Office	Telephone	Contact
J.C. Bradford & Co.	1927	Nashville	800-251-1060	N. Derryberry
Boettcher and Company	1910	Denver	800-525-3286	Tom Kovach
Alex. Brown & Sons	1800	Baltimore	800-638-2596	Bill Rienhoff
Dougherty, Dawkins	1979	Minneapolis	800-328-4085	Ron Hume
Interstate Securities	1932	Charlotte	800-937-1155	John McCabe
Edward D. Jones & Co.	1871	St. Louis	800-441-0100	Bob Beck
McDonald & Co.	1927	Cleveland	800-553-2240	David Doll
Raymond James	1965	St. Petersburg	800-248-8863	R.K. Johnson

The Municipal Bond Specialists

There are also about 500 *municipal bond firms* who make a living selling tax-exempts (and sometimes other financial products) to individual investors. Some of these boutique-like dealers are among America's oldest, some are brand new. Quite a number have built up fine reputations, while others have not. They do anothre quarter of all the tax-exempt retail unpackaged volume. Figure 19.2 lists some firms I have dealt with for many years. *Commercial banks* also deal in and sell municipal bonds to individuals, competing vigorously with Wall Street.

There are also hundreds of local *general securities firms*, and also *discount brokers*, who market many financial instruments, including tax-exempts. Usually this breed acts as a wholesaler, buying from one of the above and selling to individual investors. We may compare the general securities firms to the load funds, and the discount brokers to the no-loads, with their respective advantages of service and price.

The Institutional Dealers

Institutional houses, such as Morgan Stanley, First Boston, and Goldman, Sachs, are primarily wholesalers—they concentrate on big accounts, like the U.I.T.

Figure 19.2
MUNICIPAL BOND SPECIALIST DEALERS

Dealer	Year Founded	Main Office	Telephone	Contact
Equitable Securitites	1930	Nashville	800-251-8132	Winder Emery
Gabriele, Hueglin	1979	New York	800-422-7435	Joe Gabriele
Griffin, Kubic	1980	Chicago	800-621-5714	David Sveen
William R. Hough	1962	St. Petersburg	800-359-6864	Terry Hornsby
Lebenthal & Co.	1925	New York	800-221-5832	Jim Lebenthal
Samuel A. Ramirez	1971	New York	800-888-4086	Bill Beahan
Stone & Youngberg	1931	San Francisco	CA 800-447-8663	Sales Manager
Texas Commerce N.B.	1967	Houston	800-231-5652	Joe Lawrence
M.B. Vick & Co.	1933	Chicago	800-346-3345	Mike Vick
*Barre & Co.	1980	Dallas	214-953-0250	David Glatstein

*I am a consultant to another office of this company, so I may be prejudiced.

---

sponsors, the fund managers, and banks and insurance companies. This large volume business is highly competitive and is often conducted with tiny profit margins. Some institutional firms also service larger individual accounts. With deregulation a fact, commercial bank bond departments are now joining the front ranks of this division.

Choosing a Bond Dealer

With so many dealers to choose from, how do you pick the one for you? First, something to watch out for. Wall Street's simplest rule for its own protection is 'Know your customer'. Follow this lead, and 'Know your dealer'. If you get a call from a stranger urging you to buy some terrific bonds, don't utter so much as a "maybe". There used to be a little yellow sticky pad note at home saying, "We don't accept telephone solicitations. Please send something in the mail." Now I have it by heart. Later on we'll see someone's experience with a fly-by-night bond hustler illustrating just about the worst that can happen, an almost total loss. Most such contacts won't be that awful, just plain bad. Start by taking control—initiate the contact yourself.

☞ *WILSON SAYS*

Don't meet bond salesmen by telephone.
Make your own financial contacts.

How *do* you go about starting? If you already have an established and satisfactory connection with a dealer who knows tax-exempts, by all means continue. If you don't, look around. The best avenue is a referral. Ask freely—most people feel flattered if someone asks them for the name of their broker. If you don't have any good leads, try calling one of the securities houses listed in Figures 19.1 or 2. All of these have told me they will recognize the source of your call if you say, "Wilson sent me!". After you make contact, request coverage by an *experienced* municipal bond salesperson, as detailed shortly. Then *you* are conducting the inquiry, making them pitch themselves to you. It's your money, so take good care of it.

Registration

I strongly suggest that you meet your salesperson face to face and in the office. You can pick up a lot by seeing the environment. Wherever you get your reference, check out both the firm's and the sales person's qualifications as to *registration, capital* and *experience*. The bad old unregulated days when a bucket shop could call itself 'The Federal Reserve, Inc.' have long passed. (Imagine the president of a country bank hearing that 'The Fed' wanted to talk about his bond portfolio.) All dealers should be members of the National Association of Securities Dealers, and all salespeople *registered* with them. If you have any questions about a dealer or salesman feel free to call the N.A.S.D. at 212-839-6200.

The cash and securities of individual customers are protected by S.I.P.I.C., an industry-wide mandatory insurance plan devised after an embarrassing number of N.A.S.D. firms collapsed in the seventies. S.I.P.I.C. covers customer losses of up to $100,000 in cash and $500,000 in securities. (If your account is larger than this check a dealer's additional insurance limits.) So far the degree of protection has been exemplary; S.I.P.I.C. has experienced so few claims that it now assesses dealers only token premiums.

There are a number of extremely specific, highly detailed N.A.S.D. rules governing municipal bond firms' activities. For instance, written confirmations of purchases and sales have to be mailed out within twenty-four hours of a trade. They *must* contain: the principal amount, bond description, coupon, maturity, price, any relevant call features, yield to maturity or call whichever is lower, and the C.U.S.I.P. (bond identification alpha number). Take a careful look at the confirmation, and if anything is missing or different from your understanding, it may indicate poor compliance. Confirmations' touchiest point: the yield. It's required that yield be fully disclosed, so insist that your minimum yield be stated. Also, you should get your bonds delivered and interest payments or money due you, promptly.

Capital

An investment company's *capital* enables it to buy and offer bonds well. Many firms operate normally with only a few hundred thousand dollars, usually by doing only non-risk business, that is, selling bonds owned by other firms. However, some undercapitalized firms do strange things. Therefore, I suggest you choose a dealer with a *minimum of $5 million in capital*—not a huge amount in the financial world. Hudson's last capital report showed a hefty $600 million, but of course they needed it to support their many operations: stock, bond, and other. To soothe the feelings of some of my less well-heeled dealer friends, here's an alternate suggestion—deal only with firms that have been in business for at least five years. Many firms without large bank accounts are eminently respectable, and so if you like the looks of one that has been established for five years, give them a try. Five and/or five. Sufficient strength, either in dollars or in years.

Salespeople

Most investment writers take a suspicious and critical view of salespeople. However, once you find a good dealer firm, the key to buying bonds well is a loyal and reliable municipal bond salesperson. If you are ever going to develop a lasting, useful relationship with one you have to contribute. We all know how hard it is to get good service around home—the best plumbers and painters have more work than time, enabling them to choose between customers. I have learned to cultivate these workmen, considering their schedules, paying them promptly, and so on. Similarly, you need to create a sound working relationship with a financial professional. One basic point—unless you have an exceptionally large amount of money to invest you should do all your business exclusively with one firm and one salesperson, and not shop around with several dealers, thus wasting your, and their, time and effort.

Experience

In some basic respects an individual investor's relationship is with the firm, but more importantly it's with the salesperson. At the risk of offending over half of all bond salespeople, I suggest that in addition to dealing with a firm that has five million dollars capital or a five year life, you pick a representative with *five years experience selling tax-free bonds*. If a salesman has lasted that long he or she should have passed several tests of time, accumulated sufficient knowledge to serve customers, and long since had the callow ebullience squeezed out. Steve, from Tower Securities, pitched trusts to Joe and Marci presentably enough, but a year later he was gone. A salesperson should be a permanent employee, here today and here tomorrow. Hy was in his tenth year with Hudson & West, and for Joe and Marci's sake we can wish he will stay there a good deal longer. You pay a lot for direct investing service, so demand the best. Behind the salesperson stands the direct support staff. We also saw how Hy's assistant helped out when he was away from the office. When your R.R. is unavailable you need a backup to place an order, get a quote, send you cash, or whatever you need that minute. In addition, the firm's operations people should be able to efficiently handle such matters as securities delivery and checking on redemptions of their customers' bonds.

☞ *WILSON SAYS*

Cultivate and maintain a good working relationship with a knowledgeable municipal bond salesperson.

Dealer Relationships

Some investors really prefer to deal anonymously, keeping the contact in the background and using toll-free numbers to deal with impersonal order takers. However, those who prefer more individualized treatment receive a number of benefits. Salespeople can educate customers, supply them information, or even provide a kind of friendship. There is something nice about having a cheerful painter working in the house or a plumber with a flavorful twist to his character, and all the more so with your securities representative. You deserve not only suitable bonds at correct prices, but also a congenial person presenting them to you. Life is too short for anything but good company wherever we manage to find it. When you succeed in finding a responsible salesperson, well-informed and affable, with a sound firm, you should think carefully about keeping him, or her, happy. Meet your obligations—give them enough business to make it worthwhile servicing you, understand what you buy, and pay on time. This gives an adequate profit, a trouble-free relationship, and the cash to make everything go smoothly. Salespeople need what you do—information, good deals, and a friendly person on the other end of the phone. Perhaps most importantly, they need appreciation. Tell them when you are pleased with their work. It's a two way street and the more you give, the more you get. Now let's go on to new issues, where newborn bonds take their first breaths.

SUMMARY ** CHAPTER 19 ** SUMMARY

Introduction to Independent Investing

- Know your dealer.

- Make your own financial contacts.

- Use a securities firm with a capital of at least five million dollars, or that has been in business at least five years.

- Find and keep a registered rep with at least five years experience selling municipals.

CHAPTER 20

NEW ISSUES

The Borrowers

In my corner of Wall Street we naturally tend to think of municipal bonds as good, saleable sources of tax-free income. However, government officials don't primarily think of their securities as tax-exempts—to them bonds are a method of borrowing and also obligations to be serviced. After bonds have been sold and a facility built they have to levy and collect the money to pay for it, finally retiring the debt. Most of our public facilities are not designed in Washington, but in the fifty states and thousands of municipalities. Recognizing the need for a new school building, for example, and determining how it is to be paid for, are parts of the local American political process. After the pols decide to borrow, a bonding authorization goes to their finance experts for implementing. Many larger communities (Los Angeles and Seattle prominently among them) maintain complete departments to manage their money, to apply for grants, and, when necessary, to create bond issues. Others hire *municipal finance consultants* from the private sector to do this work. I have written about Clearwater, Florida and Kenosha, Wisconsin, both of whom are happy to use consultants.[1] U. S. municipalities are now selling new issues of bonds at the rate of about $125 billion a year, or 2% of the gross national product.

---

1.   White, Wilson. *The Municipal Bond Market: Basics,* The Financial Press, Jersey City, New Jersey, 1985.

The Lenders

In recent years individuals have been supplying most of the money for municipal bonds. As we have seen, they buy many of them through the medium of U.I.T.s and managed funds. They also buy them directly from new issues. However, new issues come in big, complex chunks, requiring middlemen—the municipal bond dealers—to distribute them in usable sizes. Issuers borrow by the millions of dollars, individuals lend by the thousands, and municipal bond dealers take up the slack in between.

The Dealer Middlemen

Of the approximately 500 dealers in municipal bonds, about half regularly *underwrite* them. To underwrite tax-exempts means to buy new issues from local governments and distribute them to investors. This process is defines the *primary market*. Primary market underwriters incur expenses for research, sales, and administration, much like the suppliers of other goods and services. The largest underwriters are organized as separate departments of publicly owned firms such as Shearson's Lehman Brothers, Smith, Barney, (or our invented Hudson & West) or of the biggest commercial banks such as Chase or BankAmerica. Most medium size and smaller firms, for example, Barre & Co. in Morristown, New Jersey, or Zahner in Kansas City, are privately owned. Dealers contest against each other in the primary market, technically according to a special set of S.E.C. and M.S.R.B. (Municipal Securities Rulemaking Board) rules, but in practice complying with a much harsher regulator, our perennially ferocious competition.

Yield Pricing

We'll be getting into new issue pricing shortly, so let's tackle some of its math and jargon right now. In Chapter 4 we saw how to calculate current yield. Just divide income by invested amount. $80 per year income on a bond at $1,000 gives you a current yield of 8%. However, at any other price, up or down from principal value, current yield does not account for the eventual loss or gain when the bonds come due. A more complete gauge of bond income is *yield to maturity*. Y.T.M. is calculated by using a complex formula which weighs current yield and adds in gains or losses to give a total return. This formula is wired into bond calculators and salespeople can figure yield with one in a few seconds. They simply push the right buttons to get numbers like those in Figure 20.1.

Figure 20.1
YIELD AND PRICES–1 YEAR MATURITY

Settlement date: 1/1/1992

Amount (M)	Description	Coupon	Maturity	$ Price	Current Yield	Maturity Yield
100	Hawaii	6	1/1/1993	100	6.00%	6.00%
100	Hawaii	6	1/1/1993	99	6.06%	7.05%
100	Hawaii	6	1/1/1993	101	5.94%	4.96%

In Figure 20.1 there are three lines but just one bond description: $100,000 principal value of Hawaii 6's due in January 1993, one year after the settlement date. While the price in the one year maturity bond falls one point, from 100 down to 99, the current yield barely moves. In the same case, the Y.T.M. rises by over a full percentage, a substantial difference. And the same from 100 up to 101, where yield to maturity shows the difference clearly, in reverse.

Y.T.M. is particularly useful when different coupons and prices are involved. In Fig. 20.2, which of the three bond returns the most: the 8% bond at 100, the 10% bond at 124, or the 5% bond at 64?

Answer: The 5% bond, yielding an 8.26%. The 10%, premium bond has the highest current yield, but the 5% bond yields the most to maturity, 8.26%.

Figure 20.2
YIELD AND PRICES–30 YEAR MATURITY

Settlement date: 1/1/1992

Amount (M)	Description	Coupon	Maturity	$ Price	Current Yield	Maturity Yield
100	Hawaii	8	1/1/22	100	8.00%	8.00%
100	Hawaii	10	1/1/22	124	8.07%	7.90%
100	Hawaii	5	1/1/22	64	7.81%	8.26%

Premium Bonds and Yield to Call

In these days of fluctuating interest rates we often find older bonds carrying high coupons offered in the market. These will naturally carry higher, *premium*, prices, that is they are now worth more than 100. Most of these can be called in, that is, redeemed before final maturity by their issuers, often at slightly over 100, 103, for instance. The true yield of these bonds can be accurately figured using a variant of Y.T.M., *yield to call*. At a time when long municipals are selling readily at 8.00%, you may be offered an 11% bond issued in palmier days, at say, 112, or 112% of face value. 11% divided by 1.12 gives you a current yield of 9.82%, much cheaper than currently available yields on long bonds and also a 9.67% to maturity, apparently providing a good deal. However, looking more closely, if you figure what your return will be if in fact the bonds are called in two years at a price of 103, then you will find that your yield will drop down to only 5.98%. The Y.T.C. formula figures in the effects of coupon income, current yield, the loss of 9 points (from 112 down to 103), and the time factor, producing the 5.98%, probability much lower than the yield you could get in the long term market.

Salespeople are required to disclose this lower yield when selling premium bonds, but make sure you ask about it. Only yesterday I encountered a deeply disappointed individual investor whose lovely 12% bonds were lost in a call, leaving him with nothing to show for two years wait. See Chapter 25 for more on callables.

The Borrowing Procedure

There are two distinct ways communities can float bonds. One is through *public competitive bidding,* the route most often chosen by smaller and more seasoned G.O. issuers. The other is by *private negotiated sale*, usually favored by larger issuers, particularly for revenue bonds. In 1990 the volume scoreboard read one quarter competitive and three-quarters negotiated.

COMPETITIVE NEW ISSUES

After a municipality decides to sell bonds at public bidding, its financial people, often assisted by an outside consultant, start designing a borrowing plan. When the timing seems right they advertise a bond issue, inviting interested parties to submit sealed bids. It's not unlike asking for proposals to paint City Hall or to provide its fuel oil, except that the product supplied is money. Although anyone may compete, in practice virtually all bids are submitted by municipal bond dealers. In recent years an average week has seen about 20 new issues of significant size sold via competitive bidding.

The Bidding Process

Municipal bond dealers usually form groups called *syndicates* to bid on new issues together. As soon as the *managers* (the dealers who lead a bidding group) see a competitive sale announced they line up a syndicate (averaging some ten dealer members) basing membership on the last public sale of this particular bond. Our illustration dealer, Hudson & West, manages some deals, but they also may appear with second billing, as a co-manager, or even lower, as a plain member. Hudson & West's municipal bond department occupies the two top floors of a post-modern building on Park Avenue. The firm's municipal syndicate, trading and institutional sales divisions are on eleven and public finance and administration on twelve.

Syndication

Shortly before a sale each group holds a *syndicate meeting* (either by telephone or at its manager's office) at which, without knowing what levels the competing groups are considering, the members set their bid. The art of underwriting lies in naming interest rates that will be just high enough to attract investors but still low enough, profit included, to beat the competition. Most municipalities issue bonds which come due over a large number of years, *serial bonds*. Figure 20.3 shows a typical kind of work sheet used during this process. Discussion focuses on what we call the *scale*, a string of yields assigned to each of the issue's maturity years. As discussed, yields usually rise as maturities lengthen, perhaps from 5.00% for bonds due in one year, 6.50% for those due in five years, out to 8.00% in thirty. After the syndicate members express their views and intentions, which often differ quite sharply, they reach a compromise, setting the scale, agreeing on a profit margin, and producing the final bid. The manager does the math, then enters that syndicate's proposal with the community.

At a specified hour the community opens all the proposals and, provided that an acceptable one is received, awards the whole issue to the bidder offering the lowest interest cost. For example, on August 21, 1990, Traverse Area Public Schools, Michigan, had put up $22 million bonds for competitive bidding. Five syndicates bid on the bonds, with a syndicate headed by Griffin, Kubik and Stevens submitting the lowest interest cost bid, at 7.2152%, and it was awarded the issue.

Figure 20.3
TRAVERSE CITY WORK SHEET

Size __22A__   Issue __TRAVERSE CITY SCHOOLS, MI__

Sold __8/21/90__   N.I.C. __7.2152__ $ __100.005__ Cover bid __7.24__   __PRESCOTT__

Dated __10/1/90__   Callable __01c 101½/04@100__ Ratings __A-1/A+__
__(+ AMBAC)__

	Amounts	Coupon	Yield	Dollar Price	Concession
1991					
92		9	6.10	104.31	1/4
93			25	106.46	3/8
94			40	108.20	
1995			55	109.56	
96			70	110.56	
97			80	111.51	
98			90	112.23	
99			7.00	112.73	
2000		7	6.90	100.68	
01			7.00	100	
02			05	99.60	
03			10	99.17	
04			15	98.70	
2005			20	98.14	
06			25	97.68	
07			NR0	96.23	
08				95.60	
09				95.00	
2010				100.993	
				100.	
				.993	

Date __8/23__   Balance __9,655__   Date Closed __10/29/90__

The winning syndicate becomes the temporary owner of the issue and its members get to work selling the bonds in smaller lots. Members are required by their syndicate contract to offer bonds only at the agreed prices. This price fixing is permitted by securities laws, helping both members and investors get a fair deal. At sale time, investor enthusiasm comes to a natural peak and customers who wish to buy place their orders with one of the syndicate members. The members in turn enter them with the managers during an *order period*, often lasting one hour. The manager tabulates the orders and then chooses which bonds to allot to which members. What happens when there are more orders than bonds? The manager decides which member gets them. New issue bonds are sold subject to completion of legalities (when issued, or W.I.), but in practice almost all deals go through as scheduled. In real life the G.K.S. syndicate proceeded to reoffer the Traverses as shown in Figure 20.4.

The Takedown System

When investors buy most securities, stocks, for instance, they pay a certain price *plus* a commission. Municipal bond new issues, however, are sold at the advertised price, *net,* with no commission. To promote sales, part of the syndicate's gross profit goes into a *takedown* system whereby members take down (buy) bonds from their syndicates at the set scale price, *less* (minus) a discount. On the Traverse issue, the price in 2001 was set as 7's at 100 (par) and the takedown was 1/2 point, or $5, so members could take down the bonds at 99 1/2, sell them at 100, and keep the 1/2% for their efforts. If, just after sale time, you had decided to buy $25,000 of those bonds you could have given your salesperson an order for them. He would have reported the order to his firms' liaison desk, where it would be entered with the syndicate manager. If the manager decided to allot those bonds to that member and if the member chose to honor your order, you would get your bonds.

Selling from Syndicate

If enough orders are entered to sell out the whole issue the bonds are all allotted, the account is closed, and the anticipated underwriting profit is made. However, if some bonds are unsold, the manager releases a report called the *run and balance,* showing which bonds remain and the group continues its sales efforts. After the order period is over, members may take down bonds according to regular syndicate terms, but now it's first come, first served, and not subject to allotments. If bonds remain in an account more than a few days the group may rethink their commitment and decide either to cut their price, thus reducing their profit, or liquidate the remaining bonds and take a loss. The Traverse Area account sold two-thirds of the issue by the end of the order period and finally closed it out on October 29, 1990. We shall see how some of the bonds entered the secondary market, where they trade according to supply and demand. Eventually, new issue managers add up the syndicate's profit, subtract the expenses, complete the bookkeeping, and send members profit checks (or bills, if there is a loss). In the example issue the syndicate earned a worthwhile profit, about $2 per bond, or $50,000, plus takedown income.

The Pros and Cons

Investors who buy directly from competitive new issues get a number of advantages. Choice names like Lake Forest, Illinois, Millburn, New Jersey, or Greenwich, Connecticut, appear so rarely in the secondary market that new issues are almost the only way to buy them. New issues are good sources of bonds priced at or near 100, the level favored by many investors. In addition, though dealers can make the takedown by selling the bonds, new issue profit margins are usually lower than those in the secondary market.

Along with these advantages come a number of special hazards. Large buyers, including dealers themselves, often snap up the most attractively priced maturities long before individual investors get a chance. Small buyers may even find an 'All Sold' sign on a whole deal before their orders are considered. Markets do change and underwriters do make mistakes, so if your broker fills your new issue order it's often because nobody else wants them and the underwriters are stuck. I suggest you consult an experienced municipal bond person before buying bonds from a competitive new issue, as you would seek the advice of a trustworthy antique dealer before venturing into a serious professional furniture auction.

NEGOTIATED NEW ISSUES

The other way new issues are underwritten is by *negotiated* sale. In a negotiated deal the issuing body and the manager's public finance department work together to develop a financing plan. The preliminary stage may take several months or even years, as political, engineering, and marketing problems are solved. Back in 1978, when a unique petroleum unloading facility, the Louisiana Offshore Oil Project, was proposed, a new state authority was created to finance it. Loops, as we now call its bonds, are secured by such elaborate contract guarantee provisions that they would have been impossible to sell at public bidding.

However, after months of negotiations a First Boston syndicate brought the deal to market and the $450 million underwriting went smoothly.

Any dealer can enter a bid at a competitive auction, but you can't just walk into an issuer's office and sign up to be its negotiated deal manager—the process of getting named for the job is difficult and expensive, and, finally, competitive. The competition doesn't come through bidding, but from other dealers' municipal finance departments who also make a pitch for the assignment. Established managers, therefore, usually try to produce the best results for the issuer, aiming to protect their existing, favored positions. Hudson & West has a fifty person municipal finance division, medium size. It competes nationally with the largest negotiated dealers, but most of its success has been in California, where it had taken over a smaller firm's public finance department several years earlier.

To Market, To Market

When a negotiated issue nears final form the issuer applies to one or both financial service *rating* agencies—Moody's or Standard & Poor's—for an assessment of the proposed bond's quality. (See Chapter 25 for more on ratings). The manager mails out 'the papers' which describe the issue's credit provisions and also often conducts *information meetings* to further describe and promote the deal and to respond to investor reactions. As sale time approaches the manager usually invites co-managers and other dealers into the party, repaying obligations and otherwise keeping peace in the municipal bond industry.

As soon as satisfactory ratings are received the manager *prices* the issue, that is, tests investor response with a tentative scale of interest rates. If demand is either too low or too high, the offering yields are adjusted, up or down, until a reasonable balance is achieved. Then the issuer and the manager may bargain for profit margins and any remaining details and the syndicate assumes the commitment. An order period follows, during which perhaps hundreds of millions of dollars worth of bonds, along with their takedown profits, are allotted at the manager's discretion. If all goes well the bonds are completely sold and the syndicate makes its expected profit. If not, the remainder is handled thereafter like that of a competitive account.

All in all, underwriting, both publicly bid and privately negotiated, is a varied and challenging job offering dealers multiple possibilities for profit and satisfaction. Beginning salaries in syndicate departments now run around $25,000 a year, possibly reaching $50,000 after five years or so. Heads of departments in medium sized firms may earn $100,000 a year. All of these may also receive bonuses, ranging from token amounts for low performance or marginally profitable years, up to six or even twelve month bonuses when things are right.

Underwriting is good sized. New issues now provide about half the funds needed for municipal construction, and sends over $1 billion a year of gross income to reward the underwriters. Hudson & West underwrote $10 billion in 1990, up 15% from the prior year. This brought the firm a $9 million profit, $2 million after expenses, or about 4% of the entire company's earnings.

The Investor and Negotiated Deals

It might appear that individual investors could get a price break in a negotiated deal, but that's not really the case. Buying from these issues is usually even tougher than from a competitive one. They are primarily designed to be resold in lion-sized blocks of $10 million or even $25 million or more. Who buys in this size? Insurance companies, U.I.T.s, managed funds, dealers (for their own speculative purposes), and also banks. If there's anything left over, it's likely to be stale chicken feed. However, the deals do get done, issuers receive effectively low rates, and the largest investors (who in most cases are intermediates for individuals) get attractive bonds. There seems to be no corruption to speak of, and few real credit-related disasters. Most of the substantial profits finally go to publicly owned corporations. The system may not be perfect, but it's huge and it works. Want to buy from a negotiated new issue? Definitely seek help.

New Issues and Old

Pick up the financial newspapers and you'll think that the municipal bond business consists entirely of new deals. The visible part of such new issues is neatly scheduled weeks in advance and makes good, comprehensible, reading. They begin life with either a dramatic bidding duel or a newsworthy negotiated offering. Their reception by investors is followed closely, often setting the tone of the municipal market day. A new issue's usual cycle is as predictable as that of a farm, starting with a regular planning period, proceeding to offering and sales, and ending with the syndicate's harvest of profit or loss. However, as we'll see in the following chapters, new issues are only one way individual investors can buy municipal bonds.

SUMMARY ** CHAPTER 20 ** SUMMARY

New Issues

- State and local government building projects are often financed by new issues of municipal bonds. These sales now total about $125 billion a year.

- Most smaller municipalities issue general obligation bonds via competitive public sale.

- Most larger communities and revenue bond borrowers issue by private negotiated sale.

- New issues are offered without commissions, chiefly for professionals.

- Individual investors rarely get good treatment buying from new issues.

CHAPTER 21

HOW DEALERS BUY BONDS—PART 1

The Trading Market

Dramatic as new issues are, they usually provide less than half of the total municipal bond transaction volume. The rest comes in the secondary, or trading, market where sales may reach half a billion dollars per working day. Each new issue's primary market phase is short—usually lasting a week or less. But for the rest of a bond's twenty or so year life it can trade only in the secondary market. There is no Municipal Bond Exchange—our hundreds of thousands of bond descriptions defy such organization. Instead, the secondary is conducted over-the-counter, in trader-to-trader, over-the-telephone bargaining. There is no central pricing mechanism and few transactions are reported. The secondary operates through an informal network of the same 500 dealers we have described earlier, in all states, but firmly centered in New York. With few exceptions, the larger Wall Street firms and many smaller ones as well, maintain active municipal trading departments. We have seen Hy at Hudson & West selling funds and we will soon see his firm's traders at work. Joe and Marci came close to the secondary market when Hy showed them some New York State Power Authority bonds, but, like many individual investors, they bought managed funds instead. To some the secondary market may seem hard to understand. We have hundreds and hundreds of traders, salesmen, and brokers, calling both each other and thousands of

197

customers all day long, with nothing published, nothing like a ticker tape. It's more like a city than a farm—crowded, fast moving, and loaded with variety. To some it's a jungle. Even bond veteran Jim Cooner, in his estimable book, says that the secondary " ... functions more like a cross between an oriental bazaar and a Charlie Chaplin movie... . If I had to choose a motto for the foggy munici- pal secondary market, it would be a toss-up between 'Let the buyer beware' and 'What the market will bear.'" However, let's turn on our fog lights and find a way through the trading alleys.

An Individual Seller

Now let me introduce you to another of my imaginary characters, one William J. Whitmore, from Jacksonville, Illinois. Although Whitmore didn't even know that the trading market exists he soon learned how useful it can be. He had invested heavily in some real estate a few miles out from Springfield and its losses unex- pectedly brought him down to the zero tax bracket; and he wanted to reduce his loan. Fortunately, the family trust just distributed some common stocks to him and also $100,000 face value of municipal bonds as shown in Figure 21.1. Whitmore had little idea what the bonds were worth, only that they were tax-ex- empt. He was particularly concerned about one of the items, an Eastern Airlines bond, which his newspaper said was bankrupt. And with his losses he didn't need tax-exempts right then.

Once in a while, we all get into fixes when we definitely need an expert but don't know where to turn. A car lock won't open or a tree falls on the front lawn. Whitmore had never owned securities himself—he didn't even have a bro-

---

Figure 21.1
WILLIAM J. WHITMORE

INVESTMENTS

(M)	Bond Description	Coupon	Maturity	Annual Income
20	Decatur, ILL. Parking Revenue	5.75%	2/15/05ca	$1,150
30	New Jersey Turnpike Authority	7.20%	1/1/18ca	2,160
25	Andover, Conn.	8.25%	7/15/97	2,063
25	Wayne County I.D.R., Mich. Eastern Airlines Inc.	5.00%	9/1/99	1,250
100				$6,623

kerage account. He didn't want to use the local bank—their old-fashioned ways didn't appeal to him, and he also hoped to avoid some of their charges. Suppose you found yourself in his predicament, what would you do? His first thought, odd though that may seem, was to look in the Yellow Pages, maybe under 'Bonds, Municipal'. Then he remembered that a friend had spoken highly of a securities dealer and thought he might talk to them. He was headed right toward the secondary market.

Bright and early one Monday morning Whitmore drove over to Springfield, walked into Hudson & West's branch office on Main, and received a pleasant reception from registered representative Frances MacComber. He was pleased that she understood that he wanted to sell some securities, not buy anything. The R.R. priced the stocks easily enough using a desktop quote machine, but the municipals were a different matter. She said she'd call New York and ask their traders to work up some numbers, which would take a few hours. Whitmore, pleased that he had access to the national market, gave her the information needed for a new account form. Getting to the secondary market isn't impossible.

Hudson & West has over 100 other sales branches, mostly located on the East and West Coasts and in the Midwest. In these branches some four thousand salespeople push the products that the firm has for sale. As soon as Whitmore left Frances called Arnie, her liaison person with H & W's retail trading desk in New York, and gave him the list for pricing. Why did she have to call Arnie? Because all decisions to buy or sell tax-exempts, and at what price, are made only at the company's home office.

Frances then spent a few minutes thinking about Whitmore, who was obviously a straight shooter from way back, but not so dumb. She reviewed her approach, guessing correctly that it was his first dealer experience, and decided she had started well—just do what he asks, at least for the time being. It amazed her what securities the cat drags in some days, but if she played her cards well, liquidating those bonds for Whitmore would put about $150 net in her wallet. Certainly better than the twenty bucks she'd get for spending an hour educating someone on an I.R.A. Then she turned her thoughts to how to land Whitmore big.

Thousands of investors all around the country find themselves in Whitmore's situation every business day. We've discussed liquidity a number of times, and this is what the tax-exempt liquid boils down to—how much can bonds be sold for in the secondary market? They will mature only once, at a fixed date in the future. To sell them before maturity someone has to pay you cash. Here bond dealers step in. They can either find a new investor and sell the bonds directly, or they can put up the cash themselves, bridging the time gap until they do. Why do people ever sell their nice, tax-exempt municipal bonds?

For three principal sets of reasons: their personal *financial situation* has changed; the *market value* of their bonds has changed; or the *credit quality* of their bonds has changed.

Three Reasons for Liquidating

Number One. Municipals aren't for everyone, or for every year either, as investment policies need adjusting. Whitmore was in the zero income bracket, where municipals made little sense for him, and besides, he needed the cash. Or, an insurance company may decide to switch part of its portfolio out of bonds and into the equities.

Number Two. The passage of time itself brings changes. We talked about this with U.I.T.s in Chapter 11 and it works similarly with unpackaged bonds. Suppose that back fifteen years ago you had bought a twenty year bond and now you see that it will come due in five years. Since short bonds usually sell at lower yields to maturity than longer ones, you may be able to sell the short bonds, reinvest the proceeds in long terms and increase your take-home pay substantially.

Bond market values fluctuate, often with amazing speed. I recently showed my young associates a chart of the bond market in 1963-64 showing how the market used to move—three points, top to bottom, in two whole years. On Tuesday of the week before this writing we saw bond prices rise up three points and then fall off five, ending down two, but traveling a distance of eight points, 8%, in one day. Dramatically or not, municipal bond prices do shift around a lot, again creating opportunities for their holders. Buy low, sell high and take a nice profit. Or, take comfort in selling an unfortunate position at a loss in order to gain a substantial tax break. I've seen investors dump bonds at 40 or 50 point losses, write them off, then swap back into other bonds and ride them up to 110, turning a sickening loss into a healthy profit. Whether for cash, for security, or profit, the secondary bond market has plenty to offer.

Number Three. The credit standing of tax-free bonds frequently changes, sometimes falling, but recently more often rising. In the last thirty years we have seen many larger urban regions suffer social and physical deterioration, accompanied by substantial bond issuance and by investor perceptions of greater credit risk. The bonds of Buffalo, St. Louis, and Kansas City, Kansas, which once brought top prices, now sell at much lower levels. Investors who are nervous about certain bonds may want to get out of them before it's too late. On the other hand, holders who bought many Southern or Northeastern bonds cheaply when they were out of favor may wish to sell them at today's good prices and look for other bargains. Investors in long term bonds bought when interest rates were high may see them refinanced, shortening their repayment dates and enhancing their credit standing, thus creating sale and replacement possibilities.

When, for any of these or other reasons investors want to sell, they go to the secondary market. One of the dealers in the trading network buys their bonds, trying to make a profit by selling to a new investor at a higher price. Like used cars, used bonds can either be traded in for new ones or sold outright. One difference, however—you can't sell bonds yourself; you have to go through a registered expert: a municipal bond dealer.

Selling to a Dealer

Many investors think that dealers don't like buying their bonds. Actually, this isn't at all correct. Dealers are often just as anxious to buy as they are to sell, and can make as much profit doing so. Dealers frequently need fresh inventory for resale, they may think the market is going up, or may even have a standing order for exactly the bonds you own. They plan to make good money buying from you, so watch them carefully. Aren't you suspicious about the motives of a shopkeeper whose sign reads 'We pay cash for old gold,' or 'Highest prices paid for estates'? It may be *you* that's doing *them* the favor, and so with either bonds or jewelry, make sure you get a good price. We return to this point in Chapter 26.

The Five Trading Parties

A typical secondary market operation involves five parties: the customer-seller; the salesperson who handles him; the house (represented by a trader); a second salesperson; and the new customer-buyer. You; the used car person who buys your old car; the auto dealer; the salesman who resells it; and the new buyer. Sometimes sales and trading are merged into one person, and in other cases more traders, often from outside firms, get into the picture. But five parties make up the most usual trade—two customers, and three dealer employees, each party needing compensation along the way. See Figure 24.1.

Taking Risks and Taking Orders

There are two ways traders buy bonds in the secondary market—going long and filling orders. *Going long* means to buy outright, taking the risk of ownership. In going long a bond the trader functions like an antique dealer who buys your old credenza, assuming the risk and expenses of ownership, in hopes of selling it at a higher price. (Going long can understandably be confused with using the term 'long', as in 'long' term maturity bonds, but it's entirely different.)

The other way traders buy bonds is by *filling an order*. This way a customer first commits to buy some bonds and only then does the trader buy them, filling the order. The only risk is that the order falls through. In a slightly different version, if a trader finds a good bargain in bonds another dealer owns, he may show them to his sales force, then, if an order comes in, buys them from the other house. Like a shopkeeper who shows a customer a soup tureen in a catalogue, and says, 'I don't have it in stock, but I can get it for you in a few days.' This is not 'going long', it's executing an order, a riskless transaction. When I can't satisfy a customer from my own inventory position I sometimes have to do this too, but it's a lot less fun, and usually less profitable as well. *Going short* is a much rarer (in municipals at least) technique, meaning selling bonds you don't own, in hopes of profiting by buying them back later at a lower price.

The Traders

We visited Hudson & West's syndicate department earlier at the company's New York City headquarters. Now we move to the north end of the eleventh floor to approach trading, a Wall Street function often much in the spotlight. About 70 people spend their time here, buying and selling bonds in the secondary market, both from customers and from other municipal bond dealer departments. Hudson & West, as do most wire houses, maintains four separate trading desks corresponding to the four classes of bonds we'll get to shortly. Two kinds of municipal bond traders work at each of these desks: *block* and *retail*. The goal of both kinds is our usual one—to make as much money as possible in the shortest possible time. However, Wall Street's ferocious competition limits achieving these laudable goals.

Block Trading

Block traders deal with institutions, such as U.I.T. sponsors, fund managers, or banks and insurance companies. All day long they work with the institutional salespeople who sit nearby, going long, going short, and soliciting and filling orders. Block traders are notoriously volatile—they may own a huge quantity of bonds or none at all, depending on how they like the market at the moment. The smaller trading firms might average under $5 million in inventory at any one time. Medium sized firms may position perhaps $25 million and larger ones may own hundreds of millions. Block traders also deal in the wholesale market, watching and waiting, buying and selling, alone and jointly with other dealers. Block trading may also be used as a speculative vehicle, to support new issue activities, or for other purposes. An average trade might be 250 bonds, $250,000 worth.

Retail traders service a dealer's individual customers. They too buy at wholesale, and also from the sales force's customers. Since smaller lots of bonds tend to be less volatile than, larger ones, retail traders operate more steadily than the block guys. They try to keep a level of inventory appropriate for their hundreds or thousands of salespeople to push, owning maybe one week's usual sales volume at any one time. Since neither salespeople nor individual customers can be expected to know their way around the current secondary market, retail traders and their supervisors have an obligation to price bonds equitably so that the customers, the salesmen, and the house all get a reasonably fair deal. If the traders function correctly chances are that the house and they will be well rewarded. At Hudson & West the retail traders sit at the same desks as do the

Figure 21.2
HUDSON & WEST'S NEW YORK MUNICIPAL BOND TRADING FLOOR

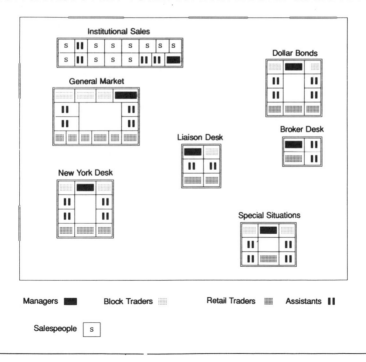

block traders but at their own end. A typical trade might involve 20 bonds, $20,000 worth, usually from the firm's own long position.

Sometimes traders, particularly block traders, are viewed as gamblers; or parasites on legitimate investors; sometimes as bumbling idiots, losing pots of money and never knowing when to quit. At other times they seem to take an inspired stand, bringing a whole department fine profits in perilous times. In plain fact, we traders do live a rich, full, life—some days heroes, some days villains. Trading is a difficult, demanding and wonderful way to make a living, especially when things are going well. And when the going gets tough we really earn our keep. Imagine being responsible for $10 million of bonds when the market's off five points and you'll see what I mean.

The Four Classes of Bonds

Municipal bonds are handled in four classes: general market names, dollar bonds, local credits, and specialties. *General market bonds* bear the larger and better known names, like G.O.'s of Mississippi or Portland, Oregon, or Chicago O'Hare Airport revenue bonds. They come in many thousands of different coupons and due dates, generally trading in yield to maturity. On one day a trading department might be offering $1 million California 6 1/2's due 7/1/08 at a 7.20%, but after they sell it this exact bond might not come into the market again for a long time. Like a house at one address which might be for sale only every ten years or more.

The *dollar bond* markets are more continuous. Dollar bonds originate from large new issues. They are *term bonds*, usually carrying a single coupon and maturity. They often trade actively, for months or years, and are closely watched on Wall Street broker television screens. As their name implies they trade in dollar prices, so that we may quote one of them at 99 1/4 (99 bid, 99 1/4 offered). Dollar bonds are more like apartments that sell frequently in a large condominium building.

Many *local bonds* tend to trade according to particular circumstances, especially the varying levels of state income taxes. New York, California, and Connecticut are currently prominent in this respect, so many houses assign trading responsibility for them to specializing traders.

The fourth category, *specialty* or *junk bonds*, covers anything that doesn't fit into the others—low grade, obscure, in default, etc. These are my kinds of bonds.

The General Market Desk

Hudson & West's *general market* desk is staffed by four block traders, the desk's manager first and foremost. Behind them sit the firm's dozen institutional tas-free salespeople. At the other end of the general market desk sit six retail traders. As noted, traders buy bonds both at wholesale and from customers, block traders from larger accounts and retail traders from smaller customers. Four assistants, who record transactions, keep track of inventory positions and work with the liaison people on communications, complete the general market team.

Dollar Bond Trading

Nearby is the *dollar bond* desk, where on one end three block traders deal in active term bonds. They spend all day watching trading screens, buying and selling against orders and also making their own markets. Three retail dollar bond traders sit on the other side, along with four assistants.

Local and Junk Trading

Farther on down the room is this office's *local desk*, which specializes in New York State bonds. The New York desk has two block traders and a head trader-manager, three retail traders, and four assistants. New Yorkers, saddled with high income tax rates and with prolific issuing bodies, find these bonds especially attractive. Many wire houses maintain separate trading departments in their most active branches but not Hudson & West. They do it their way, handling all trading from New York City.

At the end of the trading room is the *specialty desk* (often called the junk desk) where the head trader is flanked by two block traders, four assistants, two researchers, and one retail trader.

In addition to their risk-taking trading desks, H & W has two satellite centers which feed and digest information to and from the four trading positions. The *liaison desk,* a communications point, is located a few feet away from the general market trading desk. It is headed by Arnie, who with five others keeps in contact with the firm's thirty other, purely order-taking, branches, such as the one we visited in Springfield, Illinois. Among other responsibilities, the people on this desk respond to salespeoples' questions about bond offerings, get prices when customers such as Whitmore want to sell, and solve payment and bond delivery problems.

Hudson & West also maintains a *broker desk,* where four people relay information and execute trades with the dozen or so of Wall Street's broker's brokers—specialized firms that trade bonds between dealers for a small commission

SUMMARY ** CHAPTER 21 ** SUMMARY

How Dealers Buy Bonds—Part 1

- The secondary market for municipal bonds is conducted by about 500 dealer firms, over-the-counter, not on an exchange.

- Some trading concentrates on large size blocks.

- Retail trading handles the smaller sizes.

- There are four classes of bonds in the trading sense: well-known general market names; dollar bonds; bonds of various local markets; and specialty situations.

- Dealers buy bonds from customers, both institutional and retail, and at wholesale, from other dealers.

- They also take orders for bonds owned by customers and other dealers.

CHAPTER 22

HOW DEALERS BUY BONDS—PART 2

By 11:00 Arnie had finished organizing the day's second wave of requests for bond prices. Thirty different salespeople in twenty branches were clamoring for current market prices on about one hundred fifty different lots of municipal bonds. Two of Arnie's assistants had transcribed the bond descriptions onto slips of yellow paper, one for each item. Arnie then sorted the slips into four piles— general market, dollar, (local), and junk. Whitmore's bonds were all there, one in each of the piles. Arnie divided the local pile into New York-exempt and local bonds of other states, and then delivered the four piles to their appropriate desks.

Preparing a Bid

A few minutes later on the general market desk a young trading assistant there picked up their pile, among them Whitmore's Decatur bonds. The assistant then looked up the current quality ratings on all of them. Entering their descriptions into the K.I.S. Munibase, a broker-owned proprietary data base. There she found their current ratings and other information pertinent to pricing the bonds and typed this data onto each slip. Finally she sorted them into two piles, one for round lots—$100,000 and over, and one for smaller lots. That's how Hudson & West draws the line between retail and institutional—$95,000 and under for the retail end of each trading desk, and over that amount for the block traders. She took the large lots to one of the block traders and the others to the retail traders.

Making a Bid

Shortly before noon Philip, a junior retail trader specializing in general market bonds East of the Mississippi, looked at his share of the new items, eleven lots of bonds. He picked up the slip with one of Whitmore's bonds, noting the description, Decatur Parking Revenues, the maturity, 2005 (but with a new refunded, payoff date), the amount, 20, and the rating that the assistant had researched (AAA by Standard and Poor's). Philip looked at the slip carefully. What was going through his mind? He liked these bonds since they had been refunded with sufficient U. S. Government securities to pay them off in 1995. The new due date, 1995, was in good demand right then from the firm's individual customers. The amount was small, but usable. He knew that the branches could certainly use these and planned to make an aggressive bid.

But what bid to make? Consciously or no, Philip weighed about twenty different pricing factors, including the general economic background, the current government bond market yields, the level of his inventory, and his recent trading results. He picked up the sheet describing all the sales the department had made on the Friday before, and saw that five items similar to the Decatur pre-refundeds had sold, bringing profits averaging $13 per bond. Philip also noted that two similar bonds had already traded that Monday morning, at a yield of 6.80%, which converted to a dollar price of 95 1/2. Since the other bonds had sold readily at a 6.80% yield, he thought that these Decatur bonds would be an easy sale at a higher yield (cheaper price), perhaps at a 6.90%. This would be a little better buy for him—a dollar price of 95. He jotted 95 down, and subtracted the profit margin he had in mind, 1 1/2 points, or $15 per bond, producing a bid of 93 1/2. That was the price Philip was proposing that Hudson & West should pay customer Whitmore.

Philip handed this bid of 93 1/2, or a total of $18,700, to his immediate superior, the head of the retail trading desk. She glanced at it, then looked at that day's trades. Hudson & West had already sold $3 million worth of bonds, but so far had bought only $1 million. She handed the slip back and told Philip that she wanted more bonds in inventory, implying that his bids should be raised somewhat, to increase their chances of buying the items.

Although he had his doubts about how necessary it was to raise the price to a retail customer, Philip complied. He saw that Hudson & West's activity level was high, their inventory relatively light, and agreed that they should own more bonds. He raised his projected offering price by one half point, to 95 1/2, a yield of.80%. After the subtraction of the same $15 per bond profit margin, this came to a bid of 94, or $18,800, $100 more for Whitmore. Philip then bid on the other items on his desk and handed all of them to the head trader, who after looking at them changed one or two slightly. She initialled the bids and put them in the out box for one of Arnie's liaison people to send to the branches where they originated.

Customer bonds are only one source of inventory for Hudson & West's traders. The traders spend much of their day bidding the wholesale broker wires and other dealers for their bonds. This wholesale market resembles an auction where the highest bidder buys the article on the block. Whether bought directly from customers or in Wall Street's second-hand district, the traders then display their newly acquired wares for sale. They may run listings in the professional media, take out ads in the newspapers, or most importantly, release (show) them to their sales people who in turn may offer them to you, the customer.

How would have Philip's bid of 94 compared to bids he would make under competition in the wholesale market? His instructions were to make the same bids to both and he followed the rules. Other firms do it differently, some protecting the selling customer with stricter rules, while others take a greedier approach. Notice that Hudson & West is offering to take a risk on Whitmore's 20 Decatur bonds. If they buy them, no matter what happens in the market the firm will take the profit, or the loss.

The Dollar Bond Desk

We discussed dollar bonds earlier, large issues of term bonds which carry one coupon and one maturity year, suiting them for active trading. At the dollar desk the three block traders were keeping their eyes glued to an array of six screens displaying up-to-the-second markets on about 40 different active municipal bonds. New Jersey Turnpike 7.20% bonds due 1/1/2018 were the center of attention. The screen showed 96 7/8-7, that is, a Street bid of 96 7/8, and also an offering of 97. This was a difference of just $1.25 per $1,000 between bid and offering, but a normal spread for an active dollar bond.

"Wow," the head trader said, "Pikes at ninety-seven again, this thing is running!" One salesperson who covered several large fund buyers, including Olde Yankee, said that he had a customer they call Jimmy who would sell $3 million at 97, right at the quote. The trader heard that and asked the institutional salespeople sitting nearby if any of them had customers interested in selling Pikes any cheaper than that, at 96 7/8, perhaps. But after a minute of frantic phone calling, none found anyone who wanted to sell at that price. The head trader then called out, "Buy Jimmy's three million", directing his salesman to buy $3 million principal amount at 97, or $2,910,000, which he did. This way of buying is called 'taking the offering'. He thought that the market was headed up and bought the bonds at the screen's offered side, hoping that the market would continue upward. When he glanced at his screen again Pikes were flashing, showing a change, at 97 1/8. This meant that their buy at 97 looked like a good one, since the quoted bid side was equal to what they had paid, and the best price dealers could now buy them was at 97 1/8, or a little above their cost.

What was going on? Hudson & West was trading for its own account. Their traders bought these New Jersey Turnpike bonds from a managed fund at 97, probably in hopes of reselling them shortly at 97 1/2 or so, for half a point, or $5 per bond, profit. They felt that the dollar bond market had some more room to rise, and $3 million was an amount that appealed to them. Half a point on $3 million bonds would mean a profit of $15,000 for the department, a goodly amount these days. Naturally the market could go down instead of up, producing a similar, or greater, loss.

The Customer's Cost of Buying

At one point we saw that New Jersey Pikes were offered to professional traders at 97. The tax-exempt market is now so intensely competitive that many institutional accounts are routinely offered the traders' *wholesale* price. At the same time how was the *retail* end of Hudson & West's dollar bond desk handling Jersey Pikes? They were offering them at 99. Salesmen around the country could sell the same bonds to retail customers, but at two points higher. So a sale of 30 bonds would be made at 99, $20 per bond, or $600 higher than the round lot price. About one-third, $7 per bond, would be paid to the salesman, with the house keeping the rest.

Why do small customers pay more? Because the per bond expenses are much greater. The expenses both direct and indirect, of billing and delivering 30 bonds, including the services of Arnie, his assistants, the retail dollar bond trader, and the final salesperson, may well equal the expenses on a $1 million bond professional trade. It takes so much more work to produce a retail sale that most Wall Street firms have to charge more for executing small orders. To sell $1 million all the trader had to do was to say "Hit the bid," and that's that. To sell the same amount of bonds in 25 bond pieces would take thousands of phone calls over days and days, with all the expense which that would involve.

The Customer's Cost of Selling

Suppose that the inside, dealer-to-dealer Jersey Pike market was still hovering narrowly around 97. What price would a customer who wanted to *sell* 30 of these bonds receive? Probably about 96, or one point under the professional level. Why one point less than the inner dealer market? For the same reasons as on the offering side. The expenses of doing a small trade often equal those of a large one. Why only one point difference from the inside market, instead of two, as on the offering side? Because the buy side has a built-in marketing profit potential included in the price. Also because when a customer sells, she will often buy other bonds with the proceeds, and so the dealer gets two trades for the price of one.

The Retail End of the Dollar Bond Desk

Let's see what actually did happen to Whitmore's odd lot of 30 New Jersey Turnpikes. One of the dollar bond retail traders picked up a new pile of bid wanted slips and looked them over. It was a slow day for him, just 40 items, almost all familiar names, a total of 900 bonds. He wrote down his bids, in most cases about one point, or $10 per bond, lower than the current Street bid. In the case of one five bond lot, he made it two points, because Hudson & West had a $100 minimum on municipal bond trades. ($5,000 x .02 = $100.) He looked at his screen to check Jersey Turnpikes and saw them still fluttering around 97. He wrote down his bid on Whitmore's thirty bonds, 96, or $28,800. Hudson & West was offering to pay Whitmore 96 cents on the dollar for his bonds, one point, or $300 less than the level at which round lots of the same bond were trading at the other end of the desk.

He usually saw about 200 such items per day from the branches, but only about 50 result in actual trades, the rest being merely for evaluation or other casual purposes. Quotes, quotes, quotes, that's part of the routine of a retail trader's job. He dropped Whitmore's bid slip back in the pickup box along with the others in that bunch, giving them no further thought.

The Broker Desk

Now let's see what happened to the Andover, Connecticut G.O.s. As we saw earlier in this chapter Hudson & West's traders didn't especially care for this lot. Hudson & West didn't have any branches in that state, but dealers who did would probably pay a considerably higher price than he would for them, since they were exempt from that state's 14% tax. It was the firm's policy to put bonds with such special value out on the broker wires, and take a commission for selling them. In this way their selling customers get a fair shake and Hudson & West makes some money as well. Had the firm operated branches they would certainly have been more interested.

The Brokers

We mentioned municipal bond brokers earlier. In the trade we just call them brokers, and they operate strictly on a non-risk basis between dealers, earning a middleman's commissions. There are now ten of them in business, operating anonymously between the five hundred or so dealers, nationwide. Brokers such as J. J. Kenny Drake, J. F. Hartfield, and Chapdelaine transmit much of the information useful to municipal bond dealers. Several maintain wire systems whereby hundreds of dealers can be simultaneously shown bonds for auction bid. For instance, Hudson & West's Andovers. Interested dealers call their bids confidentially into the displaying broker. (If this process reminds you of the new issue public bidding mechanism you are right on target.) The broker then collates the bids, figures which one is highest, and reports the top one to the selling dealer. If this dealer decides to sell then the trade is done with the broker taking a commission, typically about $1 per bond, with a minimum of perhaps $100.

A few minutes after eleven a trader at Hudson & West's broker desk took the Andover bonds, phoned one of the brokers and asked him to take what he called a B.W.—a bid wanted—on 25 C.U.S.I.P. 034285KH8. This is the data identification number for all Andover, Connecticut 8 1/4% bonds due 6/15/97. The broker thanked him and within the hour the 25 bonds appeared on a nationwide wire system, with bids requested by two o'clock. By two all the bids were in, 11 in all, with the highest one, after subtracting the broker's commission, being 106 1/2. This bid, probably from a Hartford dealer, represented a 6.90% yield minus a few dollars margin. The broker desk trader jotted this bid down on the slip and put it where Arnie would pick it up later. Philip had been right, 106 1/2 was indeed a fine bid, higher by several points than he would have made himself. To make a profit the trader subtracted one point from the bid broker's number, making the price to the customer 105 1/2. Maybe this makes it clearer why buying bonds can be profitable to a securities firm and its salespeople, and why it can be worth your while to get a good price when you sell.

The Junk Desk

Meanwhile the specialty trader, a salty veteran, turned to Whitmore's Eastern Airlines bonds that one of his assistants had already run through the standard data base. He then looked them up in his own voluminous file of bonds, mostly obscure as to credit quality, experiencing financial troubles, or possessing special features. Although 95% of all municipals are readily tradable, the 5% remainder comprise almost as many separate names, among them Whitmore's Wayne Countys. Eastern was in bankruptcy at the time and you might think along with Whitmore, that these bonds would be poor quality indeed. However, the properties built with these bonds were located in metropolitan Detroit's thriving airport, and were so desired by other airlines that the bonds, despite their low coupon (5%) were worth almost 80 cents on the dollar. They might have stumped other traders but were easy for this desk. In fact, this exact bond appears for sale in the municipal bond marketplace about once a month and the junk desk at Hudson & West buys the majority of them. On some other items, such as many non-rated bonds, or those issued on particular multi-family housing projects, original research has to be performed. This may take a day or two to finish. In this case the trader just checked the last transactions, saw that the research was fresh—an assistant had called Detroit earlier in the month and had discovered that nothing had changed, and so he wrote down his bid, 78 1/2. This bid, too, was about the Street bid, following Hudson & West's standard operations. He dropped it in the out box, hoping that he would buy the bonds. Here again, only about 20% of all bids result in purchases, but that's a fact of a bond trader's life.

By 2:30 Arnie had picked up, among perhaps 100 others, four bids for the Springfield branch—the Decaturs (94), the New Jersey Turnpikes (96), the Andovers, (105 1/2) and the Wayne Countys (78 1/2). He checked them all over. Arnie phoned the results to Whitmore's R.R., who wrote down the bids, carefully reading them back. She then simply multiplied the prices by the amounts, and added up the totals, as shown in Figure 22.1.

Figure 22.1
HUDSON & WEST'S BIDS ON WHITMORE'S MUNICIPAL BOND PORTFOLIO

(M)	Bond Description	Coupon	Maturity	Price	Extension
20	Decatur, Ill. Parking Revenue Dated 11/1/66 CUSIP—243181BAI	5.75%	2/15/05	94	$18,800
30	New Jersey Turnpike Authority Dated 11/21/85 CUSIP—646139FW0	7.20%	1/1/18	96	28,800
25	Andover, Conn. Dated 6/15/78 CUSIP—034285KH8	8.25%	6/15/97	105.5	26,375
25	Wayne County I.D.R., Mich. Eastern Airlines Inc. Dated 1/1/68 CUSIP—944522NO3	5.00%	9/1/99	78.5	19,625
100M					$93,600

Later the same Monday Whitmore returned to Hudson & West's branch in Springfield and looked at the bond prices Frances had received from New York. He asked her what she thought. She said that the numbers looked pretty good, but that she might be able to pay him even more if he gave her a definite order to sell. Whitmore saw that if he sold all his bonds he could raise about $93,000 cash, and the stocks were worth about $50,000. This was more than he needed right then and he said he would think about it.

Whitmore took the list home and decided to sell the Decaturs, the Waynes, and the Andovers , and also some of the stocks. The three municipal bond holdings would bring in about $65,000 and the stocks $35,000, about what he needed. He would keep the New Jersey Turnpike bonds. Next morning he called Frances, told her to sell the three lots of bonds and the stocks, remembering to ask her if she could improve the bond prices somewhat. She phoned Arnie right away and asked him to try to get a little higher if possible, but to sell them at those prices. Arnie did try, but no dice. Prices in the municipal bond market were actually down about half a point, and though the three traders involved might have been inclined to lower their bids that day they agreed to pay the same prices. This accommodated their salespeople, in line with the policy of the firm, and at these prices they thought they could still make money on Whitmore's bonds. If, however, these were larger blocks, say of $100,000 or more, then their bids could well have dropped with the market (or risen, had the trend been reversed.) Arnie reported the news to Frances, who called Whitmore and confirmed his sales with the final prices. She thanked him, agreed how she would take delivery of the bonds and rang off to tell New York that the bonds were bought. 70 bonds, bringing about $150 for her, plus another $100 from the stocks. Some days things happen right.

All in all, Whitmore did quite well. He wound up, via a personal referral, at a branch office of a conscientious and efficient wire house with a well-run municipal bond system. He got reasonably good bids within a few hours; the firm renewed the bids next day and charged him standard fees.

However, he might have done better. Do you see the conflict of interest between the house and the customer? It's to the house's advantage to buy bonds as cheaply as possible, and although each of the traders made honest, market-conscious bids, other competing firms might have bid higher, perhaps by a point or two. Some firms do it differently—they pit their traders against the professional broker wires. If the Street bid is higher, then the bonds are sold at that price and the customer is charged a commission.

Whitmore could also have asked another, competing firm for bids, much as he would have for adding a room to his house, probably a smaller proposition. In this case, where the R.R. supplies minimal service, this would be perfectly ethical. When a salesperson provides a higher level of service, such as watching a customer's bonds and recommending changes, then dealing with two firms on the same item isn't fair.

Customer Whitmore might easily have done much worse. This firm's traders made conscientious, competitive bids, whereas others, either through inefficiency or design regularly attempt to buy bonds improperly, below current levels. The Decaturs and the Waynes had some tricky aspects and Hudson & West caught both, thus paying him more than they might at first glance be worth. Within the week Whitmore's trustee delivered the physical securities, all in good order, and he soon received a check for about $100,000. Let's hope he put the money to good use. For how H & W fared on the purchases, see the next chapter.

That day Hudson & West's block traders bought six lots of bonds totalling $7 million, going long $4 million and executing orders for another $3 million. The dollar bond boys bought 25 lots, $6 million in all. The retail traders accumulated 70 items; 40 from the system, including the three from Whitmore and 30 from the broker wires and other dealers. The grand total of purchases was 131 different lots with a face amount of $15 million, about an average day for this department. Thus Hudson & West's share of the whole secondary market was about 1% of the nationwide total, typical for a good sized firm.

SUMMARY ** CHAPTER 22 ** SUMMARY

How Dealers Buy Bonds—Part 2

- The municipal bond secondary market provides liquidity for existing bond holders and potential profits for dealers.

- Most dealers buy bonds for their own account directly from their customers.

- You can ask your broker to get competing bids for bonds you want to liquidate.

CHAPTER 23

HOW DEALERS
SELL BONDS—PART 1

As we saw, Hudson & West maintained several trading desks in New York to handle the various specialized municipal bond categories. Now let's see how they fared with customer Whitmore's bonds. A trader, Philip we called him, was at his desk at 8:00 o'clock on Tuesday morning, looking over the list of bonds he was responsible for—smaller size general market items. He noted one or two errors, made the corrections, and settled down to his routine. At 10:30 Arnie picked up a bunch of slips from the branch system, among them three from Springfield and brought one of these to Philip—a 'buy', that is, a purchase order, for the Decatur bonds.

A GENERAL MARKET TRADE

The New Offering

Philip looked at the Decatur slip, where he had bid 94 the day before, and saw that the customer had decided to sell them at that price. Hudson & West's rules were that all small lot bids were good through the day, so Whitmore could have sold them the bonds without question up to 5:00 Monday. But this was another day, and it was up to the trader to renew the bid or not. Back in the prior

217

sections we saw that the buying and selling prices of U.I.T.s and open end funds are set by evaluation. As we are seeing, unbundled bonds such as Whitmore's Decaturs are priced judgmentally, by traders who negotiate, strictly over-the-counter.

The Release Price

Before Philip acted on bids made to customers the day before he wanted to rethink his trading stance. Although the major quotes showed governments and municipals somewhat weaker that morning, he thought that the market was in good overall shape. He saw that his bonds were selling briskly and noted that the retail inventory position totalled only $5 million bonds. Their limit was $15 million, so he had plenty of room. His feelings on the market were constructive—it didn't seem too high and it was fairly active. What do these factors add up to? A relatively stable and brighter than average trading background. Other kinds of markets had to be handled differently. When prices are falling rapidly, retail traders try to keep their risk positions low and to sell as quickly as possible. In strong and rising markets, the challenge is to buy enough bonds to keep up with sales. Philip's conclusion about the Decaturs? To buy them at 94 and release them at the same price, 95 1/2. If the market had shifted sharply, or if his inventory position had grown too large, then he might have made an adjustment. However, things were pretty much unchanged, and on the Decaturs it was still 94 - 95 1/2, bid and offered. As you see, there's a time lag in the small lot municipal bond secondary market, but the potential profits are large enough to compensate for it. It's different with larger lots of bonds, where bids and offerings can change at the drop of a hat.

The Sales Commission

So Philip took the Decaturs from Whitmore at 94, or $18,800. Since Hudson & West pays salespeople to buy bonds, he jotted down on the buy slip a $5 per bond gross buy commission for Frances, $100, and about $35 net for her. Philip put the buy ticket in the out box where Arnie picked it up shortly. He then took the pink copy of the same slip and marked it with the re-offering price for the Hudson & West system, 95 1/2, a yield of 6.80%, which left a gross profit of 1 1/2 points, or $15 per bond, $300 total. Philip's assistant typed up a position card for the Decaturs, all details entered, and it into Philip's inventory book. Then she entered this item on Hudson & West's release sheet—their internal list of bonds available for sale to customers, with descriptions, ratings, prices, and commissions included. Salespeople could offer the Decaturs to customers at the released price. The firm's control section, their operations department, salesperson Fran, and customer Whitmore would all soon get copies.

Figure 23.1 shows what part of the release sheet looked like, with the Decatur bonds sitting there waiting for a new home. Several dozen of their salesmen would look at the new items during the day, thinking about where they could sell them. The salesperson selling them would earn a commission of 1 1/2 points, or $300. H & W would pay out about a third of this, or $100 net. Could a salesman just sell them without checking with New York? No. All transactions have to be cleared with the trading desk, making sure the item had not already sold, or changed in price. Three such sales per day would bring a salesman an annual income of $75,000, not bad these somewhat trying Wall Street days.

A Dealer Sale

During Tuesday about 25 items sold from Philip's retail general market position, and he bought 15 new blocks, bringing his inventory down to $4.5 million. He had a few 'nibbles' on the Decatur bonds, meaning that some Hudson & West salespeople had shown interest in them, but they remained unsold. So, late that afternoon, he instructed an assistant to advertise them on Wednesday's edition of both the *Munifax* and *The Blue List* nationwide wire systems, showing the offering to hundreds of municipal bond dealers. Other firms do it differently, but Hudson & West lets their branches get first crack at most new purchases. However, items which they don't sell internally the first day most often are released "to the Street". Philip set the wholesale price on his 20 bonds—a yield of 6.80%, less a 1/4 *concession* (dealer discount). This figures to 95 1/2, and less the 1/4, makes it 95 1/4. See Figure 23.2 for the yields and dollar prices.

At 8:30 on Wednesday morning, though it was only 7:30 A.M. in the Midwest, a Chicago dealer telephoned Hudson & West's general market desk, inquiring about the Decatur bonds. Philip got out the card, making sure the bonds were still available, and made the dealer an offering at the level advertised on the dealer wire—a price to yield 6.80%, less 1/4. The Illinois dealer said that he would buy them at Philip's listed 6.80 basis, but at a bigger concession, less one point ($10 per bond). Traders would say, "He was bidding a six-eighty less one." This was 3/4 under Philip's price, or 94 1/2.

A dual trading track now appeared in Philip's mind. On one track was Hudson & West's sales system, which had had its chance to sell these bonds for a day. If the system sold the bonds at 95 1/2, his desk would show a gross profit of $450, but a net profit of only about one third of that for his desk, $150, because the sales department would take a big two-thirds cut.

Figure 23.1
FROM HUDSON & WEST'S MORNING SALES INVENTORY

Settlement date: 1/2/92

Rating	(M)	Bond Description	Coupon	Maturity	Yield	Price	Sales Commission
/AAA	20	Decatur, Ill. Parking Revenue Refunded 100% U.S. Govt. Original Maturity 5/1/05 Dated 11/1/66 CUSIP—243181BAl	5.75%	2/15/97	6.80%	95.5	$12
A/A	530	New Jersey Turnpike Authority Dated 11/21/85 Callable CUSIP—646139FW0	7.20%	1/1/18	7.29%	99	17
/CCC	25	Wayne County I.D.R., Mich. Eastern Airlines Inc. Dated 1/1/68 CUSIP—233541F2O	5.00%	9/1/99	8.00%	83	25
A/	120	Marshall, Mich. Electric Rev. Dated 10/1/76 Callable CUSIP—572444CA	6.25%	9/1/99	7.40%	90.2	12
A1/A+	75	Michigan Housing Authority Rev. Dated 11/1/71 CUSIP—594649ES0	6.00%	7/1/10	7.50%	85.12	15
/BBB	255	Greater Detroit Resource Rev. Dated 12/13/84 CUSIP—391689AA4	9.25%	12/13/08 CA95 @103	8.50%	103.87	20

Philip's other train of thought concerned this potential wholesale trade. If they sold at his listed price of 6.80-1/4, his gross profit would be $250, and his net profit the same $250, because there would be no sales department cut, a better result for him than if they had been sold through the sales system. But if he sold them at the Chicago firm's bid price, (94 1/2), Philip would realize a profit of 1/2 point, only $5 a bond, $100 total. He made up his mind—to negotiate with the Chicago dealer, but to refuse to sell them cheaper than 94 3/4, showing his desk about the same profit that a retail sale would.

He guessed that the other dealer had an order from an account, possibly a bank trust department, probably at a 6.80 yield (95 1/2), so that the Chicago firm's profit would be the one point concession he was bidding. Philip thought a 6.80 yield was reasonable enough, and the market was quite firm, so he told the other trader that he would sell them to him a little bit cheaper, at a 6.80 less 1/2 point, at 94. Traders would say that Philip was "*countering* a six-eighty less one bid with an offering of less a half". The Chicago trader waited a second, then agreed to buy them, and Philip confirmed him the bonds at a six-eighty yield less a half. Bought at 94, sold at 95, a gross profit of $200. As you see, had the Chicago trader been better at horse trading Philip would have sold them at 94 3/4, so the other dealer left some money on the table.

As always, in confirming the trade, Philip went over the whole transaction, amount, description, including the C.U.S.I.P. number, the coupon, maturity and the agreed price. What price the Chicago dealer sold them was his private business, but if indeed he did have an order at a 6.80, then his firm would make the 1/2 point concession, a total of $100. The other dealer also might have sold them at higher, or lower prices, or bought them for his firm's inventory account to be sold later.

Philip was satisfied with the transaction, knowing that the better he handled the position, the better his future. Such a trader makes about $50,000 a year these days and perhaps a three, or even six, months bonus if all goes well during the year. Eventually, H & W would deliver the bonds to the Chicago dealer, be paid, and their accounts will be straight. One of Whitmore's three lots down, two to go.

Philip marked the trade on his trading card and handed it to his assistant who wrote up a sell ticket, time stamped it and put it in the processing box. Later, along with all the other sale tickets it would be taken to the back office. There the trade's exact dollar figure, including accrued interest, would be calculated and entered into the firm's processing system, from which a confirmation would be generated and electronically exchanged with the other dealer, making sure both parties agreed. There are about twenty separate steps in the operations cycle, some performed by hand, and others by computer, adding up to substantial expenses.

Figure 23.2
A WHOLESALE TRADE
(DEALER-TO-DEALER)

/AAA   20M   Decatur, Ill. Parking Revenue   5.75%   2/15/97
                Refunded 100% U.S. Govt. Original Maturity 2/15/05
                Dated 11/1/66   CUSIP 243181BAI

Transaction	Yield and concession	Dollar Price	Extension	(Potential) Profit
Tentative purchase from Whitmore	6.90 less 1 1/2 points	93 1/2	$18,700	$(350)
Purchase from Whitmore	6.80 less 1 1/2 points	94	18,800	(250)
Chicago dealer's bid	6.80 less 1 point	94 1/2	18,900	(100)
Sale to Chicago dealer	6.80 less 1/2 point	95	19,000	200
List price to dealers	6.80 less 1/4 point	95 1/4	19,050	(250)

How did Hudson & West do on this trade? The Decaturs were bought at 94, sold at 95, leaving $200 gross profit. Rep McComber was paid $30, leaving $170. If you figure $50 in direct expense per trade and another $50 in indirect expense including payments to the trading department, that leaves around $70 before tax for Hudson & West and its shareholders. Certainly not a way to get rich quick.

A LOCAL BOND TRADE

A Brokered Sale

Philip had put the Andovers on the broker J.J.Kenny's wire system the day before, and as we saw, got a bid of 106 1/2. Normally, for small lots such as these, bids are 'good' (will remain unchanged) only through the close of business on the day they are made. On the same Tuesday Arnie took the buy order on the Andovers to the broker desk to sell at 106 1/2, if possible. An assistant there called her counterpart with this proposition and the broker soon called her back saying that she could pay the same price and confirmed the trade in every detail.

The assistant then wrote up two tickets—one buying them at 105 1/2 and the other selling them at 106 1/2. In and out, one point, for a $250 profit. She wrote in Frances' commission for buying the bonds and entered everything into the firm's control and accounting systems. That day a confirmation would be mailed out to Whitmore showing that he had sold them to Hudson & West at 105 1/2. Another confirmation would go to the broker, electronically, detailing the sale in every respect. Two down, one to go.

A JUNK BOND TRADE

A Special Situation

Arnie's last stop was at the junk desk where he dropped off the slip from Springfield on the Wayne Countys. The seasoned head trader was out that day, his custom on Fridays, but the young second-in-command moved right in. She handled the department's Michigan research and knew Wayne County airports well. She decided to honor the bid from the day before, buying the bonds at 78 1/2. She wrote up a ticket and dropped it in the out box. Then she thought about a possible release price, much as Philip had on the Decaturs.

As mentioned before, the source of payments for these bonds, Eastern Airlines, was at that time operating, but in Chapter 11, voluntary bankruptcy. However, this issue was over twenty years old and Hudson & West's junk people knew that the gates and other facilities at Detroit International built with this issue were much desired by other carriers. They still were contributing net income to Eastern who had continued to make the modest payments necessary to pay off these bonds. In addition, about 10% of this issue were scheduled for early retirement, at 100, every year, through the action of a sinking fund. So, although the bonds were rated CCC (Speculative) by the services because of their Eastern name they were in fact well secured. The trader calculated that at a price of 83 they would yield 8.00% to maturity. This did indeed represent good value, and she entered them on the day's list for the sales force to offer at that price. She put down 2 1/2 points as a sales credit, fatter than on most other offerings, thus also making them particularly attractive to the sales force to sell. $25 on 25 bonds would be $625 gross for a salesperson, quite a good commission on such an appealing bond. We will see what happened to them in the next chapter.

SUMMARY ** CHAPTER 23 ** SUMMARY

How Dealers Sell Bonds—Part 1

- Several hundred municipal bond dealers buy bonds in the secondary market and sell them to customers and to other dealers.

- Most of them maintain long positions, taking risks in order to provide their sales forces with commissions, their customers with bonds, and themselves with profits.

- Gross profit margins in the trading market are determined by the level of the competition. It is usually fierce.

- Net profits come after overhead, commissions, and market losses.

CHAPTER 24

HOW DEALERS SELL BONDS—PART 2

A New Customer

Now meet A.B. Higgins, practically the last character in this book. Higgins, an executive V.P. with a device engineering company in Michigan, was facing an important investment decision. He had a substantial net worth, well over $1 million, including some options on shares of the company's stock earned as an employee over many years. However, Higgins had grown nervous about the stock, having seen its value rise, fall sharply, then rise again within five years. He had recently answered an ad in the local paper by a registered investment advisor offering a free consultation to investors with portfolios of over half a million dollars. The consulting session went reasonably well, though he didn't like telling a stranger so much about his affairs.

After a week he was sent a computer-arranged list of his assets and liabilities, including his stock options and other investments, along with their current market value and yearly income. It was obvious that he had too high a proportion of his assets in one company and the investment outfit recommended more diversification. They suggested that he sell all his stock and put the proceeds into two of their municipal bond funds, one intermediate, and one long, both tax-exempt in Michigan. Higgins didn't really like this approach, it seemed that it was just another pushy way to sell him their own product. He wanted real advice, not a fancified sales gimmick, though the 7.50% tax-free did look interesting. He noted that in his tax bracket he would have to earn almost 11% on something else to equal 7.50% tax-free.

Higgins didn't consider himself all that hard to please, but somehow he never got along very well with the securities people he had dealt with. He did have an account at a regional firm, but they kept assigning him inexperienced and over-eager people who never seemed to understand what he wanted. When the company stock was zooming upward they wanted him to sell it, and the last call he got was from still another person trying to push growth stocks, at a time when he definitely wanted to lock in some high income for his retirement days.

A Bad Experience

Higgins got to talking about investments with his daughter and the conversation turned to tax-exempts. He then told her about his one and only municipal bond purchase. Several years before, a salesman from Tennessee had called him at home one night, all friendly and earnest, with a great 13% health services bond in Florida, some county or other, tax-free. He had over $25,000 in his interest-bearing checking account, more than he really wanted there, since he knew he could earn higher interest elsewhere, but hadn't gotten around to moving it. Higgins liked the tax-free aspect and the 13% sounded great, so he asked if he could buy just $10,000 worth. The salesman said that he usually sold larger amounts, but he'd ask his sales manager to make an exception. Higgins was happy when the salesman said that $10,000 would be fine. He was a bit worried about sending his money to an absolute stranger, but since he was told that the account was insured, he sent it in and received the bonds by mail within two weeks. He enjoyed cutting the $650 coupons off twice a year and depositing them, just like a check.

Then one day the bank mailed him a debit notice cancelling out his latest coupon deposit with the notation, 'No Funds Available for Payment'. He called the dealer, but was told that that salesman no longer worked there. They were very sorry, but there was nothing they could do, the issue had gone into default. Possibly the bonds, secured by the income from a nursing home, would recover some day, but in the meantime all they were worth was 20 cents of the dollar, or $2,000, an 80% loss in only two years. Very sorry.

The daughter was glad it was only a $10,000 investment, and that maybe he should sell them, take the loss and use it against his tax bill next year. She mentioned that good municipal bonds could be bought at around 7 1/2%. She also pointed out that inflation was presently steady at 4% and that relatively high interest rates were helping to hold it down. That was enough to start Higgins doing some serious thinking. After he saw his company's stock fall five points and then recover he decided to exercise half of his options right then. After all, that was part of his retirement money. In the meanwhile, he heard about a salesman who was something of a bond specialist in Hudson & West's Birmingham, Michigan branch. He gave the man a ring and received a businesslike welcome. The salesman had some sensible ideas about estate planning and Higgins felt he was talking to someone who understood his situation. Perhaps more importantly, the two men were getting along personally. Higgins told him about the asset information that the other firm had prepared and the salesman told Higgins he'd like to see it for the record, but he'd have to be in charge of his own assets. He was just a salesman, he said, and he'd recommend the best he could, but forget that financial planning hooey, an approach which Higgins and his daughter both liked.

She showed him an advertisement in that morning's paper for an A-rated school bond issue in Michigan and they looked at its scale of maturities and yields. Higgins didn't like that particular city, knowing its past ups and downs all too well, but the scale provided him with a basis for comparing any bonds the salesman might show him. So far, Higgins was doing fine. He had located a reputable dealer, considered his tax bracket and the current inflation rate, and seen that he could buy good bonds at 7.50%. The investing highway was pretty clear. However, much depends on his next step, choosing the right bonds.

A few days later the salesman faxed part of Hudson & West's morning offering list to Higgin's office. The salesman was zeroing in on his new potential customer. The theater of operations? The secondary market for municipal bonds. Specifically (though unknown to the salesman or to Higgins), finding a new home for Whitmore's old bonds.

Going back to Figure 23.1 you can see four different offerings of Michigan bonds, including Whitmore's Wayne Countys. The salesman had spotted these earlier and thought them a particularly good offering. He knew the airport, and the bonds, saying that they were totally tax-free in Michigan, a fine businessman's risk, and a good bargain. Higgins would be in the 5% state tax bracket, so multiplying that by five (See Figure 11.2) gave him a tax advantage of 25 basis points. An out-of-state bond would have to yield 8.25% to equal the Michigan-exempt 8.00%, quite a handicap. The salesman mentioned that there would be capital gains taxes on the bonds when they were sold, reducing the yield, but that would be more than compensated for by the sinking fund provision. These two divergent facts went over Higgin's head, but he believed he'd get an 8.00% return, which would probably be the case.

Higgins wanted to compare the offering yield to an objective information source, natural for many people in his position. He remembered the school bond scale his daughter had shown him earlier, pulled it out and ran his finger to the

1999 maturity. It read 7.00% there, versus the Wayne's 8.00%. Not bad at all. Higgins liked the airport bonds—he had flown from there himself many times— and after mentally checking his daughter's cautions once more, asked the salesman if he could take $20,000 of the Waynes. The salesman recommended the whole twenty-five, saying this was a round lot. Since he hadn't pushed him too hard on the amount, and the argument sounded reasonable to Higgins, he said he'd take the $25,000. While an assistant called New York making sure the bonds were still available, the salesman spelled out the exact details of the transaction, confirmed the sale, and thanked his new customer. Higgins felt right about his purchase, told the salesman he'd think about the other bonds and rang off, glad of his accomplishment.

He had every right to be glad. He had made contact with a good company, checked out the timing factors, made a valid price comparison with a new issue scale, and perhaps best of all, started a relationship with a superior salesman. Do you see something lacking? I don't. It would be hard to invest in municipal bonds more alertly. Three stars for A.B. Higgins and daughter.

The Inner Workings

What had happened behind the scenes? The assistant in Birmingham had called Hudson & West's liaison desk in New York with the order for the 25 Wayne Countys, and the sale was approved in time to confirm it on the wire. What if the bonds had already sold somewhere else? Too bad for both the salesman and

---

Figure 24.1
A RETAIL TRADE
(CUSTOMER-TO-DEALER-TO-CUSTOMER)

/CCC   25M   Wayne County I.D.R., Mich.   5.00%   9/1/99ca
               Eastern Airlines Inc. Callable
               Dated 1/1/68   CUSIP 233541FZ0

Transaction	Yield and concession	Dollar Price	Extension	(Potential) Profit
Purchase from Whitmore	8.00 less 4 1/2 points	78 1/2	$19,625	$
Price to Sales Department	8.00 less 2 1/2 points	80 1/2	20,125	500
Price to Salesman	8.00 less 1 point	82	20,500	375
Sale to Higgins	8.00 Net	83	20,750	250
				1,125

---

that customer. However, the bonds were still available and the trade was done, bringing the salesman about $200 for his effort. And more to come from Higgins, he hoped. Two such sales a day would bring him in $100,000 a year, something like the minimum a good salesperson should be making. However, it isn't an easy life.

Two sets of tickets were written up—one in Birmingham and one in New York, where it was dropped at the junk desk for the specialty trader to check it over, seeing that all was well. Whitmore sold them to Hudson & West at 78 1/2, and Higgins bought them at 83. This was $1,125 in gross profit, of which $625 went to the sales department ($200 to the salesman) and $500 credited to the junk desk. She closed out that Wayne County Airport card, at the bottom writing $500. This profit brought the junk department's day total to $6,000 and the month to $90,000. A good start to the new year and another nice bonus. An experienced and effective head trader in such a position may earn a salary of $100,000, and, in a good year, as large, or a larger, bonus. Number two might make over half that much, on her way up.

Soon one of Hudson & West's systems would generate a written confirmation and send it out to Higgins. After five business days he would be debited $20,750, plus accrued interest, and the Wayne Countys would be held in his account. Customer Higgins might own them for five years, receiving 5%, or $1,250 a year, $625 every coupon date. Then, on the salesman's advice he might sell them back to Hudson & West. If, for example, they were sold at 95, then the actual yield might amount to about 8.50%. After paying capital gains the total return would be 8%, a fine return in most markets. Then, the salesman might persuade Higgins to use the proceeds to buy more bonds, again generating profits and commissions. What would Hudson & West do after they bought the bonds back from Higgins? Essentially the same thing as before, try to find still another customer willing to buy them at a higher price.

How did Hudson & West make out on Whitmore's three lots of bonds? The retail general market desk took a risk by going long the 20 Decaturs, and sold them to another dealer, making a profit of $200. The same desk also sold the 25 Andovers into the professional market, taking a non-risk $250. The junk desk grossed $1,125. So Hudson & West took in a total of $1,575. Frances and the Birmingham salesman were paid a total of $235, and this plus other expenses of $400 or so left about a pre-tax gross of about $500 for Hudson & West's shareholders.

Of the $15 million bonds that we saw Hudson & West going long on Monday, about one quarter were sold during Tuesday—$3 million worth through their branch system and another $1 million to other dealers. On these the firm made a gross profit of about $40,000, of which about $10,000 went to the sales force. In addition, they also sold $2 million bonds they had bought previously, making $20,000 there. They had started Tuesday with a total position of $30 million, sold $5 million and added another $7 million, thus ending the day at $32 million and were off to a reasonably good month.

SUMMARY ** CHAPTER 24 ** SUMMARY

How Dealers Sell Bonds—Part 2

- There are five parties involved in most trade cycles in the municipal bond secondary market.

- An individual owner sells them through a salesperson on orders from a trader. Then another salesperson sells them to a new investor. Customer, salesman, trader, salesman, customer.

- The customer gives old bonds and is paid cash.

- The first salesman gets a buy commission.

- The trader tries to make a profit by selling the bonds at a higher price.

- The second salesman gets a sales commission.

- The new customer pays cash for new bonds.

CHAPTER 25

HOW TO CHOOSE A BOND

The Point of Decision

We've spent a lot of time thinking and talking about unbundled municipals and seen example people buying. Now let's see if we can get you some results. You have a brokerage account all set up, and the bond market signals are right. You've investigated U.I.T.s and managed funds but have decided that plain, unbundled bonds are for you. How are you to choose among the 40 years of maturities, hundreds of coupons, and thousands of different credits? I hope you won't settle for what happens to strike your fancy some day or what some salesman is pushing, but firm up your own requirements and then find the bonds that best match them.

Since you have come this far in the book perhaps you have gained some measure of trust in my approach to bonds. So let's face something together right here. *There is something seriously wrong with the way most people buy municipal bonds.* Ask almost anybody who has bought them and you'll see what I mean. Far too few people are truly happy with their tax-exempt purchases. The reason is a little difficult to swallow, and I guarantee that most financial people will disagree with me. But the measure of theory is practice, isn't it? Why are the great majority of individual investors so displeased with their bonds? If the prevailing approach is correct most bond holders should be happy, but they aren't. And it's not their fault—being too fussy, unrealistic, and so on. It's Wall Street's fault. Conversely, why are people who have followed the theory presented in this book and this chapter glad they bought their bonds? Because the theories work. Why do most Wall Streeters and most money managers along with them continue to sell bonds that make people unhappy? It's easier, faster, more instantly profitable. Today, this month, maybe even this year they make more. But bonds are meant to be held for a long time and most sellers of municipal bonds don't have the patience. With the usual claptrap selling techniques, some programs turn out fairly well, some poorly. But that's not good enough for me. If you follow the thinking of this book, you should get superior results.

Presuming that the timing is right, what is the biggest mistake municipal bond *buyers* make? Overemphasizing credit quality. What is the biggest mistake municipal bond *sellers* make? Overemphasizing credit quality. Triple A, insured, whatnot. It's easy, plays on peoples' fears, and promises what it can't deliver. Selling high quality bonds protects reputable but uninformed bond sellers from a lot of liability. They can just say that the market went the wrong way, it wasn't their fault, and they feel protected by this position.

It must drive General Motors engineers wild to work for years developing a better fuel burning system or more reliable batteries, or whatever, only to see Ford's styling boys win the sales sweepstakes. Similarly, high gloss, high rated, or fancy sounding names on a bond are ornamental and perhaps aesthetically pleasing. But a bond provides just principal and interest, that's all. How much it pays, and how much it's worth. All else is decoration. You will get bigger coupons, longer bond lives, and higher principal value if you put bond selection values in their right order. In order of their proven contributions to higher returns and higher worth. Once you've decided to buy, it's number one, maturity. Number two, call feature. Number three, credit quality. Maturity counts for six units. Call feature for three. Credit quality for one. That's their relative importance. See Figure 25.1. Put them in their proper position and you will have an excellent chance to be happy with your bonds. Wouldn't that be the best proof?

THE THREE MAIN FACTORS

1- The Maturity Factor

How long a bond should you buy? Sometimes considerations militate powerfully for investing in *shorter maturity bonds,* for instance when you have substantial liabilities which will need financing at a certain time. Back in 1977, if you wanted to finance a college education beginning in five years and had bought

$50,000 worth of nice-looking long term A-rated California Water 5.20% bonds, by 1982 their value, after inflation, would have fallen to under $14,000, just enough for freshman year. So if you are putting away savings for a definite purpose, you should match your bonds to this need. There are other ways to achieve high liquidity, under expert care, but by far the simplest is to buy bonds due at or near the time you'll need the cash. If you are free of such constraints, then buy as long a maturity as you dare. We presented the risks and the rewards of buying fund maturities in Chapter 17, a similar task.

Short bonds are predictable, and you can be almost certain to receive their good after-tax yields. So why buy longer, riskier bonds at all?

A.) Their attractive price tags. As we have discussed, when a five year bond yields 6.00%, you can typically buy ten year maturities of the identical bond at 7.00% and longer bonds at 8.00%.

B.) The possibility that interest rates will fall. Buying short bonds solves the problem of ensuring a minimum, if lower, real return; it does not address the question of future interest rate levels making necessary at maturity time a new round of decisions. By taking a stand on the question of future interest rate levels buying long bonds ensures a higher return, but risks loss of principal value to do so. In practice, most individual investors opt for the longer bonds and higher yields. I usually recommend this approach. If you are genuinely uncertain, I would suggest buying some short, some long. Don't try to compromise with an intermediate, fifteen year maturity. They often go down when long bonds fall and sit still when they go up.

☞ WILSON SAYS

The most important factor in buying an unpackaged bond is *maturity*.
Buy as long a bond as you can live with comfortably.
If in doubt, buy some with long maturities and some with short.

---

2 - The Call Factor

The final payoff date of most municipals is fixed at a certain maturity. However, most issuers also reserve the right to retire the bonds earlier through the action of a *call feature*. Ten years from issue date at 103 is the most common deal. The second most potent factor affecting individually wrapped bonds is this call deal. This is no small proviso—it enables someone else to switch the most important factor in selecting a bond, its time schedule. Imagine if your nice low rate 30 year mortgage could be foreclosed by your lender if interest rates rose sharply. Getting your bonds called because interest rates have fallen is the same thing, in reverse. When you hold an issue with a call feature you relinquish control over maturity. Rarely are bonds called when it's favorable for the investor—calls are designed to benefit the issuer. Beware of callable bonds.

Most callable new issues are priced near 100. These are particularly bad bargains. If the market goes up, you will almost certainly lose your bonds in ten years. Even before then the price of your bonds will be held down by the potential call. Buying a long callable bond selling at 80, or 85, or even 90, makes more sense. Then, if the issuer calls them in at 103, you have made something worthwhile. This means sacrificing some current yield, a small price to pay for protecting long bonds. Where can you get long term discount bonds? Mainly in the secondary market.

You don't have much control of calls when buying a U.I.T. or a managed fund. However, with regular bonds there are many from which to pick. This is one main reason I favor unpackaged bonds. One way to win this game is to buy noncallables. Then, no matter how low interest rates go, your bonds will stay with you. In early 1986 I bought some non-callable Saco, Maine 14 3/4% bonds due out in next century for my own account, paying a premium price of 127. Interest rates fell a long way and even if they fall further the issuer cannot call them in, and so my ex-wife can enjoy their income for a long time. Unfortunately, non-callable bonds are rather scarce and usually carry lower yields. You and I aren't the only people thinking like this.

With non-callables scarce and callables near 100 undesirable, another way to win this part of the tax-exempt game is to buy callable *premium, selling over 100,* bonds, especially when they reach a price of 110 or even higher. Buy them at 119 and see them called in at 103? That's a winner? Yes, because so few investors understand the process their yields, figured to that call date and price can be quite attractive. Consult a trusted expert. Everything said about call features goes double for *housing revenue bonds,* either single- or multi-family. They can be terrible, or wonderful, depending on factors too numerous and complex to go into here. Consult a professional who knows what she is doing.

☞ *WILSON SAYS*

The second most important factor in buying an unpackaged bond is its call feature.

> Avoid buying long term callable bonds selling near 100.
> Consider buying big premium callable bonds well above 100.
> Make sure you know *all* call features before you buy.
> Especially watch call features on housing revenue bonds.

3 - The Credit Factor

Something like 3% of all municipal bonds are odd ball, junky, or actually in default. Another 2% or so are obscure, questionable or marginal. But well over 90% of all tax-exempts are sound, investment grade securities. When we say that credit quality is only the third most important factor in selecting a bond there is one governing caveat: that you *buy investment grade bonds* only. Among

Figure 25.1
AVERAGES OF LOSSES DUE TO INFLATION, INTEREST RATES AND CREDIT TROUBLES.

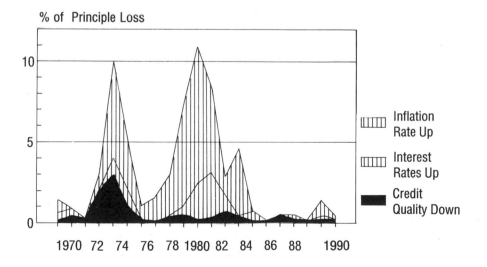

investment grade bonds there is little difference in probability of repayment. I remember one novelist, perhaps John O'Hara, writing something like, "He spent his daylight hours selling municipal bonds, exploring their finely graduated degrees of absolute certainty." I'd agree, as long as you stay within the top 95%, the regular investment grades.

Credit Analysis

At this point the reader might be expecting me to describe all the tax-free goods thoroughly, the ratios of debt to assessed valuation, the problems with hospital bonds, the credit pitfalls of housings, etc., but I don't intend to. The sources mentioned later in the chapter have already done this exhaustively and there's no point in my adding to the overemphasizing of credit. In reality, most people look at the ratings and stop there, some want to see what's been written about their bonds, and only a few want to dig any deeper. So here's a three level credit analysis approach from which to select.

Credit Research - 1

Level One, rely on the rating services. The great majority of all municipal bond buyers are justifiably satisfied by knowing the published rating. Moody's Investor Services (now a part of Dun and Bradstreet) started the rating idea back in 1909 and long dominated the field, with their particularly valuable, annually revised *Municipal and Government Manual,* huge blue books containing marvelously accurate information on thousands of individual bonds. They also publish a condensed version every few weeks, a red book, *Moody's Bond Record.* Standard & Poor's (a division of McGraw Hill) has been in the field for forty years and now challenges Moody's for the lead. S & P publishes both a handy rating and statistic book, their bimonthly *Municipal Bond Book,* which includes cogent municipal bond commentaries. Figure 25.2 shows what the grading systems mean to me.

The two rating systems are as alike as their letters; 90% of the time they arrive at similar opinions. For example, when in April, 1991, the Colorado Springs Utility system was negotiating a $340 million new issue, after weeks of intensive credit research, Moody's called it Aa, while S & P had it AA, or as we say it, double/double A, or write it, Aa/AA. If there is a difference between the two Moody's tends to weigh community debt versus liabilities, whereas Standard looks more closely at the economic backgrounds. Aa/AA is this man's opinion of the quality level of the two rater's ratings.

If you suspect that quality and rating is different you are right. In the first place, the raters are human and they do make some outright mistakes. Evergreen

Figure 25.2
THE MUNICIPAL BOND SERVICE RATINGS

Moody's	S & P	Equivalent School Mark	Explanation	Default Probability
		Investment Quality		
Aaa	AAA	A+	Highest. Gold medal. First class.	0%
Aa	AA	A	High. Silver medal.	0%
Al	A+	A-	Upper medium. Business class.	1%
A	A	B+	Medium. Bronze medal.	2%
Baal	BBB+	B	Lower investment grade. Coach.	3%
Baa	BBB	B-	Lowest investment grade.	4%
		Not Investment Quality		
Ba	BB	C	Somewhat speculative. Standby.	10%
B	B	D	Speculative, but still paying.	20%?
Caa	CCC	E	Highly speculative or in default	?%

Valley Development Corp., Maine, Series B revenue bonds were at one point erroneously analyzed as state guaranteed and rated AAA. When the lines at the ski tows the issue financed didn't fill up the bonds sold as low as 2 cents on the dollar, and flat as a hat.

At other times the raters ignore real world numbers and events in favor of abstract analytical theories. The not exactly imaginary Wayne Countys as discussed in Chapter 22 may serve as one example. And I recently saw one rater give prior lien Venice, Illinois Bridge bonds a 'Ba', upper junk rating, while I know that that little city has over 90% of the money for the whole issue in the bank and that by the time this is published all of these bonds will have been called at 100. Admittedly the past earnings of the bridge haven't been great, but how safe can you get? Let's charitably assume the service hadn't looked at this rating recently.

☞ WILSON SAYS

The third most important factor in buying an unpackaged bond is *credit quality*.

Buy investment grade bonds only.
Buy as low a quality investment grade bond as you can stomach.
If in doubt, buy medium quality.

These extremes of over- and under-rating occur only rarely, but in addition the services omit many smaller issuers. Niagara County, New York has an issue of industrial revenue bonds originally secured by payments from lower grade FMC Corp. but later escrowed in U.S. Government bonds. The ratings? Ba2/NR, junk and non-rated, because one service didn't recognize this escrow and it's too small for the other to bother with. So don't necessarily equate non-rated with low grade. Ratings are thermometers—not the weather. They indicate temperature but there is certainly a lot more to a fine fall day than the Fahrenheit. And sometimes, as when the sun hits them, their readings are cockeyed. However, ratings are excellent starting places for any level of credit study.

Credit Research - 2

Level Two, delve into the *available research.* Wall Street now employs something like 500 people with advanced degrees to dig through mountains of facts about our thousands of different bonds, write up hundreds of bond opinions, and fill file after file with collections of municipal bond data of all sorts. Dealers have access to these research reports on both general topics, such as overviews of public power systems as a whole, or on reports on separate projects, such as the Georgia Municipal Electric System. Just ask your representative for one of them.

S & P, in their *Credit Week,* publishes rationales of their ratings, available in many public and business libraries or from your dealer. If you can't get enough information from the published periodicals you can actually call Moody's or Standard yourself. I do it all the time in pursuit of information for trading purposes, and find them exceptionally helpful. Just call them and ask for the analyst for the bond in question. See Figure 25.3 for some other leads.

Credit Research - 3

Level Three is for those not satisfied with other people's ratings and reports. You can do your own *original research,* the whole thing yourself, approaching professional standards. First, study the issuers, new issue prospectuses and annual reports. Then talk to the analysts and make comparisons with other bonds. If you have a particularly serious problem, telephone the issuer's financial officer—it's surprising how readily the treasurers of even substantial municipalities make themselves available. Finally, the trustee or bond counsel may supply some of the more arcane details concerning the status of bond reserve accounts, or the community's authority to make special bond calls, etc. I don't suggest that many

Figure 25.3
MUNICIPAL BOND RESEARCH SOURCES

*The primary tax-exempt research sources are the periodicals mentioned in the text. These are available at many libraries and almost all securities firms' offices.
Most questions can be answered by first referring to these.

Source	Information Available	Telephone	Contact
Moody's	Current bond ratings	212-553-0315	Municipal Ratings Desk
Moody's	Bond data and ratings rationale	212-553-0300	Specific Bond Type Analyst (Health care, State, etc.)
Municipal Securities Rulemaking Board	New issue prospectuses (Dated since Jan.1990 only)	202-223-9347	MISL Library, in person
Public Securities Assn.	General municipal bond information, brochures	212-809-7000	Publications
Public Securities Assn.	Trends and averages	212-809-7000	Andy Nybo, or research analyst
Securities Data (Bond Buyer)	Averages and trends of past bond sales	201-622-3100	Sandy Foight, or research analyst
Standard & Poor's	Current bond ratings	212-208-1527	Municipal Ratings Desk
Standard & Poor's	Bond data and ratings rationale	212-208-8000	Specific Bond Type Analyst (Health care, State, etc.)

investors try level three, but if you have the taste for it you can turn up some worthwhile information.

Now let's get on with picking a credit type. Naturally that is strictly an individual decision, but here are few thoughts. Consider *medium grade bonds*. Some kinds of investors, such as insurance companies and banks, need the superior marketability of highgrade bonds, while others, notably bank trust departments, tend to protect themselves immoderately. Both sorts drive the price of high grade bonds up and their yields down. If you agree with my assessments of default probabilities, Figure 25.2, use them to do your own calculations. Here's one way to do it.

Suppose a few years ago you could buy either of two bonds: upper medium grade, 30 year maturity A-1/A+ rated Intermountain Power Agency of Utah 8% bonds, selling at 100; or naturally gilt edge Aaa/AAA State of New Jersey 7's also at 100. You could collect one point more interest on the I.P.A.s every year for thirty years, and come out thirty points ahead, or $30,000 on every $100,000 invested.

However, you have to deduct the 2% chance of a default, during which their holders might well suffer a loss of 50 points in principal and interest. 2% of 50 is one percent, the averaged loss probability on these bonds due to credit failure. Take the one point loss away from the thirty point gain and you're 29 points ahead. You can do all sorts of fancy tricks with these numbers, such as discounting the future value at today's interest rates, but in plain language, if you believe with me that what amounts to all of Southern California will stay solvent for the next 30 years, that medium grade IPA investment was a real bargain. For one you could get thirty. Work the numbers your way to see what you are paying for your quality preferences. But if I were you, I'd take 29 and smile.

The same reasoning applies if the spread is lower than 1%, but to a lesser degree. Sometimes both medium grade and artificially blue chip insured bonds of the same issuer are available at the same time. If you could buy either uninsured and insured Nebraska Public Power District bonds, one to yield 8 1/2% and the other 8%, we would say there's a 50 basis point spread. The difference of 1/2% a year, $5 per bond, adds up—it's 15 points in thirty years. I'd consider paying 1/4% for insurance on sound, investment grade bonds, but no more.

☞ WILSON SAYS

Avoid gilt edge bonds, *unless* their yield is close (.25%) to medium grades.

Figure 25.4
FROM HUDSON & WEST'S LIST OF MICHIGAN BOND OFFERINGS

Settlement date: 1/2/92

Ratings	M	Bond Description	Coupon	Maturity	Yield	Price
A1/AA-	125	Norway Vulcan Area Schools, Mich. G.O. Callable	7	10/1/05	7.00%	100.00
a/AA-	275	Michigan State building Authority Chippewa Corr. Facs. Callable	7.05	10/1/05	7.30%	97.84
A/AA-	275	Michigan State Building Authority Chippewa Corr. Facs. Non-callable	10	10/1/05	7.60%	120.23
a/AA-	275	Michigan State Building Authority Chippewa Corr. Facs. Px to call 10/1/95 @ 103	11	10/1/06	7.25%	114.39

Figure 25.5
FROM HUDSON & WEST'S LIST OF MICHIGAN BOND OFFERINGS

Settlement date: 1/2/92

Ratings	M	Bond Description	Coupon	Maturity	Yield	Price
A/A	115	Michigan Public Power Agency Campbell Project. Callable	5	12/1/05	7.30%	80.11
A1/AA	55	Traverse City Area Public Schools Qualified State Sch. Fund. Callable	5	1/1/05	7.70%	78.07
A/AA-	535	Michigan State Trunk Line Hwy. Rev. Orig. Yield 7.30%. Non-callable	0	8/15/05	7.30%	37.66
Ba/B	450	Highland Park Hospital Rev. Callable 12/1/96 @ 102.5	8.75	12/1/05	8.75%	100.00

The Dollar Price

As we discussed, a bond's dollar price (60, 85 3/4, 109.61., etc.) is a factor of maturity, coupon, and yield. In most markets, good grade discount (priced under 100) bonds are available at higher yields than those of exactly comparable current coupon, near 100, bonds. When discount bonds are priced 50 basis points cheaper than par bonds, that's a good time to buy them. Sometimes the spread is wider, sometimes narrower. At the time of this writing, discounts are selling higher than par bonds making them a far less attractive buy. Why buy discounts at all? Because you can buy more principal with the same amount of money, because you have an automatic profit, eventually, and because the math of bond reinvestment favors them. Their disadvantages? You have to put up with their lower current yield and when you sell them, any profit is taxed as a capital gain.

☞ WILSON SAYS

Avoid discount bonds unless their after-tax yield is greater than that of other, similar, current coupon bonds.

The same concept applies to non-callable premium bonds. Although there are no tax considerations, sometimes premium bonds sell cheap, and sometimes high. As a rule, consider premium bonds when they are available markedly higher in yield than par bonds. In sum, there are market phases when discount bonds and also premium bonds can be bargains. Compare their true yields and if you can get more for your money take a good look.

I also like ultra-high premium callable bonds, selling at 110 or above, as I mentioned before. Figuring when these are good buys is quite complicated but for the advanced investor definitely worth looking into.

☞ WILSON SAYS

Avoid premium bonds unless they are considerably cheaper than competing current coupon, offered at 100 bonds.

So this gives you some ideas about choosing different kinds of bonds in the primary and the secondary markets. When you are ready to do, get a variety of offerings, don't let a salesperson talk you into just one. Almost always he will have a whole list, but knows that customers get confused when they're shown more than one at a time. I can certainly sympathize and believe you me, when I push a bond to another professional it's the one I want to sell most, the one that makes me the most money. Naturally. But it's not your job to make life easy for securities salespeople. Insist on a variety of offerings. Don't try to make them happy—tell them what you want—there are hundreds of offerings around the market at all times. What's best for you may disappoint the salesman, but that's life.

One good control check is a new issue scale. You see them all the time in financially interested newspapers. Check secondary offerings against new issues, one of the best available guides to prevailing municipal bond prices. Another check is in the bond index that many papers carry every day. *Investors Daily* prints forty current quotes and their list makes interesting comparing.

Taxes, Taxes

Now we are at the same spots we were when choosing among all U.I.T.s or managed funds. The market is right, and you have selected your bond type—its maturity and quality. In addition you have a good idea about how to choose among discount and premium bonds. Now what? To buy at the best available after-all-taxes yield. Check Figure 11.2.

As for state (and local) taxes, on a thumbnail, multiply your top tax bracket by .05% to get the yield advantage of buying bonds exempt in your state. Let's say you are a resident of Kentucky, an average income tax state, and you are in the 6% bracket. Six times .05% is thirty basis points. It costs .30% every year for a Kentuckian to own a non-exempt bond. Suppose you find two long term maturity, medium quality bonds, a Pennsylvania bond at 8%, and a Kentucky exempt bond at 7.5%. Take away the .30% from the 8% bond and it becomes a 7.70%. This 7.70% is *higher* than the state exempt 7 1/2% yield, and so you're better off, after tax, buying the Pennsies. However, had you lived in Connecticut, under a 14% tax rate on out of state bonds, then 14 times .05 is .70%, reducing the 8% down to a 7.30%. So a Connecticut exempt 7.5% is higher here, by .20% a year. Twenty basis points better by the thumbnail method and .2727% better by formula. So those are the basic considerations in picking among unwrapped bonds—maturity, quality, coupon, price, taxes. Happy hunting, it's worth the effort. Now for a few other thoughts.

MISCELLANEOUS BOND SELECTING FACTORS

Large, well known issuers—all the states and such issuers as Atlanta, Georgia, or Seattle's King County, Washington, are undoubtedly general market names and as such have substantial investor following. The resale value of bonds like this tends to be greater than for less well known credits. Bonds of Morgan Hill School District, California, and East Baton Rouge Parish revenue bonds guaranteed by Imperial Chemical, are local in character and far fewer investors, or dealers, are interested in them, despite their A-1 ratings. If you can buy a perfectly good locally flavored bond cheaper than you can a big time name, by say 50 basis points, go right ahead. However, don't give up your liquidity without a bargain price.

☞ WILSON SAYS

Avoid local bonds unless they yield considerably more than comparable general market names.

Way back in 1978 Farmington, New Mexico sold $125 million of 6% Public Service Company of New Mexico San Juan Project revenue bonds due in 2008. This issue is typical of most long revenue bonds—they are designed with one or more big *term* maturities. Investors and dealers like term bonds because their large size draws more buyer interest and their continuing supply tends to create a more active, narrowly spread, market. This makes them relatively easy to price and to add to existing holdings. In Chapter 21 we saw Whitmore's holding of the largest term bond of all—New Jersey Turnpike 7.20's. Many term bonds are quoted in the financial newspapers, albeit with very wide retail spreads. So at the time Whitmore was considering selling his Jersey Turnpikes they might have been printed in the Journal at 96 - 99.

☞ WILSON SAYS

Consider *term bonds*.

A few of more suggestions about credit.

1.) The superiority of general obligations over revenue bonds is much overrated. If you look up the definition of a G.O. you'll see that they are supported by property taxes, a principal source of municipal *revenue*.

2.) The raters get too easily flummoxed about state bonds. States have powers, such as the ability to raise taxes without outside consent, that make them much stronger than local bonds. There should be a special rating category, State AAA, State Aa, etc., for them. The market usually confirms this, but sometimes, as when Louisiana in April 1987, or Massachusetts in the fall of 1990, get cheap, they've proven good buys.

3.) Look for bargains in depressed states or regions, carefully. Almost every place in the country has been under pressure at one time or another and subsequently recovered. Bonds in the Northeast, the Deep South, California, Texas, New York, Massachusetts, even Connecticut, have all proven excellent investments when bought during their toughest times.

4.) We mentioned the dangers of over-concentration several times. Do not put more than a fraction of your assets in the bonds of any one state, insured or not. *This most especially applies to New York.* Much as everyone hopes and prays they won't, the profound troubles of New York City, social, economic, political and financial, are highly likely to once again threaten its solvency, and its bondholders. This will spill over into the bonds of every nearby community. Much as I like the place personally, it remains this country's hottest of all municipal credit hot spots. The present investment grade ratings are absurd. Listen to someone who was in the thick of their 1975 debacle. Don't lend more than 10% of your net worth to New York City, New York State or any of their 101 borrowing aliases. Maybe another 10% if they are insured. Sell the residue now. Triple tax-exempt is no excuse. Better safe than sorry.

5.) Look at bonds subject to the *alternative minimum tax*. They usually come about 25 basis points or so cheaper than other bonds and if you are not in the A.M.T. category why not take the extra income?

6.) Zero coupon bonds can be fine for specialized purposes. Watch any that are callable.

7.) Avoid bonds of your own home town—it's impossible to be objective with them.

8.) If you are at all adventurous, look for special situations in municipal bonds. They are frequently available, but use a knowledgeable professional you can trust.

When you are about to buy your own bonds directly first get the timing right. Then plot out the maturity you prefer. Longer for higher yield and lower liquidity; shorter for lower yield and higher liquidity. Go out as far as you dare. Then look at the call feature, staying away from long callable bonds selling near 100. Next, take a good look at credit, and unless you do some powerful researching yourself, pick a medium quality bond. Higher medium (A-1 rated) for less yield; lower medium (A rated) for more yield, as low a quality as you can feel comfortable with. If you can find an attractively priced discount or premium bond, or a local bond you may know, then take one of those. If not, then look at general market bonds. Go shopping to find the highest after-all-tax yield in a bond with these requirements. It's up to you, and the best of good fortune.

SUMMARY ** CHAPTER 25 ** SUMMARY

How to Choose a Bond

- Check the market signals, 8, 3, 83.

- Pick your maturity.

- Watch the call feature.

- Plan to buy the lowest quality bond you can tolerate.

- Go shopping to find the highest after all tax yield.

CHAPTER 26

WHEN TO SELL

Just as there is a time to buy, there is a time to sell and maybe it's now. Take a good hard look at your own holdings to see if it is. Many's the time I've mentioned the three prerequisites for buying tax-exempts—cash cushion, tax bracket high enough to benefit, and lack of other investment opportunity. I'd suggest that individuals go over these points every few months to revalidate their need for the naturally lower tax-exempt returns. If you no longer benefit from municipals you can sell them and replace them with more suitable investments.

We have emphasized checking for interest rates, inflation, and spreads, to indicate the right *time* to buy. And we have discussed maturity, call, and credit as the most potent factors to consider when buying time comes. If these signals are wrong to buy, it may easily be the right time to sell.

Interest Rate Signals

First, interest rates. I have suggested 8% as the handiest long term bench mark. Over the usable past, the last twenty-five years, when individual investors have waited to buy long maturity, medium grade municipal bonds until they yielded 8% they have had superior results. From 8% down to 7% (when long bonds might rise by 10 points) you may hold on. But when they reach 7% or lower, it's time to sell. The 7% level marks territory that bonds have resisted vigorously. I'd advize selling any holding due more than five years out when the long term rates approach 7%. Again, the handiest gauge of this is the *Bond Buyer* 40 bond index seen in most financial newspapers. Then what to do? Get onto the quiet local road, waiting in money market or short term bonds until rates are up to 8% again. For yield signals on all maturities see Figure 26.1.

Another blast of caution: these numbers are valid now, in 1991, using wonderful hindsight. A simple formula like this is just one tool among many. One thing I do guarantee—interest rates will fluctuate, and it's impossible to predict how or when. 8%, that's my standard, and I'll stick to it. However, you have to draw your own line, adjusting when basic conditions change.

☞ *WILSON SAYS*

Sell long term tax-exempts when their yield falls under 7%.

Figure 26.1
MUNICIPAL BONDS
WHEN TO BUY, HOLD AND SELL

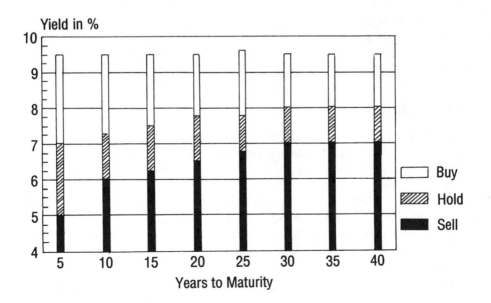

Inflation Signals

In Chapter 3 we used a 3% rate of real return (8% bond yield, minus a 5% average inflation bite) as an indicator of worthwhile income. But if inflation climbs to 6%, and bond yields stay at 8%, leaving only a 2% real return, something is wrong. We saw that long term bonds become attractive when their yield exceeds your expectations of inflation by 3% a year. So, if you figure that inflation rates are heading up, it's time to consider selling long term, less liquid bonds.

Beating inflation is a fundamental investment concept and holders of billions and billions of dollars worth of bonds also think this way. A fundamental rule of the fixed income road is to buy bonds when they beat inflation and sell them if they won't. Buy at 3% or more, sell at 2% or less, in between just hold.

☞ *WILSON SAYS*

Sell long term tax-exempts when their real yield falls below 2%.

The Spread Signal

The third signal is the ratio spread—how close long municipal bond yields are to those of U.S. government bonds of the same maturity. We have advanced an 83% spread as a buying indicator. When municipals yield over 83% they have been relatively good buys. When they have yielded less than 75% it is usually a good time to sell them.

As you may have figured out, independent investors, particularly those who handle their portfolios intelligently are my own favorite. I'm glad to sell my bonds to U.I.T. portfolio buyers and I deal with fund operators all the time, but to me it's a lot more satisfying to sell bonds to individual buyers and I try to make it a lot more profitable as well. How do I do this?   Chiefly by selling bonds to other dealers who then sell them to customers they know. (I also handle a few private investors myself, but that's an entirely different story.)

☞ *WILSON ADVISES*

Sell long term average quality municipals when their return is less than 75% of U.S. Treasury yields.

That's it for timing, now on to review your tax-exempts' maturity, call features, and credit quality, to determine if they are still suitable vehicles.

Check Maturity

First, maturity. By now you've surely received my message that bonds aren't diamonds, they are not forever. When formerly long term bonds approach maturity their investment characteristics usually change, calling for action. Ten years before maturity most municipal bonds begin to climb the yield curve quickly. Take another look at Figure 3.4. Suppose you had bought some 30 year maturity bonds back at a time one of those yield curves was in effect. You have now held them for fifteen years and if that same yield curve describes the current municipal bond market your bonds will have risen in value. How much? If it's from an 8% to a 7%, this means that their price has also risen, perhaps up from 90 to 100, automatically, *even though the market as a whole is unchanged.* Why? Because they are now ten year bonds and are more valuable to someone who needs that shorter maturity. If your needs are still to maximize income then sell them out and go get something better. Time's a-wasting.

Similarly, many long term bonds have now been pre-refunded, which means they will be paid off far in advance of their maturity. Have your bonds checked for current yields and prices so you can replace and improve.

A shortening of maturity can also be used to soothe the pain of past mistakes. Suppose that back in 1971 you bought some thirty year high grade 5% bonds at 102. They probably fell as low as 50 cents on the dollar in the early eighties, but on the same yield curve you could sell them at a 7% yield, at 85. Take the 17 point loss, use it to wipe out some capital gains, get rid of that old low coupon and re-invest in a nice fat long bond.

Taxes certainly have to be considered when selling at a profit and also when taking losses. Tax liability on profits reduces the amount you will have to re-invest. Tax credit may be of use when taking a loss. Consult your accountant. Profit or loss, look to the future and its possibilities; checking and switching your old tax-exempts can help maximize your income and clean out past mistakes.

☞ WILSON SAYS

Sell your municipal bonds when their maturity becomes shorter than you need and re-invest in higher yielding longer term bonds.

Check Calls

We discussed call features at length in Chapter 25. Take a careful look at the future calls that might occur to your existing bonds and what effects they would have. You may think you have a long term bond, but if it's callable and bears a coupon higher than the ones currently in the market for similar bonds, then you may well lose it through early redemption by the issuer. How do you figure this out? Get a quote on your bond, and if it's worth more than 100 ask your broker what yield you would get to call. This may persuade you to consider selling it now, before it's too late.

I warned against buying long callable bonds at prices near 100. Their potential is low, while their downside is unlimited. The reverse holds true. When you check your long term callable bonds and find that some are worth around 100, consider selling them, providing you can get a better deal on a replacement. For this, beware of general securities salespeople. A few may know enough about stocks and some municipals to be of help, but call features are *way* beyond 95% of them. Consult a municipal bond specialist, both in getting a good price for the old bonds and locating better values somewhere else.

☞ *WILSON SAYS*

Watch callable bonds carefully.
Watch callable bonds carefully.
Review what they will yield if called.
Sell callable bonds when their price is near 100.

Check Credit

Every three months or so, go over every bond you own to check for credit changes. Asking a good dealer is an excellent way to begin. Bonds which develop some trouble should be reviewed and decisions made at once, to hold, to sell, or possibly to add on, if they seem undervalued. Bonds whose credit has improved may seem to be no problem, but suppose a bond bought to last fifteen years gets escrowed or insured. If you can sell it at a 6% yield and reinvest at 8%, you may be better off.

☞ *WILSON SAYS*

Check the credit quality of your bonds regularly.

Once you decide to sell a municipal holding how do you proceed? We saw that Whitmore's wire house paid him correct market prices for two tricky bonds. In the hands of inefficient or devious dealers, those sales could have been badly botched. One suggestion: until you develop trust, direct your salesperson to put the bonds you have decided to sell out for the bid on broker wire, then to report the bid, and his commission, to you. Then reinvest the proceeds yourself, when you find something you like. Don't fall for a glib swap proposition—look at both sides of any proposed switch of bonds carefully.

Once you trust your salesman you can get a *quote* on your bonds, that is, an approximation of their value, not an actual bid. At the same time, ask for a suitable replacement. This may accomplish two things. It may demonstrate your wish to improve your holdings, not just to dump and buy again. And the prospect of two transactions may encourage him to work harder, bringing you better prices.

That finishes our section on unwrapped tax-exempts. Municipal bonds are probably the single most complicated investment that the public buys in quantity and so it's not surprising that so many people buy trusts and managed funds. However, for the independent minded there's nothing like the satisfaction of making your own financial decisions. And, if you do it right, a bigger payday becomes your reward.

SUMMARY ** CHAPTER 26 ** SUMMARY

When to Sell

- Check the bond market signals.

- Review your bond holdings frequently, inspecting maturity, call features and credit.

- If the market is wrong, or your bonds have changed, consider selling and replacing.

CHAPTER 27

RATING
UNPACKAGED BONDS

WHITE'S INVESTMENT RATING: ***

Overall, I'm not terribly impressed with the investment results most people have achieved with their tax-exempts. Most buying decisions are made by small investors and there are whole investment systems built on how wrong the individual buyer always seems to be. However, if individuals have a landmark to steer by I'm sure they have a better chance of investment success. My landmarks are 8, 3, 83. No matter which of the four ways to invest are chosen, if you stay on the slow safe road of short terms until long bonds are at 8%; if bonds beat inflation by 3%, and if municipals yield 83% or more of Governments, you should experience superior results.

I've spent quite a lot of time rethinking my opinions on the four paths to tax-exempt investing and find myself standing by them. To me, U.I.T.s are the first and lowest tier of municipals. Their high load, fixed portfolio, and annual charges handicap them so heavily that they will never be suitable for any but the smallest investors. One star only, definitely.

The managed funds represent the second level of investing in tax-exempts. I'm skeptical about the management advantage of funds because I've never seen much more than competence there. More often mediocrity in managing is the rule. The performance figures seem to bear it out. What ever positive result comes from their swapping bonds around is negated by their annual fees. Two stars is the most I can award. At that, the load factor should carefully be considered—is the service you get from a broker worth the diminution of income?

The third and highest tier of public tax-exempt buying is reached at the level of individually wrapped bonds. I sincerely believe that bonds well chosen for maturity and credit suitability will yield the best results for individual buyers. Bearing a fixed due date and bearing no annual fees, carefully watched unpackaged bonds should bring you out ahead. Three stars, the tops in my system.

Figure 27.1
MUNICIPAL BOND CHARACTERISTICS

Investment Quality

	Price Stability	Principal Safety	Typical Selling cost Per $1,000	Typical Relative Yields
5 year Maturity	High	Extremely High	$10	7.00%
10 year Maturity	Moderate	Very High	15	7.50%
15 year Maturity	Moderate	Very High	20	7.75%
20 year Maturity	Low	Very High	20	7.80%
25 year Maturity	Low	Very High	25	7.90%
30 year Maturity	Low	Very High	25	8.00%

Selected Lower Grades

5 year Maturity	Moderate	Moderate	20	8.00%
10 year Maturity	Low	Moderate	25	8.25%
25 year Maturity	Low	Moderate	30	8.50%

Section V
Delegated Asset Management

NOT RATED

CHAPTER 28

THE MONEY MANAGERS

The fourth path in the municipal bond investment field leads to different territory—where you delegate asset managing to someone else. Although public awareness and knowledge of investing techniques has grown remarkably in the past ten years, still many people don't have enough confidence in their own financial ability to select the right time and vehicle for their savings. Sometimes families are involved, complicating matters greatly. Or trusts or other specialized forces make investing on one's own seem perilous. Investors in these situations may turn over the decision making to someone they feel knows more about the subject. About one-fifth of all municipal bond owners choose this way, so if you're among them don't feel lonely. If U.I.T. and managed fund buying resemble guided tours of a foreign country, and direct investing independent travel, using a money manager is like viewing a travelogue. You may see a lot of landscape, but in a second-hand way.

☞ *A DEFINITION*

Money Managers

Any of various types of professionals who provide financial advice and service.

There are probably as many explanations why people delegate municipal bond investing as there are people who do so. However, in my experience two reasons are most often mentioned: 1.) That the manager knows a lot about tax-exempts, and 2.) Somehow he or she has your interest at heart. The first is rarely true. The second is never. This makes the odds about 10 to 1 against you. *The plain fact is that extremely few money managers comprehend municipals and all are primarily driven by self-interest.* Coming to understand the workings of tax-exempts is a long and difficult learning process to which virtually no money runners have ever submitted. No small managers I've known, few medium sized, and a minority of large ones know the second thing about the tax-exempt market or its bonds. Those who do put their own interest first, simply and doggedly trying to show a profit. To do so they often rely on the many clichés of investing to sell their services. Unless you like your baloney cut thick, make them convince you by superior investment results, not con you with benevolent smiles, conservative posturing and tastefully furnished offices. I can recommend no professional financial advisor who knows enough about municipal bonds to be trusted with managing them without sharp supervision. I find them no less greedy than the regular municipal bond hawker out to make a buck. What's worse, they don't admit it or even realize it themselves. If this sounds harsh, try asking some people you know how they feel about their experiences with delegating, if you, or they, dare. One outstanding fault: almost unanimously, advisors refuse to adopt imaginative investing techniques.

Since everything depends on the individual future performance of the advisor and since no figures are available for past performance, generalizations about their bond techniques are difficult to make. They seem to stick to unpackaged bonds. They rarely recommend funds and never U.I.T.s. Here are four principal sets of investment experts ready to accommodate you—financial planners, dealer managers, bank trust departments, and regulated investment companies.

Financial Planners

Perhaps you have seen advertisements in which *financial planners* offer their services. This relatively new breed serves people whom Wall Street's traditional bankers had long neglected—individuals with substantial assets who need better advice than the usual securities salesman is able to give. A financial planner reviews his or her customer's life situation and offers a wide spectrum of advice ranging from tax work, through saving plans, to investment suggestions. Many have been recruited from the usual brokerage houses, or through insurance companies where salesmen wish to add to their titles or expand their product lines. Any advice about municipal bonds should be treated just as though it were being pitched to you in the regular way. Run any suggestions through the principles of this book and make up your own mind.

The Investment Professionals

When and if your total portfolio reaches a certain size you may delegate your investment decisions to a *dealer money manager,* to a *bank trust department,* or to a *regulated investment company.* Whereas financial planners say they consider their customers' whole money situation, these specialized money managers stick mainly to investments. All three types prefer individuals with abundant assets, especially those who have little financial expertise. You get an account person to unearth your particular goals and to fabricate a lifelong plan to finance them. Once agreement is reached, the advisor puts your money into stocks, tax-exempts, or other investments, selling, or swapping them for others when the time seems right. Advertisements offering these services are generally lower-key, with pictures of little toy bulls and bears or expansive country estates, decidedly upper-class, and naturally charging fees to match.

Dealer Money Managers

The newest of this class are what used to be called high net worth salesmen. Now some dealers have separated, on paper at least, these salespeople into a department that devotes most of its energies to servicing people with portfolios of perhaps half a million dollars and up. Naturally they can be expected to suggest the dealer's own products and they are usually paid on this basis. Most of their accounts are set up as non-discretionary, that is, you the investor have to approve all transactions. Unless your situation is unusual, I'd make sure that your okay is received before a trade is done. The avowal of objectivity is a potent one, so investors should not be fooled by shallow claims. Subject any municipal bond suggestions through the usual scrutiny, just like buying bonds yourself.

Trust Departments

The investment advisor that most people and estates end up with are *commercial bank trust departments.* There are about 1,000 in the U.S.A. and they handle something like two million separate accounts. I've serviced a large number of them, including the supposedly most eminent, and as a class my guess is that they have produced poor investment results. They seldom publish reliable fig-

Figure 28.1
INVESTMENT CHARACTERISTICS OF ALL MUNICIPAL BOND CATEGORIES

	Price Stability	Principal Safety
Money Market Funds	Extremely High	Extremely High
5 Year Maturities		
Trusts	High	Extremely High
No-Load Funds	High	Extremely High
Investment Grade Bonds**	High	Extremely High
10 Year Maturities		
Trusts	Moderate	Very High
No-Load funds	Moderate	Extremely High
Load funds	Moderate	Extremely High
Investment Grade Bonds**	Moderate	Very High
25-40 Year Maturities		
Trusts	Low	Very High
No-Load funds	Low	Very High
Load funds	Low	Very High
Investment Grade Bonds**	Low	Very High
Lower Grade 25-40 Year Maturities		
Trusts	Poor	Moderate
No-Load funds	Low	High
Load funds	Low	High
Investment Grade Bonds**	Low	Moderate

**Regardless of ratings, treat as non-investment grade uninsured G.O. bonds of any
  sizable municipality where the income level of a significant portion of the population
  is far below the national average.

Selling Cost per $1,000	Annual Fee per $1,000	Convenience	Principal Safety
$ 0	1	Extremely High	6.00%
30	2	High	6.00%
0	7	High	6.75%
10	0	Low	7.00%
35	2	High	6.50%
0	7	High	7.25%
30	7	High	7.25%
15	0	Low	7.50%
60	2	High	7.00%
0	7	High	7.50%
45	7	High	7.50%
25	0	Low	8.00%
70	2	High	7.50%
10	0	High	8.00%
50	10	High	8.00%
30	0	Very Low	8.50%

ures by which to compare their lack of success with others. I know of none to recommend.

If you are stuck with a bank trust manager try to keep control over them so you can influence their decisions. I've seen trustees with full investment discretion flout the wishes of families and donors, sticking to the letter of a trust clause, thereby avoiding any legal trouble rather than be sensibly adaptable. If you have the power, I'd suggest that you engage a professional financial person to confer with the trustee to awaken the bank's best efforts.

Regulated Investment Companies

The final class of money managers are the regulated investment companies. These are licensed financial experts who have certain standards to maintain and they make it their business to advise larger sized individuals and institutions. Most of their accounts are discretionary, so that they buy and sell without individual trade authorizations. Many times they will present records of past success, which should be looked at carefully. Plenty of distortions somehow creep into most past performance charts. They do not usually sell their own products and so try to maintain the appearance of objectivity. To test this point you might ask one what percentage of their business is done with which securities dealers. Look at their annual fees as a deduction against income and see how much you give to them. Are they earning 1% of your principal every year? That may come to over 15% of your income, a hefty charge.

If you do use any kind of money manager voluntarily what can you do to improve your results? First of all, are you happy? Do you get enough to live on from your investments? I know of one lady from Pennsylvania who was left a good sized amount of one conservative stock in a trust that a bank finally came to totally control. The bank trust department left three-quarters of her assets in this stock, and over 20 years it went up slowly, fluctuating, but on average rising by about 6% a year. It paid a 3% dividend, and on this income the lady lived, well enough by most standards. I asked the trust officer if the stock should be sold to increase her income, but she didn't like the fact that there would be a big tax on the gain. I talked her into selling some of the stock, reluctantly, but she boasted that it had always earned 9%. That was phoney—two-thirds of the gain was from the compounding effect alone. I didn't want to argue the point—there was no use—but the gain came about because the bank had kept the supposed beneficiary on a lower than necessary income. Some trust! The bank re-invested the proceeds conservatively, more than doubling the lady's income, and God bless her, as soon as January came she was driving a nice safe Mercedes down to Florida.

As in dealing with any professional, it's up to you to exert final responsibility. You should definitely check periodically on how well your account is doing. And has done in the past five, ten, and more years. Did you make a fairly reasonable 15% a year on stocks, or 8% a year on tax-exempt bonds, income and profit or loss included? If not there is something wrong. You are paying a pretty penny for good advice so don't hesitate to challenge poor results.

I don't rate the money managers, since information is not available. You have to do that, armed with the records of what they have done for you.

☞ WILSON SAYS GOOD-BYE

Thank you for reading this book. I sincerely hope that you will benefit from it.

SUMMARY ** CHAPTER 28 ** SUMMARY

The Money Managers

- Beware of all money managers, especially bank trust departments.

- Never surrender control over any account if you can possibly avoid it.

- Watch your money manager's decisions closely, applying the standards of this book.

Index